WOMEN AND ISLAM

Published by:
Saurabh Publishing House

WOMEN AND ISLAM

Iqbal Qureshi

Saurabh
Publishing House
4735/22, Prakash Deep Building,
Ansari Road, Daryaganj,
New Delhi- 110002

Published by :
SAURABH PUBLISHING HOUSE

Distributed by :
Lotus Press Publishers & Distributors
Unit No. 220, 2nd Floor, 4735/22, Prakash Deep Building,
Ansari Road, Darya Ganj, New Delhi- 110002
Ph.: 23280047, 09811838000
• E-mail : lotuspress1984@gmail.com
www.lotuspress.co.in

Saurabh Publishing House is an imprint of
Lotus Press Publishers & Distributors

Women and Islam

ISBN: 81-89005-12-X

Printed by : **Lotus Press Publishers & Distributors, New Delhi**

PREFACE

The word islam is "the infinitive of the fourth form of the Arabic triconsonantal root s-l-m meaning 'to submit,' 'to surrender'"; therefore Islam effectively means "submission to God". Followers of Islam are expected to submit to God by worshipping him, following his commands as described by Prophet Muhammad, and avoiding polytheism. The word Iislam is also based upon the Arabic word for peace (salam) and could be applicible to the religion of Islam if it is taken to mean that "true peace resides in submission to God". Islam alone is condemned by many westerners as blocking the way to women's rights. And yet, though neither Christianity nor Judaism played an important role in promoting equality of the sexes, millions of Jewish and Christian women today enjoy a dual privilege full human rights on the one hand and access to an inspirational religious tradition on the other. This book offers a critical perspective on the social status of women as described in the Quran and as defined by Islamic jurisprudence. This undistorted, straightforward presentation of the facts will reveal that millions of Muslim females, under rigid and inexorable Islamic laws, have been deprived of their fundamental inalienable rights and driven into seclusion for many centuries. These humiliating laws have played an important role in creating the socioeconomic ills that still afflict the Muslim world today.

The majority of Muslim exegetes and jurisprudents, especially among modern writers and commentators on the Quran, have held that Islam actually elevated the position of women. They insist that the rights of women are well recognized and protected by Islam, more so than in other faiths. They point out that Islam put an end to such barbaric practices as infanticide of girls. They also argue that by giving a married woman the permission to dispose of her own property as she pleases, Islam has promoted her standing. Some modern interpreters of the Quran go even so far as to insist that in Islamic communities men and women are treated equally.

CONTENTS

Preface v

1. **Rights and Roles of Woman in Islam** 11
   - Introduction 11
   - Functional Distinctions on Earth 12
   - Woman is not just Biology 13
   - Darajah 15
   - Faddala 18
   - Disruption of Marital Harmony 23
   - Significance of Context and Chronology in Quranic Social Reforms for Women 27
   - Divorce 28
   - Patriarchy 29
   - Polygamy 31
   - Witness 33
   - Inheritance 35
   - Male Authority 36
   - Child Care 38
2. **Fundamentalism and Women's Rights** 40
   - Introduction 40
   - Lessons from Dar al-Islam 41
   - Lessons from the City of Women 44
3. **Quranic View of Woman** 48
   - Introduction 48

Quran Teaches the Reader through the Events in the Lives 49
Significance of the Women Mentioned or Referred to in the Quran 51
Woman as an Individual 53
Distinctions between Individuals 55
Distinctive Female Characters in the Quran 57
4. Muslim Societies and Women 62
Introduction 62
5. Woman's Seclusion in Islam 72
Introduction 72
The Will of Allah 74
Maze of Restrictions against Women 75
Treatment of Women Based on the Quran 78
Male Sexual Insecurity and the Need for Control 79
Veil as a Check on Male Sexual Desire 79
Veil and Marriage 83
Status of Woman in the Pre-Islamic Period 84
Female Infanticide in Pre-Islamic Arabia 86
Veil in the Pre-Islamic Period 88
Islam Today: Economic Disadvantages of Inequality 91
Summary 92
6. Muslim Family Law 95
Introduction 95
Women in Pre-islamic Arabia 96
Marriage 97
Divorce 108
Inheritance 117
Summary 125
7. Muslim Law and Women 127
Introduction 127
WLUML and Muslim Laws 128
WLUML and the Platform for Action 130

8. Legal Methodology for Reform in Islam	**133**
Introduction	133
Tradition and Change	133
Ijtihad vs. Taqlid	134
Distinction between Shariah and Fiqh	136
Usul Al-fiqh (Sources of Law) and Islamic Reform	136
Summary	159
9. Primitive Marriage Laws	**165**
Introduction	165
Women in Ancient Egypt	166
Women in Babylonia	167
Women in Elam	168
Women of India	169
Types of Marriage	169
Conditions for Marriage	164
Legal Age for Marriage	176
Bride-price in Marriage	179
Amount of the Bride-Price	181
Ancient Origin of the Bride-Price (*Mahr* and *Ajr*)	182
Bride-Price:Divine Revolution?	
Summary	184
10. Punishments for Sexual Misconduct in Islam	**187**
Introduction	187
First Injunction: Confine Lewd Women	188
Scourge the Adulterer and Adulteress	188
Stoning	190
Discrimination against Women in Penal Laws	194
Caliphs are Above the Law	196
False Allegations and Oath	196
False Accusation and the Controversy Surrounding	199
11. Islamic Higher Learning in Muslim Women	**204**
Introduction	204
Content of Islamic Higher Learning	208

Education and Islamic Higher Learning 211
Islamic Higher Learning in Practice 214
Islamic Higher Learning in the Platform for Action 217
12. International Organizations, Foreign Policy and Islam 221
Introduction 221
National Machinery 222
Interrelationships between the National and International Levels 226
Implementation of the Platform for Action in Muslim Societies 229
Implications of the Foreign Policy of Donor Countries 233
Bibliography 235
Index 237

1

Rights and Roles of Woman in Islam

Introduction

The text was revealed to the inhabitants of the earth, while they inhabited the earth, and we are all on the earth as we read and discuss the text. As such, our earthly existence transforms our perceptions of the text and is equally potentially transformed by the text. More importantly, because of the Quran's intention to guide the affairs of humans, a certain emphasis is placed on understanding and applying the text while we are here on earth.

In my consideration of woman on earth from the Quranic perspective, there are certain problems inherent in our understanding of what the Quran depicts. Our operations on the earth are shaped by our world-view (and vice versa). We have not yet attained the Quranic utopia. Whenever Quranic support is given for conflicting opinions on how to operate in this world, controversies arise. Many popular or dominant ideas about the role of woman do not have sanction from the Quran. Pointing these out causes problems, not so much with logical analysis of the text, but with application of the new analysis in the context in which Muslim societies operate.

Hermeneutics of any text must confront three different aspects in order to support its conclusions:

1. The context in which the text was written (in the case of the Quran, in which it was revealed);
2. The grammatical composition of the text (how it says what it says); and
3. The whole text, its *Weltanschauung* or world-view. Often, differences of opinion can be traced to variations in emphasis between these three aspects.

I will discuss selected concepts, terms or verses from these perspectives:

1. There is no inherent value placed on man or woman. In fact, there is no arbitrary, pre-ordained and eternal system of hierarchy.
2. The Quran does not strictly delineate the roles of woman and the roles of man to such an extent as to propose only a single possibility for each gender (that is, women must fulfil this role, and *only* this one, while men must fulfil that role and only men *can* fulfil it).

To demonstrate these points, I will make a detailed analysis of Quranic passages which have been interpreted to imply the superiority of males over females. In doing this, I will demonstrate a more integrated communal perspective on the rights and responsibilities of the individual in society using certain Quranic concepts.

Overall, my analysis tends to restrict the meaning of many passages to a particular subject, event, or context. These restrictions are based on the context of the verses or on application of general Quranic concepts of justice towards humankind, human dignity, equal rights before the law and before Allah, mutual responsibility, and equitable relations between humans.

One other aspect of my consideration will be to demonstrate the significance of chronological developments in the Quran. The Quran sets forth a logical progression with regard to the development of human interactions, morality, and ethics, as reflected by the growth and development of the community of Muslims who lived concurrent with the revelation. The significance of this with regard to application of the precepts concerning the role of woman will be demonstrated.

Functional Distinctions on Earth

I demonstrated how the Quran treats woman as an individual in the same manner as it treats man as an individual. Their only distinction is on the basis of *taqwa* (God-conscious piety). *Taqwa* is not determined by gender. The Quran also focuses on how we function in society. It acknowledges that we operate in social systems with certain functional distinctions. The relationship that the Quran shows between these worldly distinctions and *taqwa* is important in my consideration of equity among people. More importantly, functional distinctions included in the Quran have been used to support the idea of inherent superiority of men over women.

Functional distinctions are indicators of roles and role expectations. To what extent does the Quran delineate functions for each gender? Are there certain exceptions and exclusions for males or females? Does the Quran value certain functions above others?

Woman is not just Biology

Because woman's primary distinction is on the basis of her childbearing ability, it is seen as her primary function. The use of 'primary' has had negative connotations in that it has been held to imply that women can only be mothers. Therefore, women's entire upbringing must be to cultivate devoted wives and ideal mothers in preparation for this function.

There is no term in the Quran which indicates that childbearing is 'primary' to a woman. No indication is given that mothering is her exclusive role. It demonstrates the fact a woman (though certainly not all women) is the exclusive human capable of bearing children. This capacity is essential to the continuation of human existence. This function becomes primary only with regard to the continuity of the human race. In other words, since only the woman can bear children, it is of primary importance that she does.

Although it does not restrict the female to functioning as a mother, the Quran is emphatic about the reverence, sympathy, and responsibility due to the female procreator. 'O humankind have *taqwa* towards Allah in Whom you claim your rights of one another, and (have *taqwa*) towards the wombs (that bore you).' This verse is often interpreted as indicating respect for women in general. I specify this verse as indicating respect for the needed procreative capacity of women. I do not diminish respect from women as a class, but I do specify, from the Quranic perspective, the significance of the function of child-bearing, which is exclusively performed by women. The reverence given to the fulfilment of this function helps to explain how the Quran explicitly delineates a function for males which creates a balance in human relations.

No other function is similarly exclusive to one gender or the other. This brings to mind the popular misconception that since only males have had the responsibility of *risalah*, it indicates something special about that class. Both men and women have been included in divine communication as the recipients of *wahy*, but there is no Quranic example of a woman with the responsibility of *risalah*. However, all those chosen for this responsibility were exceptional.

This is not a biological association with males representing their primary function and expressing a universal norm for all men. In fact, given the difficulty they have faced in getting others to accept the message when these exceptional men have come from poor classes, the likelihood of failure for the message might have been greater if women, who are given so little regard in most societies, were selected to deliver the message. It is a strategy for effectiveness, not a statement of divine preference.

Besides the two functions discussed above, every other function has real or potential participation by both males and females. However, there is still a wide range of functional distinctions between individuals considered in the Quran. The questions that must be asked then are: What is the value of the functional distinctions between individuals? Do these functional distinctions and the values placed on them delineate specific values for males and females in society? Are these values intra-Quranic or extra-Quranic?

In particular, several verses from the Quran have frequently been used to support the claims of the inherent superiority of males over females. These verses contain two terms which have been used to indicate value in the functional distinctions between individuals and groups on earth. I will review these terms, how they have been used in the Quran, and in the overall context of Quranic justice.

The first term is *darajah* (pl. *darajat*), step, degree or level'. A *darajah* exists not only here on earth between people but also between the Hereafter and earth, between levels in Heaven and in Hell.

The other term, *faddala* is often used in conjunction with *darajat*. I have translated *faddala* 'to prefer', with a verbal noun (*tafdil*) meaning 'preference'. Often the preference given is spoken of in terms of *fadl*, which I translate as (Allah's) 'benevolence'.

Darajah

An individual or group can earn or be granted a darajah over another. The Quran specifies, for example, that by striving in the way of Allah with one's wealth and one's person or by immigrating for Allah, one can obtain a darajah. However, most often the darajah is obtained through an unspecified category of doing 'good' deeds.

Distinguishing between individuals or groups on the basis of 'deeds' involves problems with regard to the value of women in society and as individuals. Although the Quran distinguishes on the basis of deeds, it does not set values for particular deeds. This leaves each social system to determine the value of different kinds of deeds at will. They have always done this and 'every society has distinguished men's work from women's work'. The problem is that 'Men's work is usually regarded as more valuable than women's work, no matter how arbitrary the division of labour'.

On the one hand, the Quran supports distinctions on the basis of deeds, but on the other hand, it does not determine the actual value of specific deeds. This leads to the interpretation that the Quran supports values of deeds as determined by individual societies. Actually, the Qur'an's neutrality allows for the natural variations that exist.

With regard to the *darajah* obtained through deeds, however, the Quran has stipulated several points which should affect evaluation in society. First, all deeds performed with *taqwa* are more valuable. Second, 'Unto men a fortune from that which they have earned, and unto women a fortune from that which they have earned.' The deeds may be different, but recompense is given based on what one does. It does not matter how the deeds are divided between the males and the females in a particular social context.

Another implication of a 'fortune from what one earns' is that whenever anyone performs tasks normally attributed to the other gender in addition to his or her own normal tasks, he or she will earn an additional reward. For example, Moses meets two women from Madyan, where ordinarily the males tended the animals. However, because there was no able-bodied male in the family to perform this task according to the norm (the father being an old man), the women were required to be *extraordinarily* useful.

There is no indication that these women were immoral in their performance of this task, because fulfilling the tasks needed for survival takes precedence over socially determined roles. Similarly, in post-slavery America, the Black female was given employment instead of the Black male. In many families, she became the sole supporter. This necessity, in addition to her fulfilment of the ordinary tasks of bearing and rearing children, should have given her more. A flexible perspective on the fulfilment of necessity would have benefited her. Instead, she was subject to a double burden and, often, violence at home from a husband who felt displaced.

Each social context divides the labour between the male and the female in such a way as to allow for the optimal function of that society. The Quran does not divide the labour and establish a monolithic order for every social system which completely disregards the natural variations in society. On the contrary, it acknowledges the need for variations when it states that the human race is divided 'into nations and tribes that you might know one another'. Then it gives each group, and each member of the group the males and the females recompense in accordance to deeds performed.

This is an important social universal in the Quran. It allows and encourages each individual social context to determine its functional distinctions between members, but applies a single system of equitable recompense which can be adopted in every social context. This is also one reason why certain social systems have remained stagnant in their consideration of the potential roles of women. The Quran does not specifically determine the roles, and the individual nations have not considered all the possibilities.

As for the *darajah* which is 'given' by Allah, it is even more illusive than the *darajah* for unspecified deeds. There is a distinction on the basis of knowledge: 'Allah will exalt those who believe among you, and those who have knowledge, to high ranks [*darajat*]'. 'We raised by grades [*darajat*] (of mercy) whom we will, and over all endued with knowledge there is one more knowing.'

There are also social and economic distinctions: 'we have apportioned among them their livelihood in the life of the world, and raised some of them above others in ranks [*darajat*] that some of them may take labour from others; and the mercy of Allah is better than (the wealth) that they amass.' It is also clear, however, that wealth is not a 'real' distinguishing characteristic, but a functional distinction apparent to humankind and valued within society.

The *darajah* given by Allah serves another significant function to test the inhabitants of the earth: 'He it is Who has placed you as viceroys of the earth and has exalted some of you in ranks [*darajat*] above others, that He may try you by (the test of) that which He has given you.'

Finally, it is necessary to discuss the one verse which distinguishes a *darajah* between men and women:

> Women who are divorced shall wait, keeping themselves apart, three (monthly) courses. And it is not lawful for them that they conceal that which Allah has created in their wombs if they believe in Allah and the Last Day. And their husbands would do better to take them back in that case if they desire a reconciliation. And [(the rights) due to the women are similar to (the rights) against them, (or responsibilities they owe) with regard to] the *ma'ruf*, and men have a degree [*darajah*] above them (feminine plural). Allah is Mighty, Wise.

This verse has been taken to mean that a *darajah* exists between all men and all women, in every context. However, the context of the discussion is clearly with regard to divorce: men have an advantage over women. In the Quran the advantage men have is that of being individually able to pronounce divorce against their wives without arbitration or assistance. Divorce is granted to a woman, on the other hand, only after intervention of an authority (for example, a judge).

Considering the details given, *darajah* in this verse must be restricted to the subject at hand. To attribute an unrestricted value to one gender over another contradicts the equity established throughout the Quran with regard to the individual: each *nafs* shall have in accordance to what it earns. Yet, the verse is presumed to state what men have believed and wanted others to believe: that society operates hierarchically with the male on top.

Finally, this verse states: '[(the rights) due to the women are similar to (the rights) against them, (or responsibilities they owe) with regard to] the *ma'ruf*.' The term *ma'ruf* occurs in other instances with regard to the treatment of women in society. Pickthall translates it as 'kindness', but its implications are much wider than that. It is a passive participle of the verbal root 'to know', and as such indicates something 'obvious', 'well known' or 'conventionally accepted'. However, with regard to treatment, it also has dimensions of equitable, courteous and beneficial.

In this verse, it precedes the *darajah* statement to indicate its precedence. In other words, the basis for equitable treatment is conventionally agreed upon in society. With regard to this, the rights and the responsibilities of the woman and the man are the same. Again, the expression places a limitation rather than a universal perspective on this issue because convention is relative to time and place.

Faddala

As with *darajah*, the Quran states explicitly that Allah has preferred [*faddala*] some of creation over others. Like *darajah*, this preference is also discussed in specific terms. First, humankind is preferred over the rest of creation. Then, occasionally, one group of people have been preferred over another. Finally, some of the prophets are preferred over others. It is interesting to note, however, that 'preference' is not absolute. Although the Quran states that some prophets are preferred over others, it also states that no *distinction* is made between them. This indicates that, in the Quranic usage, preference is relative.

Like *darajah*, *faddala* is also given to test the one to whom it is given. Unlike *darajah*, however, *faddala* cannot be earned by performing certain deeds. It can only be given by Allah, Who has it and grants it to whom He wishes and in the form He wishes. Others do not have it and cannot give it. They can only be recipients of His *fadl*.

With regard to *faddala*, men and women, the following verse is central:

> Men are [*qawwamuna 'ala*] women, [on the basis] of what Allah has [preferred] (*faddala*) some of them over others, and [on the

> basis] of what they spend of their property (for the support of women). So good women are [*qanitat*], guarding in secret that which Allah has guarded. As for those from whom you fear (*nushuz*], admonish them, banish them to beds apart, and scourge them. Then, if they obey you, seek not a way against them.

Needless to say, this verse covers a great deal more than just preference. This is classically viewed as the single most important verse with regard to the relationship between men and women: 'men are *qawwamuna 'ala* women'. Before discussing this, however, I want to point out that this correlation is determined on the basis of two things:

1. What 'preference' has been given, and
2. 'What they spend of their property (for support of women),' *i.e.* a socioeconomic norm and ideal.

The translation I have inserted, 'on the basis of,' comes from the *bi* used in this verse. In a sentence, it implies that the characteristics or contents before *bi* are determined 'on the basis' of what comes after *bi*. In this verse it means that men are *qawwamuna 'ala* women only if the following two conditions exist. The first condition is 'preference', and the other is that they support the women from their means. 'If either condition fails, then the man is not '*qawwam*' over that woman'.

My first concern then is *faddala*. The verse says the position between men and women is based on 'what' Allah has preferred. With regard to material preference, there is only one Quranic reference which specifies that Allah has detemined for men a portion greater than for women: inheritance. The share for a male is twice that for the female (4:7) within a single family. The absolute inheritance for all men will not always be more than that for all women. The exact amount left depends on the family's wealth in the first place.

In addition, if verse 4:34 refers to a preference demonstrated in inheritance, then such a materialistic preference is also not absolute. This connection is often favoured because the other condition for *qiwamah* is that 'they spend of their property (for the support of women)'. Thus, there is a reciprocity between privileges and responsibilities. Men have the responsibility of paying out of their wealth for the support of women, and they are consequently granted a double share of inheritance. However, it cannot be overlooked that 'Many men interpret the above passage' as an unconditional indication of the preference of men over women. They assert that 'men were created by God superior to women (in strength and reason)'.

However, this interpretation is (*i*) unwarranted and (*ii*) inconsistent with other Islamic teachings the interpretation is unwarranted because there is no reference in the passage to male physical or intellectual superiority.

Faddala cannot be unconditional because verse 4:34 does not read 'they (masculine plural) are preferred over them (feminine plural)'. It reads *'ba'd* (some) of them over *ba'd* (others)'. The use of *ba'd* relates to what obviously has been observed in the human context. All men do not excel over all women in all manners. Some men excel over some women in some manners. Likewise, some women excel over some men in some manners. So, whatever Allah has preferred, it is still not absolute.

If 'what' Allah has preferred is restricted to the material (and specifically inheritance), then the extent and nature of the preference is explained by the Quran. Even if 'what' Allah has preferred is more than just the preference given in inheritance, it is, nevertheless, still restricted to 'some of them' over 'some others' by the wording in this context:

> 'men are '*qawwamun*' over women in matters where God gave some of the men more than *some* of the women, and in what the men spend of their money, then clearly men as a class are not '*qawwamun*' over women as a class.

However, further understanding of this distinction requires further explanation of *qawwamuna 'ala*. What does it mean, and what are the parameters of its application?

As for the meaning, Pickthall translates this as 'in charge of. Al-Zamakhshari says it means that 'men are in charge of the affairs of women'. Maududi says 'Men are the managers of the affairs of women because Allah has made the one superior to the other.' Azizah al-Hibri objects to any translation which implies that men are protectors or maintainers because 'The basic notion here is one of moral guidance and caring' and also because:

> only under extreme conditions (for example, insanity) does the Muslim woman lose her right to self-determination. Yet men have used this passage to exercise absolute authority over women. They also use it to argue for the male's divinely ordained and inherent superiority.

Some questions beg asking concerning the parameters of application: Are all men *qawwamuna 'ala* all women? Is it restricted to the family, such that the men of a family are *qawwumuna 'ala* the women of that family? Or, is it even more restricted, to the marital tie, such that only husbands are *qaunmmuna 'ala* wives? All of these possibilities have been given.

Generally, an individual scholar who considers *faddala* an unconditional preference of males over females does not restrict *qiwamah* to the family relationship but applies it to society at large. Men, the superior beings, are *qauwamuna 'ala* women, the dependent, inferior beings.

Sayyid Qutb, whose discussion I will consider at length, considers *qiwamah* an issue of concern for the family within society. He restricts verse 4:34, in some ways, then, to the relationship between the husband and the wife. He believes that providing for the females gives the male the privilege of being *qawwamuna 'ala* the female.

He gives *qiwamah* a decided dimension of material maintenance. The rationale behind restricting this verse to the context of husband and wife is partly due to the fact that the remainder of the verse discusses other details of concern to the marital relationship. In addition, the following verse uses the dual, indicating that it is concerned with the context between the two: the husband and wife. However, preceding verses discuss terms of relations between male members of society and female members of society.

I apply this verse to society at large but not on the basis of inherent superiority of men over women, or of Allah's preference of men over women. Rather, I extend the functional relationship, which Sayyid Qutb proposes between the husband and the wife, towards the collective good concerning the relationship between men and women in society at large. My main consideration is the responsibility and right of women to bear children.

Sayyid Qutb says, 'The man and the woman are both from Allah's creation and Allah never intends to oppress anyone from

His creation.' Both the man and the woman are members of the most significant institution of society, the family. The family is initiated by marriage between one man and one woman. Within the family, each member has certain responsibilities. For obvious biological reasons, a primary responsibility for the woman is childbearing.

The child-bearing responsibility is of grave importance: human existence depends upon it. This responsibility requires a great deal of physical strength, stamina, intelligence, and deep personal commitment. Yet, while this responsibility is so obvious and important, what is the responsibility of the male in this family and society at large? For simple balance and justice in creation, and to avoid oppression, his responsibility must be equally significant to the continuation of the human race. The Quran establishes his responsibility as *qiwamah*: seeing to it that the woman is not burdened with additional responsibilities which jeopardize that primary demanding responsibility that only she can fulfil.

Ideally, everything she needs to fulfil her primary responsibility comfortably should be supplied in society, by the male: this means physical protection as well as material sustenance. Otherwise, 'it would be a serious oppression against the woman'.

This ideal scenario establishes an equitable and mutually dependent relationship. However, it does not allow for many of today's realities. What happens in societies experiencing a population overload, such as China and India? What happens in capitalistic societies like America, where a single income is no longer sufficient to maintain a reasonably comfortable life-style? What happens when a woman is barren? Does she still deserve *qiwamah* like other women? What happens to the balance of responsibility when the man cannot provide materially, as was often the case during slavery and postslavery US?

All of these issues cannot be resolved if we look narrowly at verse 4:34. Therefore, the Quran must eternally be reviewed with regard to human exchange and mutual responsibility between males and females. This verse establishes an ideal obligation for men with regard to women to create a balanced and shared society. This responsibility is neither biological nor inherent, but it is valuable. An attitude inclined towards responsibility must be cultivated. It is easy enough to see the cases in which it has not been acquired.

However, such an attitude should not be restricted to mere material *qiwamah*. In broader terms, it should apply to the spiritual, moral, intellectual, and psychological dimensions as well. Such a perspective on *qiwamah* will allow men to truly fulfil their *khilafah* (trusteeship) on the earth, as ordained by Allah upon human creation. Such an attitude will overcome the competitive and hierarchical thinking which destroys rather than nurtures.

Men are encouraged to fulfil their trusteeship of the earth – especially in relationships with women, the child-bearers and traditional caretakers. What women have learned through bearing and caring for children, men can begin to experience, starting with their attitudes to and treatment of women.

Disruption of Marital Harmony

Finally, with regard to this verse, I will discuss whether this portion,

> So good women are *qanitat*, guarding in secret that which Allah has guarded. As for those from whom you fear [*nushuz*], admonish them, banish them to beds apart, and scourge them. Then, if they obey you, seek not a way against them means that a woman *must* obey her husband, and if she does not, he can beat her (here translated 'scourge'). I believe the passage intends to provide a means for resolving disharmony between husband and wife.

First, the word *qanitat* used here to describe 'good' women, is too often falsely translated to mean 'obedient', and then assumed to mean 'obedient to the husband'. In the context of the whole Quran, this word is used with regard to both males and females. It describes a characteristic or personality trait of believers towards Allah. They are inclined towards being co-operative with one another and subservient before Allah. This is clearly distinguished from mere obedience between created beings which the word *ta'a* indicates. Sayyid Qutb points out that this choice of words indicates that the Quran intends there to be a personal emotional response rather than the external 'following of orders' which the *ta'a* (obey) would suggest. As for the use of that word *ta'a* and the remainder of the verse, 'As for those (feminine plural) from whom you fear *nushuz*', it should first be noted that the word *nushuz* likewise is used with both males and females, although it has been defined differently for each. When applied to the wife, the term is usually defined as 'disobedience to the husband'. With the use of *ta'a* that follows. Others have said this verse indicates that the wife must obey the husband.

However, since the Quran uses *nushuz* for both the male and the female, it cannot mean 'disobedience to the husband'. Sayyid Qutb explains it as a state of disorder between the married couple. In case of disorder, what suggestions does the Quran give as possible solutions? There is:

1. A verbal solution: whether between the husband and wife (as here in verse 4:34) or between the husband and wife with the help of arbiters. If open discussion fails, then a more drastic solution;
2. Separation is indicated. Only in extreme cases a final measure;
3. The 'scourge' is permitted.

With regard to regaining marital harmony, the following points need to be raised. First, the Quran gives precedence to the state of order and emphasizes the importance of regaining it. In other words, it is not a disciplinary measure to be used for disagreement between spouses. Second, if the steps are followed in the sequential manner suggested by the Quran, it would seem possible to regain order before the final step. Third, even if the third solution is reached, the nature of the 'scourge' cannot be such as to create conjugal violence or a struggle between the couple because that is 'unIslamic'.

It appears that the first measure is the best solution offered and the one preferred by the Quran, because it is discussed in both instances of the word *nushuz*. It is also in line with the general Quranic principle of mutual consultation, or *shura*, being the best method for resolving matters between two parties. It is obvious that the Quran intends a resolution of the difficulties and a return to peace and harmony between the couple when it states: 'it is no sin for the two of them if they make terms of peace between themselves. *Peace is better.*' It is peace and 'making amends' that are the goals, not violence and forced obedience.

The second solution is, literally, to 'banish them to beds apart'. First, the significance of 'beds apart' is possible only when the couple continually shares a bed (unlike polygamy when husband and one wife do not), otherwise, this would not be a meaningful measure. In addition, 'beds apart' indicates that at least one night should pass in such a state. Therefore, it is a cooling-off period which would allow both the man and the woman, separately, to reflect on the problem at hand. As such, this measure also has equally mutual implications.

As one night apart can lead to many nights apart before any resolution is made, this separation could go on indefinitely. This does not indicate that a man should then begin to physically abuse his wife. Rather, it allows for a mutually found peaceable solution, or a continued separation divorce. Divorce also requires a waiting period, and beds apart is characteristic of that waiting. Thus, this measure can be taken as part of the overall context of irreconcilable differences between the married couple.

It cannot be overlooked, however, that verse 4:34 does state the third suggestion using the word *daraba,* 'to strike'. According to *Lisan al-'Arab* and Lanes's Lexicon, *daraba* does not necessarily indicate force or violence. It is used in the Quran, for example, in the phrase '*daraba Allah mathalan*' ('Allah *gives* or **sets** as an example'). It is also used when someone leaves, or 'strikes out' on a journey.

It is, however, strongly contrasted to the second form, the intensive, of this verb *darraba*: to strike repeatedly or intensely. In the light of the excessive violence towards women indicated in the biographies of the Companions and by practices condemned in the Quran (like female infanticide), this verse should be taken as prohibiting unchecked violence against females. Thus, this is not permission, but a severe restriction of existing practices.

Finally, the problem of domestic violence among Muslims today is not rooted in this Quranic passage. A few men strike their wives after completely following the Quranic suggestions for regaining marital harmony. The goal of such men is harm, not harmony. As such, after the fact, they cannot refer to verse 4:34 to justify their action.

Finally, the word *ta'a* in this verse needs a contextual consideration. It says 'if they obey (*ta'a*) you do not seek a way against them.' For the women, it is a conditional sentence, not a command. In the case of marriages of subjugation the norm for Muslims and non-Muslims at the time of the revelation wives were obedient to husbands. The husbands are commanded 'not to seek a way against' wives who are obedient. The emphasis is on the male's treatment of the female.

The Quran never orders a woman to obey her husband. It never states that obedience to their husbands is a characteristic of the 'better women', nor is it a prerequisite for women to enter the community of Islam. However, in marriages of subjugation, wives did obey their husbands, usually because they believed that a husband who materially maintains his family, including the wife, deserves to be obeyed. Even in such cases, the norm at the time of the revelation, no correlation is made that a husband should beat his wife into obedience. Such an interpretation has no universal potential, and contradicts the essence of the Quran and the established practices of the Prophet. It involves a severe misreading of the Quran to support the lack of selfconstraint in some men.

With regard to the relationship between maintenance and obedience, it can be observed that even husbands who are unable or unwilling to provide for their wives, believe they should be obeyed. In fact, this widespread characteristic of Muslim marriage is only one example of the association of men as natural leaders deserving obedience.

This belief in the need to obey the husband is a remnant of marriages of subjugation and is not exclusive to Muslim history. It has not progressed, although today couples seek partners for mutual emotional, intellectual, economic, and spiritual enhancement. Their compatibility is based on mutual respect and honour, not on the subservience of the female to the male. The family is seen as a unit of mutual support and social propriety, not an institution to enslave a woman to the man who buys her at the highest price and then sustains her material and physical needs only, with no concern for the higher aspects of human development.

If the Quran was only relevant to this single marriage type, it would fail to present a compatible model to the changing needs and requirements of developing civilizations worldwide. Instead, the Quranic text focuses on the marital norm at the time of revelation, and applies constraints on the actions of the husbands with regard to wives. In the broader context, it develops a mechanism for resolving difficulties through mutual or extended consultation and arbitration.

In conclusion, the Quran prefers that men and women marry. Within marriage, there should be harmony mutually built with love and mercy. The marriage tie is considered a protection for both the male and the female: 'They (feminine plural) are raiment for you (masculine plural) and you are raiment for them.' However, the Quran does not rule out the possibility of difficulty, which it suggests can be resolved. If all else fails, it also permits equitable divorce.

Significance of Context and Chronology in Quranic Social Reforms for Women

With regard to matters related to the subject of women, like divorce, it is apparent that the order in which verses were revealed in the Quran is more significant than for some other issues. The Quran responded to particular circumstances in Arabia at the time of the revelation. It is interesting to note that there are no references made in the Quran to specific rights, responsibilities and treatment of women until the Madinan period. 'They consult you concerning women. Say: Allah gives you decree concerning them. If a woman was mentioned in the Makkan period, she was a generic example for all humankind.

In the Madinan period of revelation, the particular social reforms introduced were related to the existing practices. In this respect, it is also interesting to note that most reforms were for the benefit of the females. No equivalent reforms benefiting the males were instituted, ostensibly because the existing androcentric norm greatly provided for male needs and wants. The Quranic responses were directed towards the pressing need for reforms regarding women.

Although the Quran responded to the need for reform with regard to women in the Madinan *surah*, these responses have implications for later communities. However, the particulars on which these verses focus provide clear indications about the norms in that context. In matters regarding gender, seventh-century Arabia was far from ideal. However, even Quranic reforms were not fully implemented. Such rapid changes met with some difficulty and reluctance. This observation has been made by twentieth-century authors with regard to some of the details in Quranic social reforms. We will examine these details and some of the modern observations below.

Divorce

Divorce is a lawful option for irreconcilable differences between married couples. However, the condition discussed above, which allows the male a *darajah* or an advantage over the female, has been pointed out as indicating an inequity in the Quran that is, men have the the power of repudiation. Unlike women, they may state: 'I divorce you' to begin the divorce procedure.

This power of the male has received some attention in modern Islamic legal reforms. In some instances, the male is required to come before the courts prior to such repudiation. In Malaysia, for example, both the husband and the wife who find difficulty in their marriage must come before the court to express their complaints. The court then acts as, or assigns, an arbiter for counselling.

Because this is similar to the traditional position for the woman, she faces no additional problem. However, when any stipulation is made in regard to what is believed to be a male privilege, men reject it as being too difficult; such a hardship should not be imposed over their rights, thus decreasing the empowerment they feel. Such a stipulation creates greater parity between the rights and responsibilities of both. The males are able to experience the matter from the point of view of the woman. Yet few men use this experience to provide for a more mutually beneficial solution.

Another consideration with regard to this verse again involves the evolution of marriages. Since women are no longer the subjects of marriage, but full, willing partners, our focus shifts to the broader Quranic wisdom which aims at harmonious reconciliation: 'it is no sin for the two of them if they make terms of peace between *themselves. Peace is better.*' 'Either take them back on equitable terms or set them free on equitable terms, do not take them back to injure them, or to take unfair advantage'.

Again, this consideration of repudiation is clear in view of the practices as they existed at the time of revelation, and not only for Muslim marriages. There is no indication that the unilateral right to repudiation needs be continued, or if continued, that it need be only for the husband. Although the Quran stipulates conditions for equitable separation or reconciliation, it does not make a rule that men *should* have uncontrolled power of repudiation. Men *did* have this power, over which the Quran places conditions and responsibilities.

Although the Quran makes no reference to women repudiating their husbands, it has been used to conclude that they cannot. This later conclusion was drawn in contrast to the custom in pre-Islamic times when a woman had simply to turn the entrance of her tent to face another direction to indicate her repudiation of conjugal relations with a man. There is no indication in the Quran that all power of repudiation must be removed from women.

What is important is mutual and peaceable reconciliation or separation. The Quran applies explicit measures to prevent abandonment and misuse of women, who were subject to the whims of husbands in marriage and divorce. It also stipulates measures of protection for the honour of both lines of parentage.

Patriarchy

The established order within the Arabian peninsula at the time of the revelation was patriarchal: a 'culture built on a structure of domination and subordination' which 'demands hierarchy'. It was a culture with an androcentric bias, one where the male and the male experience are looked upon as the norm. (With such a bias, statements like 'All men are created equal', are left to individual whims which can interpret the term 'men' as human beings including women, or as exclusive to male humans.)

In androcentric cultures, females are looked upon in terms of their utility to men, which is primarily reproductive. That such a cultural bias was the context of Quranic revelation has serious implications for later communities which try to understand the social ideal the Quran was attempting to establish in that community. The Qur'an's accommodation of various social contexts has been viewed as implying support for the particular social order that existed in seventh-century Arabia.

Some argue that Islam is essentially a variation of patriarchal ideology. Others argue that Islam is above worldly ideology, including Patriarchy; for as the word of God, it transcends all ideology. Among these, we can distinguish two groups: those who believe that Islam as it is today is fair and just to women, and those who believe that Islam *as it is practised today* is utterly patriarchal, but that *true* Islam is not.

The implication of this patriarchal context must be understood in relation to the greater Quranic principles and their ultimate intent of harmonious and equitable relationships in society. It is this ultimate Quranic intent which reveals its true 'spirit'. Muslim thinkers in the twentieth century use this Quranic 'spirit' to argue against literal application of some Quranic statements.

It is clear through the chronological progression of the text, that the Quran sets out guidelines. Following these guidelines to their natural conclusions will not lead backwards in time to the same level of difficulty experienced by the first community. Rather, the Quranic guidelines should lead the various communities towards progressive change within the context of universal Quranic guidance. To restrict future communities to the social shortcomings of any single community even the original community of Islam—would be a severe limitation of that guidance.

I propose that the way to believe in 'the whole of the book' is to recognize that 'spirit' of the book and accept its worldview, vision, and ultimate intent. In examining the Quran, we need 'to accurately determine the rationales behind its statements, comments and injunctions'. 'Even when the reason for a certain command is not explicitly stated, it is not difficult to guess it.' Thus, to arrive at that ultimate intent requires the same level of pure commitment, devotion, and intellectual striving as the members of the earliest community. However, in the context of a technologically advanced world, such a commitment will require a broader, global perspective activated in, but not limited to, one's local context.

Although in some instances the Quran proposed immediate abolition of certain ill practices, most of the time it advocated gradual reform. Few reforms were completely implemented before the final revelation. 'If all these customs had been entirely abolished by God, several problems would have ensued, not many of His commandments would have been obeyed'. However, the means for completing others were provided for by the flexibility and intent of the text itself. 'It was considered wise not to totally abolish some of the reprehensible traditions such as polygamy [or slavery], as there were so many difficulties involved.'

In particular, some reformation which benefited the status of women was allowed to progress slowly because of the contexts in which these changes were to take place.

God's permissibility only showed man's cruel heart, his inability to submit to truth and justice, and his immoral character, acquired from the worst pre-Islamic customs. Had it not been for the viciousness in his mind, his misguided soul and cruel heart, God would not have granted him then such allowances that He disliked and which were meant to vanish with time.

It is continuing that natural evolution in society which is indicated in the Quran that explains why many Muslim countries have instituted further legal and social reforms with regard to women. These reforms operate outside the literal content of some Quranic passages and make modifications on the basis of greater Quranic intent with respect to such issues as repudiation, polygamy, inheritance, and the rules for witnessing, etc.

Polygamy

Many Muslim nations which now consider polygamy unconstitutional have justified such changes in legislation on the basis of the overall Quranic perspective on marriage, as well as on modern Islamic perspectives of marriage. The marriage of subjugation at the time of revelation was premised on the need for females to be materially provided for by some male. The ideal male for a female child was the father, and for the adult female, the husband. This economic perspective of marriage as indicated by several verses discussed above will also be reviewed here with regard to polygamy.

If you fear that you will not deal justly with the orphans, marry women of your choice, two, three or four. But *if you fear that you will not be able to do justly (with them), then only one*, to prevent you from doing justice.

First, this verse is about treatment of orphans. Some male guardians, responsible for managing the wealth of orphaned female children, were unable to refrain from unjust management of that wealth. One solution suggested to prevent mismanagement was marriage to the female orphans. On the one hand, the Quran limited this number to four, and on the other hand, the economic responsibilty of maintaining the wife would counterbalance the access to the wealth of the orphaned female through the responsibility of management. However, most proponents of polygamy seldom discuss it within the context of just treatment of orphans.

In fact, as far as they are concerned, the only measurement of justice between wives is material: can a man equally support more than one wife? This is an extension of the archaic idea of marriages of subjugation, because fairness is not based on quality of time, equality in terms of affection, or on spiritual, moral, and intellectual support. These general terms of social justice are not considered with regard to just treatment with wives.

It is especially clear that this verse is concerned with justice: dealing justly, managing funds justly, justice to the orphans, and justice to the wives, etc. Justice is the focus of most modern commentaries concerned with polygamy. In the light of verse 4:129—'You are never able to be just and fair as between women ...' —many commentators assert that monogamy is the preferred marital arrangement of the Quran. Surely, it is impossible to attain the Quranic ideal with regard to mutuality ('They [feminine plural] are raiment for you [masculine plural] and you are raiment for them', and with regard to building between them 'love and mercy', when the husband-father is split between more than one family.

Finally, with regard to three common justifications given for polygamy, there is no direct sanction in the Quran. One is financial: in the context of economic problems such as unemployment, a financially capable man should care for more than one wife. Again, this assumes that all women are financial burdens: reproducers, but not producers. In today's world a lot of women neither have nor need male supporters. For one thing, it is no longer accepted that only men can work, do work, or are the most productive workers, in all circumstances. With regard to work outside the home, *i.e.* paid employment, the market is based on productivity. Productivity in turn is based on a number of factors, and gender is only one of them. Surely, polygamy is no simple solution to complex economic problems.

Another rationale given for a man having more than one wife centres on the woman who is unable to have children. Again, there is no mention of this as a rationale for polygamy in the Quran. However, the desire for children is natural. Thus, consideration for the barren man and the barren woman should not exclude either from the chance of marriage, nor from the care and upbringing of children. What possible solution is mutually available when the wife or husband is sterile and the couple cannot have their own children?

In a world of war and devastation, there are still orphaned Muslim (and other) children who would benefit from the love and care of childless couples. Perhaps caring for all of the earth's children might be practised by Muslims in the light of global catastrophes still unresolved. One's own blood relations are important, but perhaps not in terms of the final judgement of one's ability to care and nurture.

Finally, the third rationale given for polygamy not only has no sanction in the Quran, but is clearly un-Quranic as it attempts to sanction men's unbridled lust: that if a man's sexual needs cannot be satisfied by one wife, he should have two. Presumably, if his lust is greater than that, he should have three, and on until he has four. Only after this fourth are the Quranic principles of self-constraint, modesty, and fidelity finally to be exercised.

As self-constraint and fidelity are required at the onset for the wife, these moral virtues are equally significant for the husband. It is clear that the Quran does not stress a high, civilized level for women while leaving men to interact with others at the basest level. Otherwise, the mutual responsibility of *khilafah* (trusteeship) would be left to one half of humanity while the other half remains near the animal state.

Witness

Another consideration in contemporary discussion on the issue of women in the Quran focuses on the woman as a potential witness. Is one male witness equal to two female witnesses and, therefore, one male equivalent to, or as good as, two females absolutely? In the related verse, a 'record in writing' 'when a debt is contracted' calls for two witnesses, 'if two men be (not at hand) then a man and two women, of such as you approve as witnesses, so that if the one errs (*tudilla*) the other can remind her'. In the wording of this verse, both women are not called as witnesses. One woman is designated to 'remind' the other: she acts as corraborator. Although the women are two, they each function differently.

In addition, there are some contextual considerations regarding the need for more than a single witness in the first place. The purpose is to see to it that there is no error intentionally or unintentionally regarding the terms of the contract. Fazlur Rahman takes exception to the application of the literal wording of the verse in all future transactions as follows:

> . . . since the testimony of a woman being considered of less value than that of a man was dependent upon her weaker power of memory concerning financial matters, when women become conversant with such matters—with which there is not only nothing wrong but which is for the betterment of society their evidence can equal that of men.

Thus the verse is significant to a particular circumstance which can and has become obsolete. However, I have found no commentary which considers the matter of intentional error. The call for two witnesses 'of such as you approve as witnesses' in the first place indicates an attempt to prevent corruption. If one goes wrong, or is persuaded to give untrue testimony, the other is there to support the terms of the contract. However, considering that women could be coerced in that society, if one witness was female, she would be easy prey for some male who wanted to force her to disclaim her testimony. When there are two women, they can support each other especially in view of the term chosen: if she (*tudilla*) 'goes astray', the other can (*tudhakkira*) 'remind' her, or 'recall her attention' to the terms of agreement. The single unit which comprises two women with distinct functions not only gives each woman significant individual worth, but also forms a united front against the other witness.

In addition, one male witness plus this two-female unit, does not equate to a two-for-one formula because otherwise, four female witnesses could replace two male witnesses. Yet, the Quran does not provide this alternative. Despite the social constraints, at the time of revelation inexperience and coercion of a woman was nevertheless considered a potential witness.

Even at that time of severe social, financial, and experiential constraints, the Quran recognized the potential of women's resources. In this modern era, such revolutionary consideration of women's potential should lead to greater promotion of her contributions to a just and moral social system, and end exploitation of her and others in society. Such a social system can be attained only through the encouragement of learning and experience for the male and the female.

Finally, the consideration regarding witnesses in this verse is specific to certain types of financial contracts. It was not meant to be applied as a general rule. Whenever the Quran does not specify gender in terms of a witness, androcentric interpretation concludes it to mean the male witness, exclusively. As such, the formula applied requires twice the number of females not only for witnessing but for other aspects of woman's participation as well.

This limitation regarding financial transactions does not apply in other matters. The call for two women and one man for witnessing financial contracts is not a general rule for women's participation, nor even for all witnessing. Other requests for witnesses should be for unspecified gender. Therefore, anyone deemed capable of witnessing has the right to be one.

Inheritance

The mathematical formula of two-to-one has been albeit erroneously reinforced through oversimplification of the Quranic discussions regarding inheritance. Although the initial Quranic statement, in verses 4:11-12, makes 'the share of the male equivalent to the portion of two female (siblings)', a complete look at this same verse enumerates a variety of proportional divisions between males and females. In fact, if there is one female child, her share is half the inheritance. In addition, the consideration of parents, siblings, distant relatives, as well as offspring is discussed in a variety of different combinations to indicate that the proportion for the female of one-half the proportion for the male is not the sole mode of property division, but *one* of several proportional arrangements possible.

Such variety of possibilities emphasizes two points with regard to inheritance: (1) In no way are females, including distant ones, to be disinherited. This is especially true for the pre-Islamic customs still prevailing today, which give the inheritance of even female offspring to some male relative, no matter how distant. (2) All distribution of the inheritance between the remaining relatives must be equitable. According to these verses, such 'equity' in distribution of inheritance must take the actual *naf'a* (benefit) of the bereft into consideration.

The full extent of the Quranic provision requires a look at other details which can lead to a redistribution of the inheritance according to the circumstances of the deceased and of those who inherit. The division of inheritance requires a look at all of the members, combinations and benefits. For example, if in a family of a son and two daughters, a widowed mother is cared for and supported by one of her daughters, why should the son receive a larger share? This might not be the decision if we look at the actual *naf'a* of those particular offspring.

The Quran does not elaborate all possibilities. However, by providing a variety of scenarios, it is clear enough that many combinations can and do exist, which must be considered for the equitable distribution of inheritance. Finally, one-third of the wealth can be bequeathed, with no restrictions upon whom the beneficiary is and without decreasing the divisions of the remaining wealth. In fact, the proposal is quite flexible provided, of course, equity is met.

In short, the matter of inheritance involves these considerations; (1) distribution to both male and female surviving relatives; (2) some wealth can be bequeathed; (3) consideration must be given to the circumstance of the bereft, their benefit to the deceased, and the benefits of the wealth inherited.

Male Authority

Although the basis of Quranic discussion on society was particular to the existing system, it also gives general principles from which to derive solutions to social problems in other contexts. With regard to authority, the prevailing attitudes were patriarchal. As with other matters in society, the Quranic solutions to social problems reflect the prevailing attitudes in ancient Arabia.

The general principle for leadership in the Quran is similar to the rule for fulfilling any task, that it should be filled by the one 'best suited'. That person is the one best suited on the basis of whatever qualifications or characteristics are necessary to fulfil that task: biology, psychology, education, finance, experience, etc. This principle works in a number of complex social arrangements: the family, society at large and leadership.

With regard to leadership, the ancient (and modern) Arabian patriarchy yields certain advantages for men. Certainly where males had public privileges, experiences, and other advantages, they were best suited to operate in the political and financial arena. It was erroneously concluded that men would always have the advantages that would make them most suitable for leadership. Yet these advantages were not restricted to men in the Quran. Provided the woman has the motivation, opportunities should be made available. Her capacities to become 'best suited' for a number of tasks not common fourteen centuries ago should have greatly increased by now.

Despite this difference in opportunities between men and women, even at the time of revelation, there is nothing implied or stated in the Quran which supports the opinion that males are natural leaders. Even in the context of patriarchal Arabia, the Quran gives the example of a female ruler. Bilqis, she is depicted extremely well in the Quran. In fact, other than the prophets, she is the *only* ruler in the Quran who is given favourable consideration. The Quran refers to her characteristics of wisdom and independence as a leader.

The Quran does not restrict the female from being in authority, either over other women or over both women and men. However, there is the implication that the Quran inclines towards seeing necessary tasks fulfilled in society in the most efficient manner. Neither male nor female will be equally beneficial in every situation. To force even modern patriarchal societies to submit before a female ruler would be detrimental to the harmonious welfare of that society.

However, choosing the one best suited for the tasks at hand is a dynamic process. Continual assessment of a current situation should yield sufficient information about the qualification for fulfilling any task. A more independent and insightful woman might better lead a people into their future endeavours. Similarly, a husband may be more patient with children. If not predominantly, then perhaps temporarily, such as when the wife falls ill, he should be allowed to fulfil that task. Just as leadership is not an eternal characteristic of all males, child caring is not an eternal characteristic of all females.

Child Care

Again the prevailing system in many societies has determined that the responsibility of caring for the children is appropriate to the female. The convenience of this in many families and with many women who have a 'feminine' temprament inclined towards nurturing has reinforced this man-made determination as if it were inherent.

The Quran gives rights to both parents with regard to the children and equally allows for their emotional attachment: 'A mother should not be made to suffer because of her child, nor should he to whom the child is born (be made to suffer) because of his child'. It allows for the mother to suckle a child, but leaves it to her own discretion: 'Mothers shall suckle their children for those who wish to complete the suckling'. If instead a couple or a mother decides 'to give [the] children out to nurse, it is no sin for you'. Thus the basic nurturing of even the very young child is optional.

Yet, the tendency has always been to attach all forms of child, care and in addition all forms of housework to the woman. Although this division of labour suits some families, especially when the father is working outside the home and provides materially for his family, it is, nevertheless, only one solution and does not have explicit Quranic ordinance.

In families where both husband and wife are providing for the material maintenance of the family, it is an unfair burden for the woman to be solely charged with all housework. If she has managed to increase her good deeds, then there are similar opportunities for the man to increase his by participating more in the housework and child care. In addition, this demonstrates to the children the ultimate Quranic system of evaluation which does not specify the deed: 'Whoever does good, whether male or female and is a believer, all such will enter Paradise'.

Such a flexible, integrated, and dynamic system of co-operation benefits a multiplicity of societies and family types. It places proper recognition on the single-parent households of today. If it is headed by a woman, then full responsibility, authority, and *qiwamah* are placed on her shoulders. Similarly, daughters may also assume the responsibilities of extended relatives and disabled husbands.

When the Quran is viewed in its entirety and not atomistically, the concern for the role of woman in society and the potential she has, would necessarily be broadened from the demeaning and meaningless existence which renders her no greater than a procreating animal able to function only as a domestic servant. Likewise, her skills and participation on the home front would be acknowledged as significant and meaningful, such that all who aim at performing good deeds would rush to fulfil the same tasks.

If the aim of Islamic society is to fulfil the intentions of the Quran with regard to the rights, responsibilities, potentialities, and capacities of all its earnest members, then those who truly believe in the Quran would equally wish for the woman the opportunities for growth and productivity which they demand for the man. The man would equally be charged with nurturing and caring for the family over and above attending to its material concerns. In short, both would be well-rounded and mutually beneficial to each other, to the family, and therefore to society at large. Only then is the true potential of the *khilafah* cultivated. The family acts as the initial arena of practice. Surely, as the Prophet says, 'The best of you is he who is best to his family'.

2

Fundamentalism and Women's Rights

Introduction

The world have marked the emergence of the "world community" with a "new world order." This order is based on a democratic model of the polity and on human rights as defined in the *Universal Declaration of Human Rights* adopted by the first fifty-one members of the United Nations in 1948. Although the intrinsic good intentions of such norms seem beyond question, the very historical process by which they have been expanded geographically poses the fundamental conceptual and methodological problems of the universality of any humanly devised norms.

The popularity of such gatherings coincides by and large with the end of colonial dependencies and the emergence of postcolonial social dynamics in about three-quarters of world societies. Although the colonies had been established and managed by Europeans whose humanist tradition and Industrial Revolution experiences included democratic ideas and human rights, for them the colonial experience was one of confrontation and destruction rather than of civilization and liberation. Africa and the Middle East are still grappling with the immense discrepancies between the institutional and the normative dynamics that developed in the aftermath of national liberations.

Recalling colonial history is not meant here as yet another rant against colonialism or imperialism but is meant to situate historically the emergence of concepts such as "world community" and "universal human rights" and to identify the conditions that surround reactions today to universal programmes by various social groups. It is necessary to emphasize that in the West these norms were the result of centuries of often painful transformations and debates. It took the Inquisition, the theological rifts within Christianity, the Enlightenment, the French and American revolutions, colonialism, and two world wars for the concepts of human dignity and human rights to emerge as a universal enfranchisement. Only late and reluctantly did this enfranchisement encompass Western women, colonized peoples, African Americans, and South Africans. The Western powers who advocated human rights were themselves ambiguous about their application the same powers that today are urging world societies to adopt this normative system without delay.

The long and painful process of thinking and discussion that produced humanist norms in the West is denied to other societies. The universalization of modernization processes did not provide opportunities for local civil bodies to debate, formulate, and implement their own notions of modernity. This inductivist stance has produced resistance and questions in Muslim societies as elsewhere. Indeed, the adoption of a discourse as complex and comprehensive as that of human rights should not be taken lightly. The export of human rights is carried on under conditions of post-cold war globalization, and this is as problematic as the model of economic and social development introduced by the newly independent states of the early 1960s. The procedures of the changes were not derived from local developments and were not coordinated with local cultural practices but obeyed the immediate demands for particular social relations within the unitarian nation-state and international business interests. Little was said then about the democratization of the polity and of society, let alone about human rights. It is not surprising that the developmental philosophy of these induced policies produced strong reactions.

Lessons from Dar al-Islam

The ambiguities in applications of human rights by their original champions pose the problem of credibility. Why is it that the very powers that had shown so little concern with the rights of others to human dignity yesterday, today demand respect for human rights from everybody? How is one to reconcile the skepticism toward human rights as a political programme with other elabourate discourses with universalist claims such as the Islamic one? How is one to do justice to the great variety of reactions to the introduction of the human rights discourse in culturally diverse Muslim societies?

The importance of the recognition of this diversity is emphasized in three prominent historical moments in the encounter between Muslim and Western ideas and their implication for the issue of human rights:

- The Arab cultural Renaissance (*nahdha*) of the late nineteenth and early twentieth centuries.
- The culturalist religious Awakening (*sahwa*) of the Islamic Brotherhood and related organizations since the 1950s.
- The struggle for a culture of humanism within the "City of Islam" by Muslim women.

The reaction of the thinkers of the Arab-Islamic Renaissance to the import of European Christians' ideas was extremely favourable, for it was expected to bring liberating notions and strategies that could help to end the tyranny of the decadent, stifling Ottoman monarchy. Mohamed Abdu and al-Afghani, for example, visited various European cities, self-confident and rooted in their rich theological and intellectual tradition, to find out about the societies of the West that reportedly had successfully reconciled matter and mind by liberating the individual. Their writings exemplify the Muslim intellectual curiosity that started the Arab-Islamic enlightenment quest with hope and vigour. This quest was stifled by the military and administrative colonial powers that soon occupied the region.

By the end of the colonial period not much was left of the lively encounters between intellectual equals that Abdu and al-Afghani had enjoyed in their travels. In their place among Arab intellectuals were a profound confusion, paradoxically created in the wake of the forceful expansion of the Western educational system, and a bitter feeling of loss and self-doubt. In this intellectual climate the newly established postcolonial civil societies generated various debates from within about human rights as citizens' rights (rather than as universal rights). This can be viewed as a second attempt to create a renaissance from within Muslim societies in the late 1950s and early 1960s. It, too, was crushed, this time by techno-military elites within the new states, posing as sole interpreters of the ideal society that they planned to establish. By then most regimes had signed various international conventions, including the *Universal Declaration of Human Rights*, although the majority of their populations never had heard about them and were far from benefiting from them.

The more recent culturalist claim of Islamic revivalism emerged from the confusion induced by unitarian nationalism. As the ideological eclecticism of the new states' elites legitimized the systematic violation of citizens' rights, salvation politics seemed the last resort for the increasingly younger, dissatisfied populations of Muslim societies. Their legitimation had to come from an authoritative, transcendental source. Unlike the earlier Renaissance thinkers who were trained in the classical traditions of Islamic institutions, the Awakening ideologues since the 1950s had a double education, that of state-run schools and the universities of the West, which alienated them from their own traditions. For example, Abbassi Madani, the leader of the main Islamist party, the Islamic Salvation Front (which had won the municipal election in 1990 and was expected to win the legislative elections in 1992), is himself a product of the secular educational system in the 1950s and London University in the late 1970s. He characterized what he saw as the basic principles of the Western epistemological tradition as doubt and chaos in human spirits. Atheist ideology has replaced faith in the West, leaving the individual in a quagmire of doubts. This idea indirectly expresses concern for the increasing blurring of gender roles and the increasing allegiance to the state as the regulator of society.

The adherents of the Awakening movement identify the West not only as a cultural invader bringing estrangement but as detrimental to the divine order, which relies on a clearly defined gender-based cosmology. In Algeria the emergence of the so-called Islamic fundamentalist movement as a primarily culturalist claim coincided with the access of thousands of Algerian households to European and American cable television programmes. These were simultaneously watched and condemned strongly by Muslim youths, who criticized especially what they perceived as immodest behaviour between men and women in films and the high profiles of female characters. Their opinion was formed without the mediation of the cultural commissars of the administration. It was heard and it created debates in all levels of the society.

Postulates of gender equality and individuation of women have triggered passionate debates and resistance to the implementation of laws and programmes designed to achieve these goals. The implementation of the Beijing Platform for Action likely will meet with similar objections, especially so as the notion of human rights is rejected altogether; both "human" and "individual" in this humanist-universalist discourse are seen as faithless, non-Islamic concepts. But the discussion of this issue has not ended. It is shifting to the discussion of the rights of the human being as a believer in the context of all kinds of global developments.

Lessons from the City of Women

In Muslim societies women's rights as human rights constitute the single most important topic of debate and confrontation between state and civil society and among different groups within the civil society. Indeed, the problematic of rights is embedded in the debates over citizenry. For example, the political riots of October 1988 started a period in the country when an active citizenry with highly divergent social ties and interests started to press its claims. Islamist fundamentalists, cultural Berberists, and secular feminists all voiced demands. The 1989 constitution recognized all claims but ambiguously declared the state to be both religious and secular. The first officially recognized political parties were those with agendas to build an ideal Islamic society: the Islamic Salvation Front, with a programme of establishing a pure Islamic social order, had mass appeal and attracted young men and women; Hamas, *Harakat al-mujtama' al-islami,* used a more moderate rhetoric about the gradual establishment of the Islamic society and was more popular with older professionals; Nahdha, a reformist group, was active only locally.

The culturalist Berberist movement, which demands the recognition of the native languages of Algeria as national languages, is divided into two groups: the Front of Socialist Forces, Front des

Forces Socialistes (FFS), with a nationalist agenda; the Gathering for Culture and Democracy, Rassemblement Culture et Democracie (RCD), active locally in the northern Kabylia region and in some urban areas.

Of all groups it was the women's movement of the early 1980s that first drew attention to the contradictions within the state ideology which, on the one hand, granted enfranchisement since 1963 in various versions of the constitution to all citizens and, on the other hand, denied women decision power in matters of family and personal life. The early feminists were the first to practice civil disobedience when small groups of professional women and women war veterans publicly protested in front of the then National Assembly in 1981 and 1983. Their protests led to the adoption of the Family Code of 1984.

The reaction of the City of Women to family legislation based on extreme patriarchal injunctions remains the most radical expression of modernity in Algerian society. The unpublished literature produced by the various women's associations at that time very much is about human rights as citizen rights: the right to participate in all affairs of the society, to make decisions in the private and the public realms. The ideals of equal citizenry, free individual expression, allegiance to a national society are to be realized in a modern republic. Before the women's protests, these issues were blurred within the populist social contract of Algerian socialism.

The ambiguity was also debated by Islamists who contested the state's monopoly over the political life in the nation and advocated the establishment of an Islamic republic. This political programme appealed to masses of young people between eighteen and twenty-four years of age (in a society where 70 per cent of the population is younger than thirty), including many young women students, who found in this ideology a comforting affirmation of femininity that the emphasis on genderless citizenship of the feminists lacked.

However much traditional patriarchal ideals and practices are expressed in these agendas, they give young women the chance to exercise political choice, to transcend the confinement of close kin networks. Their participation in a political movement is an act of active citizenship. It enables them to become involved in the interpretation of the scriptural legacy and in more or less learned theology and encourages them to acquire skills in debates and argumentation. The cumulative effects of these activities and opportunities cannot be ignored. Eventually, these young women in Islamist movements will come to interpret scriptures and laws to their benefit and will become articulate in pressing for their advances.

These activities are an exercise of human rights, including debates about women's rights, that come from within rather than from outside, from lived experience within certain ideological and political circumstances rather than from an Enlightenment that posited universal rights that ignored women and many other groups until those groups started to fight for their own rights.

After family laws and personal status laws in Algeria had been changed to conform to a particular version of Sharia law in the early 1980s, feminists and Islamists alike were alarmed. Feminists criticized the de facto treatment of women as minors with no legal voice in decisions affecting marriage, divorce, or child custody, for example, while Islamists demanded that Sharia law replace all laws, not only those pertaining to the family. Even within the Islamist movements young women used their authority as members of religiously grounded groups to challenge restrictive paternal authority and to insist on their right to choose a political stance. Women found themselves the centre of arguments and included in confrontations and debates. Thus, the struggle for humanism within the City of Islam was taken up by women. The opinions of young militants of religious parties, despite their backing by impressive religious ahistorical justifications, failed to impress a great many women. During the period between the general civil disobedience protests of October 1988 and the army intervention in January 1992 thriving debates took place and various political and ideological positions about women's issues and including women were formulated. Women war veterans and young, self-declared secularist feminists faced representatives of the Islamic parties, notably Abassi Madani, on television shows in heated debates on any and all subjects.

After the Arab Renaissance and the Awakening movements, this was the third most important moment in Algeria's modern history: social actors, facing each other directly, without the mediation of some myths of unifying nationalism, and fighting over their rights and responsibilities, that is, over human rights. These are painful debates, but they are necessary for the kind of liberation that can be sustained and can flourish within the cultural boundaries of a society. Only this way can contestations lead to new understandings of human rights of Muslims and can negotiations lead to compromises that will hold.

The Beijing conference, the NGO discussions, and the U.N. forum witnessed various groups with different programmes come to terms with each other over the issue of the philosophy underlying women's emancipation. The total and comprehensive enfranchisement and empowerment of women are moral and structural imperatives in today's societies, but they cannot be demanded from outside. They must be demanded from within, forged in debates, in conflict and consensus in every Muslim society. Those seriously concerned with the implementation of the Beijing Platform for Action must encourage debates in Muslim countries over the issues raised in the platform to create the momentum of local engagement and activism without which social change benefiting women is difficult to achieve.

3

Quranic View of Woman

Introduction

The Quranic treatment of the subject of woman must include a review of the roles fulfilled by the female characters mentioned, whether explicitly or indirectly, in the text. Vrhat is the significance of these women in the circumstance in which they have been mentioned? Are they mentioned for women in particular or for all readers, to fulfil the Quranic purpose of guidance? Does the Quran propose a single uniform role that women should play in society?

I propose that the Quran does not support a specific and stereotyped role for its characters, male or female. The roles of the women who have been referred to in the Quran fall into one of three categories:

1. A role which represents the social, cultural, and historical context in which that individual woman lived without compliment or critique from the text.
2. A role which fulfils a universally accepted (*i.e.* nurturing or caretaking) female function, to which exceptions can be made and have been made even in the Quran itself.
3. A role which fulfils a non-gender specific function, *i.e.* the role represents human endeavours on the earth and is cited

in the Quran to demonstrate this specific function and not the gender of the performer, who happens to be a woman.

Quran Teaches the Reader through the Events in the Lives

The Quran is a moral history. It proposes moral values, which are 'extrahistorical' and 'transcendental' in nature, such that 'their location at a point in history does not exhaust their practical impact or, one might say their meaning'. The time-span for the Quran is not limited to this present world. It is not limited to observable facts and events. It includes not only information about the actual events which occurred, but also about the intent behind such events and about their psychological effect. We have no sure indication for many accounts to determine if they are historical or metaphorical, literal or allegorical.

There are two significant concerns in our look at female characters mentioned in the Quran: the Makkan and Madinan chronological periods of revelation, and the references to known historical events. It has been argued that the detailed discussions during the Madinan period indicate accommodation towards the existing community and in some instances limit the universal objectives of the Quran. To overcome such a limitation, Muslim jurists and thinkers should give precedence to the universal revelations from the Makkan period.

A hermeneutical model which derives basic ethical principles for further developments and legal considerations by giving precedence to general statements rather than particulars could solve many problems in application. However, there is no indication that all general principles were introduced in the Makkan period and all Madinan revelations were specific. Thus, although an analysis is needed which gives precedence to general principles over specific statements, it will not necessarily follow that this will be only a chronological consideration of the difference between Makkan and Madinan passages.

As for references in the Quran to well-known historical events, a significant part of Quranic exegesis is knowledge of *asbab alnuzul*, often translated as the 'reason(s) for revealing (a particular verse or verses)', should more accurately be the 'occasions upon which (or, sometimes, because of which) a certain verse was revealed'. This distinction broadens the application of underlying principles.

If the 'reason' for a verse is a specific incident, then the universal 'extrahistorical' nature of the Quran is removed. It becomes a history book in the limited sense of a record of events. However, remembering that the Quran was revealed at a particular time in history and within a certain social context helps one to understand the significance of some verses, without implying in any way a restriction of the Quranic principles to that context.

The Quran is quite selective about historical details which help to fulfil its purpose of universal guidance. It promotes the application of the precepts exemplified by those characters mentioned in the verses rather than merely gives a record of the events themselves. For if the reader assumes he is reading a record, what he reads may be insignificant to his own life. The Quran gives just enough – but not too much – details in order to facilitate its purpose.

The Quran does not distract the reader from the moral principles by overburdening him with details about particular individuals. Thus, a process of interpretation that gets at the significance of the references to particular characters needs to be applied. Fazlur Rahman proposes that 'the process of interpretation consists of a double movement from the present situation to the Quranic times, then back to the present' because the Quran is the divine response, through the Prophet's mind, to the moral-social situation of the Prophet's Arabia. The Quran and the genesis of the Islamic community occurred in the light of history and against a social-historical background. The Quran is a response to that situation, and for the most part it consists of moral, religious, and social pronouncements that respond to specific problems confronted in concrete historical situations.

In particular, he defines that double movement of interpretation to be from the specific a study of the historical situation of the problem which the statement addresses, in order to understand its import or meaning to the general 'generalize the specific answers and enunciate them as statements of general moral-social objectives that can be "distilled" from specific text in the light of the socio-historical background.'

Significance of the Women Mentioned or Referred to in the Quran

I have tried to demonstrate the significance of particular female characters mentioned in the Quran to the modern context, because 'if the results of understanding fail in application now, then either there has been a failure to assess the present situation correctly, or a failure in understanding the Quran.' To do so, however, I first demonstrate the significance of these women in the context of the text.

I have divided all of the women whether mentioned explicitly or referred to in passing into two major categories. Those with no independent significance I have placed into category 1. This category I have divided into two levels: those with very slight mention and those women who performed functions characteristic of the 'proper' role for a woman. At both levels the women are inconsequential to the overall Quranic purpose of guidance, but are necessary for the coherence of a story or event. At the second level of this category, the women functioned in accordance to the social constraints of their particular circumstance. The Quran does not portray them as universal 'examples'.

Quranic examples provide concrete information about the application of moral precepts. In order to apply the moral principles of the Quran, a reader must have some practical understanding. Practices are rooted in contexts. Readers who interpret the significance of the women cited in the Quran often come to the text with notions of appropriate functions for women. When these are supported on the surface of the Quranic portrayal, they do not look further at the examples. This has led to a great deal of oversimplifications and contradictions when the perspective of the individual exegete is superimposed on to the Quran itself.

The Quran is not a manual of directives which only commands the individual reader to perform certain actions or fulfil particular characteristics. By citing concrete events, it makes conceptual ideas tangible. The female and male characters are particularly important to demonstrate certain ideas about guidance. The characters and events in the Quran should always be examined in the light of this overall goal.

It should be noted that all references to female characters in the Quran use an important cultural idiosyncrasy which demonstrates respect for women. Except for Mary, the mother of Jesus, they are never called by name. Most are wives and the Quran refers to them by means of a possessive construction (the idafah) containing one of the Arabic words for wife: *imra'ah* (woman), *nisa'* (women), or *zawj* (spouse, or mate) pl. *azwaj*, and the name of a particular male; for example, the *imra'ah* of Imran, or the *zawj* of Adam.

Even an unmarried woman or one whose husband is not mentioned is linked with some male: Ukht-Musa, the sister of Moses; Ukht-Harun, sister of Aaron, another name for Mary; Umm-Musa; the mother of Moses. However, this particular manifestation of respect is restricted to that context. The general principle that women should be addressed respectfully is intended for those who read the Quran at other times.

The Quran presents examples through several methods. A specific event is spoken of in general terms and the general application of the principles which underlie the verse is emphasized. 'The Quranic *ayah* is intended as a continual reality independent of the individuals (mentioned), and the individuals are merely examples of this reality.'

Other verses include information about very specific incidents, but the moral lesson to be drawn from the incidents can be generally applied once they have been interpreted. 'The method the Quran uses in this type of incident is to describe the activity which occurred and to describe with that activity, the apparent and hidden legalities (to be deduced from that incident).'

In *Surat-al-Tahrim*, the Quran points directly to some women as models:

> Allah cites an example for those who disbelieve: the wife of Noah and the wife of Lot, who were (respectively) under two of our righteous servants, yet they were betrayed them so that they (the husbands) were of no avail to them against Allah and it was said (to them): 'Enter the fire along with those who enter!'

And Allah sets forth an example to those who believe: the wife of Pharaoh when she said 'My Lord! Build for me a home with You in the garden, and deliver me from Pharaoh and his work, and deliver me from evil doing folk.

And Mary, daughter of Imran whose body was chaste, therefore we breathed therein something of *Our ruh*. She put faith in the words of her Lord and His scriptures and was among the *qanitin*.

These 'examples' which Allah specifically 'cites' for the readers are usually interpreted as being exclusively for women. Yet the verse identifies them as examples for 'those who believe' and 'those who disbelieve'. In other words, they are non-gender specific examples in this case, of the individual responsibility towards belief. No one is helped to salvation because of an affiliation with someone who strives for good no matter how intimate that affiliation. Each person must strive for good, or, at the very least, as with the wives of 'righteous servants', must not strive against the truth, and be condemned to the Fire.

Finally, on rare occasions, some incidents mentioned in the Quran have exclusive application. There is some historical information which can be extracted from them with very little or no significant application beyond that incident. These are Madinan verses, and the information includes something exclusive to the Prophet Muhammad and his household.

Woman as an Individual

In my discussion of woman in the Quran, I have considered the difference between woman as an individual and woman as a member of society. For the most part, the Quranic consideration of woman on earth centres on her relationship to the group, *i.e.* as a member of a social system. However, it is also important to understand how the Quran focuses on woman as an individual because the Quran treats the individual, whether male or female, in exactly the same manner: that is, whatever the Quran says about the relationship between Allah and the individual is not in gender terms. With regard to spirituality, there are no rights of woman distinct from rights of man.

With reference to the individual, the Quran most often uses the term *nafs*. On earth, the individual is given responsibility and capacity. Both determine the recompense of the individual in the Hereafter.

Individual capacity is expressed as follows: 'Allah does not tax a *nafs* beyond its scope. For it (is only) that which it has earned, and against it (is only) that which it has deserved'. There is no distinction between the male and the female with regard to individual capacity. With regard to their potential relationship with Allah, they are the same. With regard to personal aspirations, they are also the same. This is important because:

In every society, in every century, people have assumed that males and females are different not merely in basic anatomy, but in elusive qualities of spirit, soul and ability. They are not supposed to do the same things, think the same way, or share the same dreams and desires.

When various social systems determine differences between men and women, they conclude these differences as indications of different values as well. There is no indication that the Quran intends for us to understand that there is a primordial distinction between males and females with regard to spiritual potential. Therefore, whatever differences existing between males and females could not indicate an inherent value, or else free will would be meaningless. The problem arises in trying to determine when and how these differences come into being.

Sayyid Qutb says that 'the fitrah [primordial nature] makes the man a man, and the woman a woman', but he goes on to emphasize that this distinction has no inherent value. Al-Zamakhshari, on the other hand, says that men are 'preferred' by Allah over women in terms of 'intelligence, physical constitution, determination and physical strength', although he cites no place in the text which states this. Such an assertion cannot be erased by saying that 'men have no right to overcome women by coercion, or display arrogant behaviour towards them'. Al-'Aqqad says that men deserve preference over women.

I hope to demonstrate the negative effects of interpretations which place an inherent distinction between males and females and then give values to those distinctions. Such interpretations assume that men represent the norm and are therefore fully human. Women, by implication, are less human than men. They are limited and therefore of less value. Such interpretations encourage the stereotypes about women and men which severely hamper the potential of each. In addition, these interpretations justify the restrictions placed on the woman's right to pursue personal happiness within the context of Islam. Most troubling is the tendency to attribute these interpretations to the Quran itself rather than to the authors who hold them.

I do not hold such views, nor do I find support for them in the Quran. It is interesting to note that even those Muslim authors who issue these interpretations accept that the Quran aims to establish social justice. However, it is obvious that their interpretation of social justice does not extend fully to women. It is like Thomas Jefferson and the writers of the American Constitution saying that 'All men are created equal' without intending in the least to include equality between black men and white men.

I propose that the Quran depicts human individuals as having inherently equal value by looking at three stages in human existence. First, in the creation of humans, the Quran emphasizes the single origin of all humankind: 'He created you (all) from a single *nafs*'. Second, with regard to development here on earth, the Quran emphasizes that the potential for change, growth and development lies within the *nafs* of the individual (or the group) as well: 'Allah does not change the condition of a folk until they (first) change what is in their *anfus*. Finally, all human activity is given recompense on the basis of what the individual earns.

This leaves me to ask the following questions: Is there any way to understand the distinction between individuals? Do these distinctions reflect a particular value system? Do they follow clearly delineated lines between the two sexes?

Distinctions between Individuals

The Quran does make distinctions between things and between people. It establishes that the Hereafter is of greater value than this world. It also distinguishes within the Hereafter and on this earth. The value of the distinctions between humankind on earth can be clearly summed up by the Quranic statement in *surat Al-Hujarat*: 'We created you male and female and have made you nations and tribes that you may know one another. *Inna akramakum 'inda Allah atqa-kum* [Indeed the most noble of you from Allah's perspective is whoever (he or she) has the most *taqwa*].'

This term *taqwa*, one of the most essential in the Quranic *Weltanschauung*, has various translations and definitions. For this research I will consider it to mean 'piety', that is, a pious manner of behaviour which observes constraints appropriate to a social-moral system; and 'consciousness of Allah', that is, observing that manner of behaviour because of one's reverence towards Allah. In the Quranic *Weltanschauung*, this term always reflects both the action and the attitude. I do wish to reiterate that this multidimensional term is essential in the Quran.

The Quranic passage above reconstructs all the dimensions of human existence. It begins with creation. Then, it acknowledges the pair: male and female. These are then incorporated into larger and smaller groups, here translated as 'nation 'and 'tribe' respectively 'That you may know one another', or simply that being distinguishable allows identification. If we were all alike, with nothing to distinguish us, we would have no way of knowing each other or being known.

The culmination of this verse and its central aspect for this discussion is: 'the most noble of you from Allah's perspective is whoever (he or she) has the most *taqwa*.' The distinguishing value from Allah's perspective is *taqwa*. Provided that *taqwa* is understood in both its action and attitude dimensions, this verse is self-explanatory. Allah does not distinguish on the basis of wealth, nationality, sex, or historical context, but on the basis of *taqwa*. It is from this perspective then that all distinctions between woman and woman, between man and man, and between woman and man, must be analysed.

It is worth noting here that this verse follows verses which reprimand the individuals of both genders for mocking, defaming and backbiting one another. One might attribute greater or lesser value to another on the basis of gender, wealth, nationality, religion or race, but from Allah's perspective, these do not form a valuable basis for distinction between individuals (or groups) and His is the true perspective.

Finally, I wish to point out that the three commentators whose exegetical works were consulted for this topic all state that the apparent and worldly things which humans use to judge between one and another are not the true criteria for judgement. They do not agree, however, on what is included in these apparent things. In analysing this verse, only Sayyid Qutb acknowledges that gender is used as a basis for mockery and defamation, which then must be denounced as a false, worldly aspect of superiority. He states that the verses are inclusive of all the variations among humankind: gender, colour, etc., 'because all will return to single scale, that of *taqwa*'.

Al-Zamakhshari mentions that the references to both males and females, with regard to mockery, is more emphatic than the omission of both would be, but does not go on to conclude explicitly that gender could be used erroneously for distinction or superiority.

Maududi says that in these verses 'The whole of mankind is addressed' in order to prevent a great evil which is universally disruptive, and that is prejudice due to 'race, colour, language, country and nationality'. He does not include gender. He quotes Ibn-alMajah as saying, 'Allah does not see your outward appearances and your possessions, but He sees your heart and your deeds.' I believe that the heart and deeds are genderless on the basis of this verse: 'Whoever does good, from male or female, and is a believer, all such will enter Paradise'.

Distinctive Female Characters in the Quran

I will discuss only three Quranic female characters: the mother of Moses, Mary, and Bilqis, the Queen of Sheba. The details in the lives of these women are very different but their stories have been retold by exegetes without the female vision and without focusing on that which transcends their femaleness.

Moses was born at a time when Pharaoh was slaughtering all male Jewish infants. Allah decrees that this child will fill the office of prophecy.

And we inspired the mother of Moses, saying: Suckle him and, when you fear for him, then cast him into the river and do not fear nor grieve. Lo! We shall bring him back to you and shall make him (one) of Our messengers.

The first pronouncement in this verse speaks soft words to the mother of Moses. It promises to return the suckling child to her. Then it announces that Allah will make him a messenger. Note the tenderness the Quran demonstrates towards this woman's desire to nurture her child. Although the child is living under the threat of

Pharaoh's orders to slaughter such children, the child is saved to fulfil the decree of Allah. The desire of his mother towards the child is not directly part of that decree. Yet, the Quran details that aspect-in fact, mentions it first.

Returning the child so that he might suckle at the mother's breast will fulfil her maternal need, and presumably make it easy for her to remain silent about the child. Here sacrifice and struggle to fulfil Allah's commandments are tempered with sympathy and tenderness. She is not just a believer, she is a believer with love and concerns, fears and anxieties.

Not to be underestimated in its significance is that the Quran states that Umm-Musa received *wahy*, thus demonstrating that women as well as men have been recipients of *wahy*. Thus Umm-Musa demonstrates the point that women are distinct with regard to some aspects, but universal with regard to others.

As I mentioned before, Mary is the only woman referred to by name in the Quran. This is because in the Quran, Jesus was created in the womb of Mary by special decree and not by normal biology. He is called 'the son of Mary' to demonstrate the significance of his birth. Family relations in the Quran are labelled in term of the father or a male ancestor, but since no father is mentioned for Jesus, he cannot be called in this manner. Most important, from the perspective of the Quran, he was not the son of God. Although Mary is called by name in the Quran, she is also given one of the honorific titles common at that time in Arabia and employed in the Quran when specific women are mentioned: she is called 'sister of Aaron'.

In her story, a messenger appears before her carrying Allah's message that she is to bear a child. She responds, 'How can I have a child and no mortal has touched me, neither have I been unchaste?'. Once she has accepted the decree, the Divine ruh is blown into her, and she bears the child.

When the time for delivery comes, the Quran describes her pains of labour and her statement: 'Would that I had died before this time and been long forgotten (rather than to feel such pains).' She is like every other woman who bears a child. Then the Quran demonstrates Allah's sympathy for her predicament: 'Grieve not!' and she is asked to eat, drink, and be comforted.

Despite the centrality of Jesus to Christianity, no similar affirmation of the unique experience of childbirth is given such detailed consideration in any Christian theological work not even in the Bible. That special function is elevated to the status worthy of detailed mention to attest to its significance in the Quranic worldview. We are not left to just take it for granted.

Again, in this instance, as with Umm-Musa cited above, it is generally considered necessary only that a certain child be delivered to birth or to safety. Yet, the Quran includes these details to highlight the fact that the priority of saving the child, in each case, is also viewed in the light of the concern for the respective mothers.

Finally, one simple grammatical consideration with regard to the significance of Mary to all believers. The Quran classifies her as 'one of the *qanitin*', using the masculine plural form of the word that indicates one devout before Allah. There is no reason not to use the feminine plural form except to emphasize that the significance of Mary's example is for all who believe whether male or female. Her virtue was not confined by gender.

Finally, I will discuss Bilqis, the Queen of Sheba. Despite the fact that she ruled over a nation, most Muslims hold leadership as improper for a woman. The Quran uses no terms that imply that the position of ruler is inappropriate for a woman. On the contrary, the Quranic story of Bilqis celebrates both her political and religious practices.

Although the verse does point out (perhaps as peculiar) that she was 'a woman' ruling, this is nothing more than a statement quoted from one who had observed her. Beyond this identification of her as a woman, no distinction, restriction, addition, limitation, or specification of her as a woman who leads is ever mentioned.

The Quranic story continues: she was powerful, well provided for, and 'has a magnificent throne.' However, she and 'her people [worshipped] the sun instead of Allah'. Solomon sends a letter to the Queen of Sheba 'In the name of Allah' and invites her and her people to submit to worship of only Allah. When she reads the letter, she says to her advisers: 'Lo! there has been thrown to me a noble (*karim*) letter.' She then asks them to advise her in this affair of hers for 'I decide no case until you [advise me (on it)]'.

Although she operates within the normal protocol and asks her advisers for consultation on this matter, she has already given an indication of her perspective by describing the letter as karim. Thus, her postponement of the decision on this case is not for lack of decisive ability, but for protocol and diplomacy.

'They said: we are lords of might and lords of great prowess, but it is for you to command; so consider what you will command. She said: 'Lo! kings, when they enter a township, ruin it and make the honour of its people shame. Thus will they do. But lo! I am going to send a present to them, and see with what (answer) my messengers return.'

Solomon rejects the gift, stating that he has no need because Allah has given him a good position in both worldly and spiritual terms. In verse 42, the story resumes after she has decided to pay him a personal visit. As she is a ruler, such a decision carries importance. It means that she has determined that there is something special and unusual about this particular circumstance which warrants her personal attention and not just that of ambassadors. Perhaps it is his first letter which is written 'in the name of Allah' or because he rejects her material gift.

While she is *en route* to him, Solomon has her throne (the same one mentioned above) miraculously transported to him and uses it to test her wisdom. She is led to it and asked, 'Is your throne like this?' She answers, '(It is) as though it were the very one.' The existence of a throne so like hers, or of her throne itself, indicates something of the beyond-worldly power which Solomon commands. She goes on to say, 'Knowledge was bestowed on us in advance of this, and we have submitted to Allah (in Islam).'

Some interpret her decision to send a gift rather than to show brute strength as 'feminine' politics. I place both her worldly knowledge of peaceful politics and her spiritual knowledge of the unique message of Solomon together on the same footing to indicate her independent ability to govern wisely and to be governed wisely in spiritual matters. Thus, I connect her independent political decision despite the norms of the existing (male) rulers-with her independent acceptance of the true faith (Islam), despite the norms of her people.

In both instances, the Quran shows that her judgement was better than the norm, and that she independently demonstrated that better judgement. If her politics were feminine, then her faith was feminine, which, by implication would indicate that masculinity is a disadvantage. Her faith and her politics may be specific to females, but they both were better. They indicate one who has knowledge, acts on it, and can therefore accept the truth. This demonstration of pure wisdom exhibited in the Quran by a woman can hopefully be exhibited by a man as well.

4

Muslim Societies and Women

Introduction

When the Taliban militia seized Kabul in 1996, their extremist ideology and their cavalier disregard for international opinion created shock waves. The Taliban leaders initially offered no apology for their so-called Islamic policies of excluding girls from educational institutions, barring women from employment including in crucial fields such as medicine and beating up females not swathed in all concealing *burqas*. They made no efforts to conceal the harsh and discriminatory features of their policies because they were not self-conscious about how their policies deviated from international human rights. The very unusualness of the Taliban's attitude shows how influential the principles of women's international human rights actually have become. By 1996 ideas emanating from the Beijing conference had spread to most parts of the Muslim world, albeit maybe not to Qandahar, the home base of the Taliban.

Although universal compliance with women's international human rights still seems an elusive goal, the impact of the Beijing conference more often than not has placed opponents to women's equality on the defensive. Muslim leaders now seem reluctant to state squarely that they believe women are precluded from enjoying equality in rights by reason of their sex. Indeed, already during preparatory stages of the Beijing conference governments showed an awareness of the inadvisability of appearing to block the path to equality for women. Thus, Saudi Arabia preferred not to appear at the Beijing conference at all rather than to have to declare publicly that women should be segregated and supervised by male guardians. Obviously, Saudi leaders calculated that any defence of their policies toward women would expose them to fierce challenges and to ridicule. Unlike the naïve Taliban, Saudi Arabia's leaders had learned enough about the authority of women's international human rights to feel uneasy about admitting how they treated women.

After the Beijing conference, the clashes of diverging views on women's rights seem to have intensified, with Islam being appealed to both by Islamic feminists and by foes of women's rights. The sharp confrontations over how Islamic requirements affect women's rights reveal a religious tradition in turmoil as Muslims variously react with enthusiasm or with hostility to the message of Beijing. While some Muslims have reacted by stretching and straining Islamic rationales for the subjugation of women, others, who are equally opposed to women's human rights, seem to consider it unwise to invoke Islam as the reason for denying women's rights. I review relevant women's rights issues involving Libya, Pakistan, Egypt, Sudan, Iran, and Afghanistan to illustrate the repercussions of Beijing and the variety of "Islams" that have emerged in its turbulent wake.

Some regimes are backing away from the Islamic reservations to the *Convention on the Elimination of All Forms of Discrimination Against Women (CEDAW)*, reservations that have attracted much negative comment. In response to such reservations the Beijing Platform for Action called for all governments to "limit the extent of any reservations to *CEDAW*; formulate any such reservations as precisely and as narrowly as possible; ensure that no reservations are incompatible with the object and purpose of the Convention or otherwise incompatible with international treaty law and regularly review them with a view to withdrawing them."

The revision of Libya's *CEDAW* reservation, timed to coincide with the Beijing conference, seems to have anticipated that sweeping reservations would be challenged. The original Libyan reservation had attracted criticism. It read: [Accession] "is subject to the general reservation that such accession cannot conflict with the laws on personal status derived from the Islamic Shariah." The broad reservation placed compliance with Islamic law above *Libya's* commitments to *CEDAW* without specifying the consequences. On 5 September 1995 Libya notified the secretary-general of its revised reservation, which is worded to suggest that Libya- aims to protect women's rights:

> Article 2 of the Convention shall be implemented with due regard for the peremptory norms of the Islamic Shariah relating to determination of the inheritance portions of the estate of a deceased person, whether female or male.
>
> The implementation of paragraph 16(c) and (d) of the Convention shall be without prejudice to any of the rights guaranteed to women by the Islamic Shariah.

Instead of the original vague reference to Islamic personal status law, now there is a specific reference to inheritance rules with language that suggests that the rules apply equally to the estates of females and males. This is misleading because according to the Sharia male heirs are entitled to two times the share of female heirs. The inherently discriminatory apportionment of estates in Islamic law is not likely to be obvious to the average reader of the Libyan reservation. With regard to *CEDAW* ART. 16(c) and (d), the new reservation implies that the application of *CEDAW* could compromise Libyan women's rights as if Libya's Islamic laws guaranteed women rights superior to those provided by *CEDAW* concerning marriage and divorce and parental rights and responsibilities. The confusing formulation suggests that Libya had been embarrassed by the negative reception of its original broad reservation and was eager to put the best possible face on its policy of retaining Sharia personal status rules.

After protracted debates over possible Islamic reservations, Pakistan finally ratified *CEDAW* on 12 March 1996, appending this "declaration": "The accession by [the] Government of the Islamic Republic of Pakistan to the [said convention] is subject to the provisions of the Constitution of the Islamic Republic of Pakistan." The hidden meaning of this innocuous-sounding declaration will probably be obvious only to those familiar with U.S. RUDs (treaty reservations, understandings, and declarations) to human rights treaties. These consistently qualify U.S. obligations by upholding the supremacy of U.S. domestic constitutional standards over any contravening principles in international human rights conventions. Pakistan may have taken its cue from the United States, which disguises what are, in fact, reservations to treaty provisions by placing them under milder-sounding rubrics such as "understandings" or "declarations." U.S. "constitutional" reservations to international human rights treaties so far have not been subjected to the same degree of critical appraisal that Islamic reservations have provoked. For Muslim countries, a "constitutional" reservation can serve the same purpose as an Islamic reservation because almost all constitutions of Muslim countries establish Islam as the state religion, and many contain references to Islam. Examination of the Pakistani Constitution reveals that in addition to the ART. 2 provision that makes Islam the state religion, other Islamic features provide ample grounds for treating Pakistan's alleged "constitutional" reservation as an Islamic reservation in disguise one that can accommodate Pakistan's practice of allowing Islamic law to relegate women to subordinate status. The recourse to such circumlocution suggests that Pakistan was becoming uneasy about advertising that its Islamic laws stood in the way of full implementation of *CEDAW*.

As Pakistan was playing down the Islamic factor, controversial court cases were using Islamic rationales to roll back women's rights. Several cases in 1996 involved adult Pakistani women who were legally entitled to contract marriages but found their marriages challenged on the grounds that their male guardians (usually their fathers) had not consented to them. In past centuries Ḥanafi jurisprudence prevailed on the subcontinent, but Pakistan seems to have abandoned the old Hanafi rule of *kafaa*, which said that a woman's marriage could be nullified by her guardian on the grounds that she had married beneath her. Behind this rule stood the idea that a woman was a marker for male prestige: her marriage to a man of lower status than her father's would humiliate her family, and, thus, her guardian could sue to terminate the marriage. The Lahore High Court proved quite ready not only to resurrect the prerogatives of the marriage guardian in Hanafi law but to expand them to permit the voiding of a valid marriage simply on the grounds that the woman's father had not been consulted.

In the most sensational of these cases, Saima Waheed, a university student from an affluent family in Lahore, found her marriage to a teacher nullified by the court at the behest of her father, Abdul Waheed Ropri, a leader of a conservative Islamic sect. Her father's suit was not based on claims that his son-in-law was of low status but on objections to his daughter having married without his consent. The father had his daughter locked up in the family home where she was beaten and starved. Saima Waheed finally escaped. Determined to fight to be reunited with her husband, she sought advice from Asma Jahangir, a prominent women's rights activist. Like other Muslim women, Waheed realized that women's human rights addressed her concerns and that they gave her alternatives. Jahangir sheltered Waheed while her father tried to have her returned to his custody.

Islam was appealed to but inconclusively so because Islamic authorities disagreed on which side was right under Islamic law. The father's lawyer advised the court that it was "the father's obligation to restrain his wayward children" and that, even though she was an adult, Saima "cannot be left to roam around the Mall Road (a major Lahore thoroughfare) at will." The mentality revealed by one judge as he justified the dissolution of Saima Waheed's marriage was transparently reactive. Siding with the father, he saw himself as defending morality endangered by "the West": "Following the West blindly had caused many proplems in our society, leading it to moral bankruptcy. The race to modernize and catch up with the West, apart from achieving its desired motives, also led to the import of bad values." The ruling dissolving the marriage essentially endorsed the idea of general female incompetence and the need for male guardians to control female wards regardless of their maturity.

Interestingly, however, Abdul Waheed Ropri did not baldly assert that he was entitled to order his daughter around. Instead, he feigned solicitude for his daughter's free will. After having imprisoned and starved her, he insisted that his daughter had been coerced by others: she had been abducted by her husband and compelled to marry him and had then been "brainwashed" by Asma Jahangir. Thus, he pretended that his aim was to save his daughter from those who had forced her to marry against her will. Even this dyed-in-the-wool reactionary had come to appreciate that it was inadvisable to acknowledge frankly that he considered his adult, educated daughter a delinquent child. Toward the end of 1996 the Supreme Court suspended the High Court ruling that had dissolved Saima Waheed's marriage, leaving the final outcome of this case uncertain, but it was clear that both supporters and foes of women's rights in Pakistan had been mobilized by the controversy.

Recent rulings by Egyptian courts show the potentially harmful, dismal consequences that constitutional provisions that accord special stature to Islam and Islamic law can have for women's rights. After adopting a constitutional amendment in 1980 that made Islamic law the main source of legislation, the government showed little enthusiasm for doing more than "studying" Islamization. This amendment, however, encouraged Islamic activists to use litigation to establish the supremacy of Islamic law.

Many observers seem to discount as trivial Islamic personal status rules such as the ban on Muslim women marrying non-Muslims. In the hands of reactionary fundamentalists and like-minded judges, however, such Sharia rules can have devastating results for women's rights as the notorious case of Nasr Hamid Abu Zaid shows. Abu Zaid, a professor at Cairo University, became a target of fundamentalist ire after he presented a scholarly thesis in 1992 proposing innovative ways of approaching the Quran as a literary text. In 1995 Islamic activists persuaded a court to rule that Abu Zaid was an apostate. This decision was affirmed by the Cairo Court of Cassation in August 1996 in a ruling that sparked intense controversy The plaintiffs claimed to follow *hisba*, the Quranic injunction to enjoin the good and forbid the evil. They brought their suit against Abu Zaid and his wife Ibtihal Yunis as a personal status case in order to exploit the provision in Egyptian personal status law that judges may turn to Hanafi jurisprudence for guidance in the absence of a code provision. Because nobody had anticipated a claim that hisba principles entitled litigants to sue to void the marriages of unrelated parties, there was no personal status code provision covering the issues raised by Abu Zaid's foes. Referring to Hanafi jurisprudence, the courts ruled that hisba could be invoked even by strangers to separate a married couple. The courts decreed that Abu Zaid's scholarship contained heretical ideas that entitled them to rule Abu Zaid an apostate. Being declared an apostate meant the termination of his marriage to a Muslim woman. Had the couple continued to live together in Egypt after this "divorce," they could have been prosecuted for illicit fornication.

Abu Zaid was punished for his dangerous suggestion that religion should be an open system rather than a means for upholding tradition and a rationale for censorship. Most attention has focused on the curtailment of freedom of expression and on the courts' use of Islam as a tool of censorship and intimidation. The symbolic importance of this ruling for women's rights, however, can scarcely be overestimated. The case could just as well be named after Ibtihal Yunis, who also is a university professor. Neither the plaintiffs nor the courts accorded the slightest weight to Yunis's opinion about whether her marriage should continue. Just as in Pakistan, in Egypt the courts, in ostensibly "Islamic" rulings, terminated the marriage of an adult woman without regard for her views, thereby treating the woman like a mindless object.

Before this case, one hardly would have anticipated that Egypt would disregard an adult woman's consent to her marriage. In theory, marriages between Muslims are based on the consent of the spouses, and the medieval Hanafi jurists' rule that male guardians may nullify their female wards' marriages to men of lower status is no longer in force. For Egyptian women who thought that *kafa* principles were a thing of the past, however, the *Abu Zaid* case provided a rude awakening. It told them that Egyptian courts were ready to take unprecedented measures to shore up patriarchy. In expansive readings of Islamic law prerogatives once enjoyed by a woman's guardian were broadened. No longer was the issue the protection of a family from the shame of a daughter's mésalliance. Now the grounds for marital dissolution had been expanded to include strangers' disapproval of a Muslim husband's religious ideas, making any man's opinion that a certain husband was unfit to be in charge of his Muslim wife grounds for divorce. In the process wives were treated like incompetent minors subject to a general patriarchal tutelage.

That such a blow could befall Egyptian women in 1995-96 is striking evidence of how fragile are the gains that women have achieved and how the failure to modernize Egypt's personal status laws can render women's rights illusory. Significantly, the blow to Ibtihal Yunis was administered by Egypt's secularized court system.

Even though the ability of private individuals to bring such hisba claims has been curbed by subsequent legislation, this will not reform the attitudes exhibited by the courts in the Abu Zaid case. As in Pakistan, there is disturbing evidence that in the post-Beijing world seemingly modernized judicial institutions are ready to endorse extremist ideas that inflate Islamic rationales for subordinating women. Both the Egyptian and Pakistani rulings are in flagrant violation of norms of modern jurisprudence and of women's international human rights, probably quite deliberately so, because the views of educated urban women were being overriden in both countries.

In making Islamic reservations when ratifying *CEDAW*, Egypt had pretended that the impact of the Sharia on women's rights was benign. What connection should one draw between the Abu Zaid ruling and *Egypt*'s Islamic reservations to *CEDAW*? It would be an oversimplification to say that the dissolution of Ibtihal Yunis's marriage directly resulted from *Egypt*'s reservations to *CEDAW*. The ruling, however, ties in with *Egypt*'s adoption of the idea that women's human rights can be qualified by Sharia principles and that married women are to be treated as dependents of their husbands. Yet nowhere had Egypt's Islamic reservations claimed that women had impaired contractual capacity. Dissolving Ibtihal Yunis's marriage contract was breaching a *CEDAW* principle to which Egypt had never made an Islamic reservation, that is, the principle of equality in contractual capacity in ART. 15.2, which provides that "States Parties shall accord to women, in civil matters, a legal capacity identical to that of men and the same opportunities to exercise that capacity. In particular, they shall give women equal rights to conclude contracts and to administer property and shall treat them equally in all stages of procedure in courts and tribunals."

The Egyptian courts had in fact ruled as if women were lacking in contractual capacity. Ibtihal Yunis's marriage, a civil contract under Egyptian law, was retroactively invalidated on the premise that this university professor did not have the capacity to determine that her husband's ideas rendered him unfit to be married to her, a Muslim woman. Male strangers of no standing in the field of Islamic jurisprudence were treated as having superior ability to grasp the relevant Islamic principles and, therefore, as being entitled to make this determination on her behalf as if she were their ward.

In what way is this Islamic? One of the traditions of which Muslims have been justifiably proud is that, contrary to the old Western traditions of denying women contractual capacity and legal personality, Islam from the beginning recognized women's legal personality and, with minor exceptions, has granted women the ability to enter into contracts on a par with men. It has upheld their lawful contracts, barring only unusual situations such as breaches of the rule of *kafa*. Thus, one would not have expected to hear that there were Islamic grounds for objections to *CEDAW* ART. 15.2. The courts, treatment of Ibtihal Yunis and Saima Waheed actually was a sharp deviation from Islamic standards and an endorsement of views prevalent in premodern European laws. Instead of moving toward embracing *CEDAW* standards, some Egyptian courts were moving in the opposite direction and in the process distorting Islamic precepts regarding women's contractual capacity. Reactionaries, so quick to decry any signs of Westernization when seeking to delegitimize women's human rights, are mimicking alien Western concepts where these compromise women's rights. As Islam is being twisted almost beyond recognition to serve retrograde agendas, opportunities for exposing the cynicism and political contingency of such aberrant "Islams" are growing fast.

Egyptians' disparate views regarding the role of Islam in practices affecting women's rights showed in the mixed responses to the practice of female genital mutilation (FGM). Historically, Muslims have differed widely in their views about whether FGM is required or even allowed by Islamic law. The restricted geographical spread of FGM proves that is has no intrinsic connection with Islam. Christians and animists in northeastern Africa practice FGM, whereas Muslims in most regions of the world reject the idea that Islam approves, much less requires, genital mutilations that jeopardize women's lives, health, and psychological well-being. In Egypt disputes about the Islamicity of FGM intensified in the wake of strong condemnations of the practice at the 1994 Cairo population conference and later at the Beijing conference. After the head of al-Azhar, Sheikh Gad al-Haqq, ruled in 1994 that female "circumcision" was an Islamic obligation, a mere two years later his successor, Sheikh Muhammad Sayyid Tantawi, proclaimed that it was not. This was a remarkable turnaround by the head of the preeminent institution of Sunni Islam and indicative of the degree of doctrinal tumult with which al-Azhar was trying to cope. Ignoring Tantawi, other Egyptians insisted that Islam required FGM, including Sheikh Yusuf al-Badri, a member of the Higher Council for Islamic Affairs. A group sharing his opinion decided to sue Egypt's health minister for having banned FGM in public hospitals, claiming the ban violated Islamic law. This was not a call for respecting a custom of a traditional community but for allowing professionals in the public hospitals of a modern metropolis to excise women's and girls' genitalia in operations that the physicians knew to be hazardous and potentially life threatening.

5

Woman's Seclusion in Islam

Introduction

The Muslim clergy, theologians, and fundamentalist believers argue that, on the basis of passages in the *Quran* and the tradition of Muhammad himself, a woman should not be permitted to leave her house in the first place, and if she has to go out, she must shroud herself in a loose garment, cover her hair, and must not reveal any ornaments or make-up that she may have used. Most of the jurisconsults of the Islamic world maintain that a woman should not leave her house and go into the streets unless it is absolutely necessary. She is excluded from outdoor activities and is lodged in special quarters, segregated from all men except those closest to her, such as her father, brother, and husband.

The wearing of the veil was instituted by Muhammad in the early days of Islam.Within about one hundred years of his death, the institution of veiling and seclusion had been spread all over the Middle East by invading Muslims in pursuit of plunder from the once rich and independent countries of that region: "One and a half centuries after the death of the prophet, the system was fully established, with all the appurtenances of the harem, in which amongst the richer classes, the women were shut off from the rest of the household under the charge of eunuchs."

The use and significance of the veil have gone through many different phases and interpretations in the course of Islamic history.

One of the most orthodox Islamic schools, the Hanbali in Baghdad, objects to the appearance of women in the streets even if they are veiled. The followers of this school firmly maintain that no woman should ever be seen outside the home.

One Egyptian caliph ordered all the women in his empire to stay in their houses, and no woman was ever permitted to go in the streets. He took pride in this instruction and boasted that he was restoring the original Islamic practice. According to him, the veiling of women meant their complete confinement and seclusion. Many Western travellers' accounts show that even as late as the turn of the century, noble women in Egypt were proud of not having left their houses after marriage. It is also reported that an Egyptian caliph ordered the manufacture of ladies' shoes to be stopped so that no woman could leave her house and go outside.

The complete seclusion of woman in some Islamic countries of Asia is called *purdah,* a Persian word meaning curtain or veil as well as privacy and seclusion. In practical terms, it means the total veiling of women from head to foot when they are outside the home and the segregation of males from females in the house. A great majority of Muslim women in fundamentalist countries, whether in Asia or Africa, the two most predominant Muslim continents, practice the law of veiling and seclusion. And every Muslim male considers it a religious command to have his close female relatives cover themselves completely.

For generations women in Islam have submitted with little complaint or protest to the Quranic rule of the veil. The law is very rigid and very few women, in the long history of Islam, have dared to defy it. In fact, at the turn of the last century, almost all Muslim females used the veil. "One can generalize," says Jones, "without fear of inaccuracy of saying that at least 95% of Muslim women, perhaps even more, observe *purdah* constantly and logically." The figure may not be that high in Muslim communities today because the validity and usefulness of the veil were challenged in the 1930s in countries like Turkey and Iran, where *purdah* was then officially abolished.Unfortunately, there are places like Pakistan, the Persian Gulf states, and some North African communities where the seclusion of women is rigorously observed by the inflexible laws of the governments and severe punishment is prescribed for those who do not comply with the Quranic rule.

The Will of Allah

The inflexible laws of Islam have deprived half of the population of their equal rights. The male is in charge of the female and the subjugated half is led to believe, through Islamic teachings, that the supremacy of the man is the will of Allah and it has been predestined for women to live as submissive, obedient wives. They have been forced to accept that women are inferior to men; that their testimony is equal to only half that of the man; that they should inherit one-half of the male share from the deceased; that Allah does not want to see any woman unveiled in the street; that she may not converse with men except her father or brother; that any conversation with a man other than her close kin should be carried out from behind a curtain; and that woman is not supposed to have a position or a job in which men would be working for her and take direct orders from her.The only job for her is to be secluded at home, preparing the food, washing the clothing, and keeping her husband's bed warm.

The majority of Muslim women are brought up with the conviction that it is Allah's command for them to be under male dominance. Their fates are interwoven with that of their men. They accept their inferiority without any regret or malice. Jones says, "The pitiable thing is that the great majority accept the seclusion with a kind of fatal resignation, explaining anything and everything to their satisfaction with such a remark as 'It is our custom,' 'It is our fate,' 'It is our religion.' "

Yet the Muslim clergy and jurisprudents are disturbed over the cries of equality between the sexes heard among educated Muslim women who believe that the rising tide of modernism will eventually triumph over the prejudices of the Dark Ages.The apologists know that if they don't protect the Quranic law of the veil, segregation, and women's seclusion against the liberal minds of the opposition, the institutions of polygamy and *purdah* will be abolished. As a result, their indisputable positions as the supreme guardians of Allah's ordinance will be at stake. For this and similar reasons, they present such views as the following: "Man and woman are like fire and cotton whose meeting together is always destructive."

Other apologists try to base their arguments against the liberation of women on observations of modern science. The faithful are led to believe that the inequality of male and female is based on their apparent physical differences. Proponents maintain that women's inferiority is genuine and natural because of the way she is created, especially in regard to menstruation, pregnancy, child birth, and breast feeding. They regard all these natural phenomena as signs of inferiority. The Muslim clergy hold that the male, being the stronger, should prevail and the female, being the weaker sex, therefore must be subordinate. These arguments are obviously specious and have little relevance to modern society, where the determinants of progress are mental factors such as intellectual ability, talent, drive, and education, not physical strength or the temporary indispositions of the female reproductive system.

Maze of Restrictions against Women

In orthodox Muslim countries today every aspect of life is regulated to ensure strict segregation of the sexes. This separation is observed both in public and private life. In some countries, the women are separated from the men even on public transportation.

Of course, today's system of transportation is quite different from what it was during the time of Allah's apostle. Instead of camels and litters, cars and buses are standard. Nonetheless, the old style of seclusion of the women is more or less preserved: bus and train compartments provide separate seats and areas for women that conceal them from the gazes of male travellers. In some of the oil-rich Arab countries, the private cars of the well-to-do families are curtained and severe punishment is meted out to any inquisitive outsiders who try to look inside the cars.

In places where women are not permitted to drive a car, middle-class women must ask their husbands or close male relatives to give them a ride. The lower class of women must take public transportation, which, as has been mentioned, has a special closed section for them.

When a woman leaves her house to go shopping or to visit her folks, she is to veil herself completely. The garment she uses for veiling is different in the various Muslim communities. In North Africa she wears what is called a *burqa*. This is a long garment, usually black, covering the entire body of the woman from head to foot. There are two holes in the headcover for the woman's eyes. Fine embroidery or netting ornament these holes. In this way the woman is able to see where she is going but no one can see her eyes, much less her face.

The old style *burqa* is perhaps the most effective means of concealing a woman, for it consists of a circular piece of material with its center intricately embroidered to create a skull cap, which drops right down to the garment around the woman, giving a rather ghostly impression. The effect of all these garments is the same, though; for the woman is rendered anonymous, a non-person, unapproachable, just a silent being skulking along, looking neither to the right or left. To those who do not know her personally, she is nameless and faceless.

A woman wearing such a horrible garment is not only a nameless prisoner in the street, but she is a taboo. No one dares talk to her or even ask a simple question lest her close male kin get suspicious and cause trouble. The faceless creature is doomed to wear such a garment whenever she enters the street.

We might describe the burqa as the combination of the early Islamic headcover mentioned in *Quran* 33: 59 and the curtain referred to in *Quran* 33: 53, which was meant to separate the man from the woman. This combination of veil and curtain, through a long, slow period of reverse evolution in fundamentalist Muslim societies, could not have produced a more loathsome and senseless outer garment. Through this special dress, half the population of the Muslim world is deliberately and maliciously cut off from the rest of the community.

This segregation does not disturb most Muslim men, as their attitudes are reinforced by almost all of the Muslim theologians, who maintain that the first and most important duty of a woman is toward her husband: to prepare his food, wash his clothes, and satisfy his sexual desires. In other words, she is a loyal and faithful provider of service to her master. Disobeying one's husband is a punishable crime in the *Quran*, as we shall see later. If a man wants to take his wife out to a friend's or relative's house, she most probably cannot refuse, even if she abhors the idea.

In such a gathering, the men sit separately from the women. If they are not in another room, the women's veils are kept on at all times and they are not supposed to be lifted at any time. The women's table is separated and sometimes the men are served before the women. The formality is stiff. Women, if they are permitted to speak, should cast down their eyes and speak in a low tone, as loud laughter or conversation is considered unethical. In some orthodox Muslim countries, such as Saudi Arabia, any social gatherings attended by both men and women are considered morally wrong.

When a woman is taken ill, no male physician is allowed to examine her except in special cases. A female doctor is usually consulted even though she may not practice the right speciality. In some cases, the man may prefer that his wife or daughter not see a doctor at all.

In many instances, if a male doctor is in attendance, a sick woman will keep her veil wrapped around herself while her physician examines her. In some communities the doctors feel the woman's pulse through the veil!

There have also been recorded instances in which two lovers have met secretly and had sexual contact without removing the veil from the woman's face. In the eyes of the uneducated fundamentalist girl, revealing her face to a man who is not her next of kin is an unforgivable crime. In fact, it is a capital crime, much more serious than adultery or fornication. Unbelievable as this may sound, it is true.

A Muslim harem is taboo for males. No man is permitted to enter the quarters housing the wives and daughters, and no male except the father and brothers is allowed to see the faces of these girls. After marriage only the husband has this privilege.

In some Islamic universities, especially in the Arab countries of Southwest Asia, women are separated from the male students by a curtain drawn in the classrooms. The female students are not allowed to talk directly to their male instructors, and most of their conversation is carried out from behind a curtain that separates the instructors from the female students.

Arrangements may allow females to use the classrooms on odd days while the male students use them on even days. For example, the university library in Saudi Arabia is allocated to the girls twice a week and no male student is allowed to use the library on those days.

In most Muslim countries, coeducation does not exist at any level of schooling. It is especially rare at the high school level. No mixed sports or recreation is allowed. According to some schools of thought, women are not allowed to attend the mosques for praying. In other traditions, women may attend the mosques, but they must line up behind the men and boys. This arrangement ensures that the rows of teenaged boys will isolate the women from the men. In the mosque the man cannot see a woman's face, as he is always facing forward toward Mecca.

Treatment of Women Based on the Quran

Despite the obvious disparity between men and women in Muslim societies, some Muslim apologists attempt to show that the founder of Islam was very much in favour of equality. They cite one of the *hadiths* (traditions), according to which Muhammad said: "All people are equal, as equal as the teeth of a comb. There is no claim of merit of an Arab over a non-Arab, or a white over a black person, or a male over a female. Only God-fearing people merit a preference with God." This passage is indeed very egalitarian, and for this very reason it is difficult to attribute such sentiments to Muhammad because they contradict numerous statements in the *Quran*.The following verses from the *Quran* prove that this *hadith* is incomplete disagreement with Islam's holy scripture.

1. "And Allah hath favoured some of you above others in provision. Now those who are more favoured will by no means hand over their provision to those (slaves) whom their right hands possess, so that they may be equal with them in respect thereof."

   This verse is clear, explicit, and unequivocal, and it contradicts the above-mentioned *hadith* completely. According to the *Quran*, people are not created equal, because Allah has established the special superiority of master over slave. It is clearly indicated that some people have privileges over others in acquiring wealth, and Allah wants it that way.

2. "Allah coineth a similitude: (on the one hand) a (mere) chattel slave, who hath control of nothing, and (on the other hand)

one on whom We have bestowed a fair provision from Us, and he spendeth thereof secretly and openly. Are they equal?"

We notice once again that Allah does not equate a wealthy master with a destitute slave. The last sentence is manifest proof of the inequality, as it asks, "Are they equal?" The answer is of course obvious. The slave does not equal his master.

3. "He [Allah] coineth for you a similitude of yourselves. Have ye, from among those whom your right hands possess [slaves], partners in the wealth We have bestowed upon you, equal with you in respect thereof, so that ye fear them as ye fear each other ... ?"

The above verse clearly shows the inequality between master and slave, which was taken for granted in Muhammad's community. Such details about everyday life in the Prophet's day are enough to repudiate the tradition claiming that Muhammad urged all people to be treated equally, like "the teeth of a comb." Islam accepts the institution of slavery and it is evident that any community in which slave- trafficking is practiced cannot treat people equally.

Regarding the inequality between men and women, the *Quran* states: "Men are superior to women because Allah has made the one of them to excel over the other and because man provides the subsistence for women."

What other proof do we need? These are supposedly the words of Allah revealed to his Prophet.Claims for equality of the sexes under Islam contradict its sacred scripture.

Male Sexual Insecurity and the Need for Control

Why is Islam so obsessed with keeping men and women apart? Why have Muslim men gone to such great lengths to maintain control over women? Let us first consider the role of male sexual attitudes dating back to Muhammad, and then we will contrast the status of Muslim women with the role of women in pre-Islamic and ancient Near Eastern cultures.

Veíl as a Check on Male Sexual Desíre

The following quote is attributed to Muhammad by a number of *hadith* collectors: "A woman is a pudendum [*awrat*] which is proper to hide and cover; therefore when a woman goes out Satan looks at her and desires to carry her from the road." In the eyes of Muhammad, according to this quote, all male believers are potential "Satans" who might try to take unconcealed women for themselves. When this statement was made, most of the residents of Medina were Muhammad's followers, and most of the nonbelievers had been either driven out of the town (like the tribe of Banu Nadir) or butchered (like the Banu Qurayza). Therefore, "Satan" can refer to none other than the Muslim occupants of the town.

It should also be noted that Muhammad himself was one of the men who were unable to control their lust upon looking at women. Recall that he visited the home of Zayd, his adopted son, and there saw Zaynab, Zayd's wife, half naked. Muhammad's obvious desire for the woman eventually led to the divorce of Zayd from his wife, and shortly thereafter Muhammad married her himself.

It is related by a great number of chroniclers that in the early days of Islam both free and slave women appeared unveiled in the streets, and there was no way to distinguish between the two classes. Therefore, the ordinance of the veil was revealed because in this way the free woman, who was veiled, could be recognized and no one would bother her.

The law of the veil is not only humiliating to women, but it is an insult to men. It is a clear indication that, in the eyes of Muhammad, all Muslim males were sexcrazed. The obvious implication is that seeing a woman without a veil would cause the typical Muslim male to lose all control and that unveiled women would constantly be subjected to unwanted sexual advances. One would think that Islam does not trust its own followers to adhere to its teachings of piety, submission to Allah, abstinence, and kindness.Despite all the good deeds that a Muslim male is commanded to do, he is not to be trusted to see an unveiled woman. "Women should not shake hands with men and vice-versa, as that practice is psychologically unsound."

A faith that is so unstable as to be threatened by a handshake between a man and woman is totally out of touch with reality. Maybe the Arabs of the early Islamic period were uncontrollable and Muhammad, out of jealousy or some other personal reason, did not trust them. The contemporary Muslim men who travel to or study in Western countries today and see and meet thousands of young, sometimes beautiful, unveiled non-Muslim women do not seem to be disturbed or out of control. They shake hands, talk, dance, play, and interact with members of the opposite sex without any unseemly conduct. Their own intellect guides them to adapt to the laws of the host countries and to respect the women there.

It is immature to believe that the veil is capable of preventing men from developing sexual desires. The method of protecting the fruits of the orchard from theft or intruders is not to raise a thick, high, impenetrable wall around the garden. The wise and proper way is to declare the owner's rights to his property, apprehend trespassers, and punish law-breakers. To force women to wear the veil is to punish the innocent majority because of a few unstable individuals who might be tempted to commit sexual crimes by the sight of the female form.

This mistaken, ineffective practice of hiding what is desirable is dictated by the *Quran*:

> And tell the believing women to lower their gaze and be modest [literally, "guard their sex organs"] and to display of their adornment only that which is apparent.

According to this unequivocal command, the woman is instructed by Allah to cast down her eyes and never look directly at a man, lest he be moved by passion and develop a desire to possess her. In fact, Muhammad was obviously not convinced of the effectiveness of his teachings: in spite of all his pious preaching and the promise of heavenly rewards for Muslims who are clean in their attitudes toward others, he still believed that a glance at a woman's face or her uncovered hair might destroy a man's faith, shattering his will to submit to Allah.

In order to further protect his male faithful from the conflagration of desire caused by a woman's appearance, Muhammad commanded men also to lower their gaze and not to look at women, though they be shrouded from head to foot: "Tell the believing men to lower their gaze and be modest [literally, 'guard their sex organs']."

This admonition to the faithful to guard their sex organs resulted from ancient styles of clothing. Apparently, the nomadic, pre-Islamic Arabs, unlike the people of the civilized empires such as the

Babylonians, Assyrians, Persians, and Egyptians, did not have any use for underwear the climate was too warm for such garments to be practical. Instead, they wore long linen shirts, a head cover to protect them from the intense heat of the desert sun, and a sandallike shoe made from goat skin. The primitive Arab male and female did not know about trousers, much less underwear. It was not until after the conversion to Islam and the subsequent invasion of Iran that Arabs were introduced to the practice of wearing trousers, which they subsequently adopted.

As they did not wear any kind of trousers, when they moved about to mount a camel, for instance their genitals were sometimes exposed. This was probably one of the reasons that Muhammad had ordered his followers, male and female, to keep covered and to "guard their sex organs." (The Arabic word in the above verses is *furuje, meaning genitals.)*

Not only does the Quran specify that a woman may not look at men other than her blood relatives, but it also does not permit her even to talk with a strange man in a soft, charming voice, since this might stir his passions: "O ye wives of the Prophet! Ye are not like any other woman. If ye keep your duty (to Allah), then be not soft of speech, lest he in whose heart is a disease aspire (to you), but utter customary speech."

Many jurisprudents, based on the above verse, maintain that even if a woman is talking from behind a curtain or closed door, she must twist her tonality in such a manner so as not to reveal her age or looks to the listener. She is not to converse in the usual soft female voice, lest the man get excited and develop a desire for her.

The prevailing opinion among orthodox Muslim men seems to be that men and women are like fire and gunpowder: in close proximity they're liable to explode from unchecked sexual desire. They should therefore be kept as far apart as possible (through both veiling and seclusion) to reduce the potential for social evils. They criticize Western societies for having prostitution and sexual anarchy, which they believe results from the interaction of the sexes.

This reasoning is certainly without any foundation. Men and women have lived together from the age of primitive tribal communes through the Middle Ages up to the present day. No explosion ever occurred in ancient Egypt, Iran, or China in the past when women lived natural lives unsequestered from men. One cannot say that social evils in countries like France, Germany, and England, where the women are not veiled and kept apart from men, are more rampant than in Pakistan and Bangladesh.Certainly no evil is going to spring up if the Muslim female is freed from the captivity of rigorous religious laws.

As long as the equality of men and women is supported by law, no harm will result from the proximity of male and female. As soon as the supremacy of one sex over the other is perpetuated by the religious laws, however, and the female is driven out of society, screened behind the walls, and subjugated to the male, then the follies and evils begin to show themselves.

Veil and Marriage

Since legal puberty for a Muslim female, according to the tradition, is attained when she is nine years old, marriage at this age is not uncommon. It is at the age of puberty that females must observe the rule of *purdah* and cover themselves in some sort of overgarment or veil. "For Muslim women *Purdah* in the sense of complete veiling seems to operate after puberty in relation to all men except very close kin." Since girls are forced to veil themselves when they are still children, a prospective bridegroom usually cannot see or even talk to his future wife before the marriage.Marriage in such communities is performed with the help of a female broker, usually an elderly woman who is approached by the man or his parents. The prospective groom explains to her what physical characteristics his future wife should have and what his feminine ideals are.

The broker, after hearing the description of the prospective bride, starts to look for a girl with such qualities, which she can usually find within a few days. The broker gives an appealing description of the girl to entice the future husband, and the marriage contract is initiated. All too often, however, on the wedding night, after all of the marriage ceremonies are complete and the girl is handed over to her husband in the bedroom, he finds out, much to his amazement, that she is completely the opposite of what he had requested. Such a blind marriage is all too common in Islamic communities and sometimes ends up in a quick divorce before the marriage is consummated.

Prior to the wedding, the girl is as eager to find out about her future husband. The parents of the boy who initiate the blind marriage naturally lead the girl to believe that he is the best possible choice for her and not infrequently she is lured into accepting a man who is altogether unfit. Either he is much older than his description or he has none of the fine qualities that were detailed by his parents. For example, three of the women who married Muhammad were so ill at ease after entering his bedroom that they declared, "I take refuge in Allah," a way of nullifying the marriage agreement, and he was obliged to divorce them the very same evening.

The fate of some girls in blind marriages is much worse than that of those three brides, however. Some women find that their husbands are as old as their grandfathers, and if they cannot get a divorce which in most cases is not possible because they have no right to divorce they are bound to live a miserable life.

Status of Woman in the Pre-Islamic Period

The inequality of the sexes was not always the standard in Arabia.Among the early desert dwellers of North Arabia and the bedouin before the time of Muhammad, women wore a simple head covering, which was wrapped around the head and tied at the back of the neck. Complete concealment as it is practiced today did not exist. Arab women were their mates' partners in peace and war, and they accompanied men everywhere. "In ancient Arabia we find many proofs that women moved freely and asserted themselves more strongly than the modern cast."

In short, "The use of the veil was almost unknown in Arabia before Islam nor did the harem system prevail in the days of idolatry." Since most Arabs of this time were "nomads of the desert dwelling in tents," it would have been impractical for the women to live in concealment. It would have been impossible for them to carry a major share of the day's activities in the midst of the desert if their whole bodies had been wrapped in a cloak. Working-class women, who brought water from distant springs, prepared flour for bread, and were busy with numerous household tasks in and around their simple mud dwellings, did not use a veil other than a simple head covering to protect them from the intense heat. "The veil and seclusion were, by these, unknown and unneeded."

The position of pre-Islamic women was comparatively high and they certainly were not regarded as slaves or chattel, but as equal partners. Among the women of ancient Arabia one could find poets, judges, and business partners. They took part in tribal disputes and in some instances, they were as active as their men in the battles against their adversaries. By reciting lyric poems and beating on tambourines, they encouraged their brothers, husbands, and sons to fight and persevere in battle. Even in the early days of Islam, whenever there was a feud between the pagans of Mecca and Muhammad's followers, the pageantry of these women could be seen in the battlefields. For example, in the battle of Uhud, Hant, a Meccan woman who had lost some of her close male relatives in previous skirmishes, is described as going from one side of the battlefield to the other, encouraging the soldiers of Mecca to defeat the Muslims. The wife of Muhammad's most powerful adversary, one of the Quraysh chieftains of Mecca, she promised to free her strong African slave if he disposed of Hamza, Muhammad's fearless and youngest uncle. He did so and thus earned his freedom.

Women at that time were really free and enjoyed a better life than was later offered by Islam.They were the assets of the tribes because they were the mothers of future generations, as well as a source of income. Therefore, by bringing more women to the tribe, either as captives or otherwise, men were able to increase their numbers, thus adding to the physical strength of the tribe. In fact, each woman was treated as the mother of a future swordsman. In terms of their economic worth, recall that a bride-price was paid when a marriage was contracted. Thus, fathers welcomed newborn daughters as a potential source of wealth. Even when a father gave his daughter away for a specified bride-price, two conditions or unwritten rules were usually observed. First, the marriage had to be made on the basis of an equal match and second, the bride was not to be sent away against her consent. For these reasons, tribes would raid each other with the objective of capturing as many women as possible. Thus, women were considered the most valuable possession and were carefully guarded. We have already noted that Muhammad raided neighbouring tribes in the early days of Islam to capture as many women and children as he could. In this aim he was instinctly following the customs of his forefathers.

Pre-Islamic women also enjoyed far more sexual freedom than Muslim women today. At times they even "entertained" their husbands' friends:

> A panorama of female sexual rights in pre-Islamic culture reveals that women's sexuality was not bound by the concept of legitimacy. Children belonged to the mother's clan. Women had sexual freedom to enter into and break unions with more than one man.

Naturally, in the context of such matrimonial rites, some of which may be considered too liberal even by today's standards in industrialized societies, there was no place for the veil.

Archaeological evidence also indicates the relatively high status of Arab women before Islam. Zwemer says, "According to Nöldeke and Grimme,.the Nabathian and South Arabian coins and inscriptions prove that women held an independent and honourable position."

Pre-Islamic Arab women had the right to choose their mates and to divorce them whenever they wanted to. Muhammad's first wife, Khadija, is a good example of the freedom of the woman to find her own man. She was the one who offered her hand and proposed marriage, through a middleman, to Muhammad, who accepted immediately because of her wealth and prestige.

Khadija, however, may have been among the last group of Arab women to have such freedom. In fact, the advent of Islam and the introduction of Allah's divine law has certainly worked against women's freedom and driven them out of society's activities. The veil, the curtain, and seclusion ordained by Allah in the *Quran* have caused the position of woman to deteriorate. "The place of the woman," writes Smith, "in the family and in the society, has strictly declined under his [Muhammad's] law."

Female Infantícíde ín Pre-Islamic Arabia

The evidence that women had more rights in pre-Islamic Arabia than they do under Islam, many Muslim apologists insist that the lot of women was improved by Muhammad.To back up this claim they refer to the cruel custom of female infanticide, which had been practiced in pagan Arabia.They point to *Quran* 60: 12, which describes an oath of allegiance that fugitive women from idolatrous tribes had to take to Muhammad: among other things they were enjoined not to kill their children.Muslim clerics and commentators on the *Quran* take great pride in this ordinance.They credit Muhammad with stopping a savage rite.

Many Muslim writers relate very sad stories about this practice. Hundreds of accounts are related in which the father of the female child, after burying the child alive, would regret the act. 'Uthman, one of Muhammad's sons-in-law and the third caliph, is reported to have said that he could never forget the sight of his daughter's burial, because when he put her in the ditch and started to cover her with sand, she reached up and touched his face with her hand to brush off some particles of sand in his beard.

Stories such as this are enough to move anyone in favour of a man who is said to have stopped such cruelty. However, contrary to what Islamic writers claim about female infanticide in pre-Islamic Arabia, there is reason to believe that the practice was not common at all.

First, based on the number of women in pre-Islamic Arabia, it does not appear that the female population was intentionally curtailed in any way. In fact, at times there seem to have been more women than men. One of the reasons given by Muslim apologists in favour of polygamy was that there were far more women that men. This would indeed be paradoxical if female infants were frequently killed by their fathers.

Furthermore, in a society where women are regarded as valuable booty in tribal raids, a father would have no motive for killing his daughters. If men raided other tribes to acquire more women than they naturally had, it stands to reason that women were highly valued. Daughters were a source of income for the family since each one represented a certain bride-price for future bridegrooms. Some historians have suggested that in some cases in which the men were not capable of defending the tribe against more powerful marauders, they would kill their young daughters rather than face the disgrace of seeing them abducted. This may have occasionally happened, but was certainly not the norm.

Finally, what we know of pre-Islamic poetry indicates that women were frequently celebrated, along with wine and camels, as a source of pleasure and pride. In addition, as noted above, pre-

Islamic women had more rights than women under Islam. In such a context, it seems unlikely that female infanticide would have been sanctioned.

In every society, of course, there are parents who cannot afford to have more children, and in desperate situations caused by famine or drought, such impoverished people might resort to infanticide. But this was a rare event and certainly not the standard of behaviour. A verse in the *Quran* (6: 152) makes it clear that when infanticide did occur, it was caused by poverty: "Slay not your children, fearing a fall to poverty. We shall provide for them and for you. Lo! the slaying of them is a great sin."

Perhaps the notion of widespread female infanticide in pre-Islamic Arabia came from the well-known story of Qays, chief of the Temim tribe. He was defeated in battle and his daughter was captured by Nu'man, the prince of Hirrah.Later the girl fell in love with her captor and refused to go back to her father, even though he was eager to ransom her. It is said that the father in anger swore an oath that he would kill any future daughters that he might have and subsequently buried ten female infants.

Even if this story could be proved true, it was one case only and does not imply the widespread practice of infanticide. It seems that Muhammad has been credited with abolishing a savage custom that at its worst was a rare phenomenon.

Veil in the Pre-Islamic Period

Some chroniclers attribute the order of the veil to 'Umar, Muhammad's father-in-law and close friend. It is written that 'Umar told Muhammad it is proper to order his wives to wear veils because some men who enter his house may have wicked minds. Another story relates "that one day Muhammad was seated with Aisha when a passerby Arab admiring her beauty offered Muhammad a camel for her and this produced the order for veiling." But even if these stories are true, the custom of wearing a veil for one reason or another dates back to the ancient Near East, many centuries before the time of Muhammad.

Fakiki, one of the authorities in Islamic history, states that in the pre-Islamic period a type of head covering was worn by married Arab women to distinguish them from eligible single women in public places like the Ka'aba, the Okaz (a commodities market), or at the annual fair held between the cities of Taif and Nakhlah. In such public gathering places, suitors would seek young women as prospective brides. In those days the veil was simply a large scarf which the woman wore over her head and shoulders. A broad band of fabric was worn loosely over the head, about the neck, and sometimes around the waist. The face and hands of the woman remained uncovered. Thus, the veil was originally more a garment of class distinction, intended as a means of distinguishing married women from unmarried girls. Only free women wore the veil; slaves were not required to and in most cases were not allowed to.

This insignia separating married from unmarried women and free women from slaves did not originate in Arabia.The custom can be traced back to ancient Assyria.In the Middle Assyrian Law, promulgated in the fifteenth century B.C.E., we find ordinances pertaining to the wearing of the veil. Law 40 of this Assyrian code stipulates that every free woman must wear a veil:

> If the wives of a man, or the daughters of a man or his women go out into the street, their heads [are to be veiled. As for widows their heads are to be veiled.
>
> When [they go out] into the streets ... they shall veil themselves. The concubines (captured women) who go to the streets apart from their mistress are to be veiled.
>
> The (sacred) prostitute, whom a husband has married, is to be veiled in the streets. But one whom a husband has not married is to have her head uncovered in the streets. She is not to veil herself; her head is to be uncovered.

The one who sees a veiled harlot is to seize her, secure witnesses, (and) bring her for the judgement of the palace. Fifty blows they shall inflict upon her. Bitumen they shall pour on her head.

The following similarities between this ancient law and ordinances in the *Quran* are noteworthy:

1. In Assyrian law wives and their daughters are instructed to cover their heads when they leave the house. *Quran* 33: 59 has a nearly identical instruction: "O Prophet! Tell thy wives and thy daughters and the women of the believers to draw their cloaks close round them (when they go out). That will be better so that they may be recognized and not bothered."

2. In Assyrian law, the concubines of a man who go out into the streets must have a veil; according to Islam, all the concubines of a man are to veil themselves outside of their homes.
3. In Assyrian law, if a man married a prostitute, she must behave like a chaste woman by veiling herself; in Islamic law, when a man marries a harlot, she is to repent from her past and veil herself.
4. In Assyrian law, prostitutes are not to veil themselves; according to the jurisprudence of Islam, an unveiled woman is regarded as a prostitute.
5. Assyrian law enjoins that any prostitute who veils herself will receive fifty blows and pitch shall be poured on their head; according to most Islamic exegetes, if a woman does not veil herself properly she will be flogged and her hair shorn.
6. In Assyrian law captive women or slave girls are not permitted to be veiled; in Islamic jurisprudence veiling of captive women is not ordained.
7. Assyrian law designates the veil as the visible sign distinguishing a married woman or noble girl from a prostitute. Thus, men on the streets would know not to make sexual advances to veiled women. Likewise, the *Quran* explicitly states that married women and their daughters must wear veils when they go out "so that they may be recognized and not bothered."

Further comparisons can be drawn regarding the treatment of captive women. Ancient Assyrian law specifies the rules for marrying a captive girl:

> If a man wishes to veil his concubine, he shall have five or six of his neighbours present (and) veil her in their presence (and) say, "She is my wife," (thus) she is his wife. A captive girl who is not veiled in the presence of the men, whose husband did not say, "She is my wife," she is not a wife. She remains a captive woman. If the man dies not having sons by his veiled wife, the sons of the captive woman shall be their sons; they shall receive a portion (of the parental estate).

In Islamic law if a man marries a captive woman, he must do it in the presence of the witnesses and then veil her so that it becomes formal and everyone knows that she is married to him. An example from the life of Muhammad is the taking of his wife Safiyya (the widow of a chieftain whom Muhammad had defeated and killed). The event, as related by al-Bukhari, illustrates some parallels with the Assyrian law:

> Anas narrated [as follows]: The prophet stayed for three days between Khaybar and Medina, and there he consummated his marriage to Saffiya.The Muslims wondered, "Is she considered as his wife or slave?" Then they said, "If he orders her to veil herself, she will be one of the mothers of the believers [meaning Muhammad's wives], but if he does not order her to veil herself, she will be a slave-girl." Muhammad threw his own mantle on her in front of everyone, and took her to his own harem.

Assyrian law ordains the veil for the captive girls and prostitutes who get married; Quranic law requires the same thing. Therefore, it is not unreasonable to suggest that Muhammad perpetuated a pagan law under the banner of monotheism. In any case, the very law once practiced by the ancient Assyrians found its way into the *Quran* and is being applied even today by all Muslims.

Islam Today: Economic Disadvantages of Inequality

Because of the deep-rooted conviction in the Muslim societies of the Middle East and Africa that women are destined only to bring up children, whereas men are responsible for earning a living and providing for their families, women's employment outside of the home is a rare exception. Some of these Muslim communities are at poverty level and finding employment for men is difficult, if not impossible, so employment for women in these places is out of the question. Yet the irony is that the underdeveloped Muslim countries are disadvantaged due to the fact that half of their population namely, the women are merely consumers who are not permitted to produce anything because of religious restrictions. Poverty is a social ill that should be overcome through sustained economic growth. However, economic growth is not possible if the total consumption of goods and services exceeds their total production. It is a vicious cycle: the country is underdeveloped because the Gross National Product (GNP) is low. Therefore, the per capita income is low and personal savings are reduced with the result that the level of investment is low, ending in unemployment. In the absence of full employment, the overall GNP will fall. The capitalist countries, on the advice of their economists, have devised different methods for improving the overall economic outlook of their people, but progress is hindered by religious tenets.

Women, by taking part in the social activities of their communities and by sharing the responsibilities with men in the modern and advanced countries, can contribute to the betterment and welfare of the land they live in, and thus improve the standard of living in their own countries. This fact must be acknowledged and acted upon for true progress to take place.

A few Islamic countries, such as Saudi Arabia, Kuwait, and Iraq, have prospered because of their oil deposits. The sale of oil brings in billions of dollars each year into their economies. Those countries, thanks to the oil needs of the world, have been able to increase their per capita income to such a level that in some cases it exceeds that of the United States, Western Europe, and Japan.But material prosperity is the only similarity between these Islamic nations and their wealthy Western trading partners. Aside from their incredible oil incomes, high standards of living, and modern facilities such as telecommunications, transportation, and factories, these countries suffer from the same social ills as the poor Islamic countries. Despite wealth and grandiose projects, the female half of the population in these lands is deprived of basic freedoms: the freedom to choose a husband; to choose the colour of her garments; to move around in society; to pursue a chosen occupation; to initiate a divorce when she is subjected to domestic cruelty; to participate in political activities; to vote and to run for political office.

Summary

The struggle between the upholders of women's seclusion and the advocates of women's emancipation is not over yet. In fact, it is just beginning to manifest itself. The proponents of seclusion maintain that sexual desire is an uncontrollable phenomenon and both sexes must therefore be kept apart. They believe that a man and woman together are like "a live ember by the side of a mine of gun powder." In the eyes of such people, men and women have no willpower at all and their proximity will end in catastrophe. To them such restraining influences as the civil code, law enforcement, education, self-discipline, morality, and religion, in short, everything that historically has checked unbridled sexual passion, are without effect. These people reject the science of psychology and repudiate the ability of human minds to acquire refined behaviour. To them men and women are like beasts in heat who will explode with sexual passion as soon as they see each other. Thus, they must be kept apart.

The defenders of the veil imply that the female sex is by nature inferior. By this way of thinking, creating equality between the sexes would upset the balance of nature and nothing in society could be accomplished.

If both of them [men and women] are equal in power and no one has dominance or control over the other, neither of them will accept the effect of the other, and no action will then take place at all. If the cloth has the same hardness as the needle, no act of sewing will at all be accomplished. If the earth were so hard and impervious as not to accept the effect of the plough or pickaxe, agriculture or architecture would not be possible.

Thus it is the inequality of man and woman that enables any work to be performed at all. Without this inequality nothing would get done! This apologist and others like him think that human society is composed of two classes, one active, dominant, and strong (the men), and the other passive, submissive, and weak (women). Needless to say, this sort of reasoning is promoted to prove the Quranic law, which regards man as the superior sex. This same author prophesies a perilous future for any society in which the "natural" division of labour is abolished and women perform similar jobs as men. For such communities he foresees destruction: "Any civilization that tries to abolish this division of labour may temporarily achieve some degree of progress or glory, but its ultimate destruction is inevitably certain." No reason is given for this prophecy.

Of course, we don't know what the future might hold for a civilization in which all men and women enjoy equal rights. But it is certain that as long as Islam secludes women from society, no real socio-economic progress is possible. How can a society advance when its influential religious leaders continue to make statements like this: "Nature has given man superiority over woman. For her there is only slavery, and know it well that she cannot be emancipated from his bondage"?

6

Muslim Family Law

Introduction

Family law, which includes such important Areas as marriage, divorce and succession, has enjoyed pride of place within the *Shariah*, a prominence that reflects the *Quranic* concern for the rights of women and the family. Thus, the traditional family social structure as well as the roles and responsibilities of its members and family values, may be identified in the law.

The *Quran* introduced substantial reforms affecting the position of women by creating new regulations and modifying existing customary practice. These *Quranic* reforms, as well as customary practice, constitute the substance of classical family law.

Where *Quranic* reforms and values were incorporated, they served to raise the status of women and the family in Muslim society by establishing the rights of family members. In order to provide a background against which *Quranic* reforms and customary influences can be appreciated, this chapter will begin with a survey of women and the family in pre-Islamic Arabia. This will be followed by a presentation of the major regulations for marriage, divorce, and inheritance in classical family law according to the Hanafi school, which is the official school of Islamic law in the Middle East and South Asia.

Women in Pre-islamic Arabia

Women's status in pre-Islamic Arabia was reflected in the predominant marriage agreement, a contract that closely resembled a sale through which a woman became the property of her husband. She was obliged to follow him to his tribe and to bear children who were considered to be of his blood. The wife's tribe relinquished its rights to her and to her future children by receiving a price or gift called *mahr* (dower). Strong emphasis was placed on the chastity and potential fidelity of the woman. Therefore, her family strictly limited her behaviour in order to insure her reputation and consequently the family's honour. Since a woman would eventually leave the family, her value consisted primarily in the dower (*mahr*) her family received at her marriage sale. In addition, any possibility of her right to inheritance from her family, especially inheritance of fixed property such as land, which would in effect be transferring family wealth to another tribe, was out of the question. And, the married woman's status in her new family was not improved. As a wife she became totally subject to her husband and to his kindred and totally dependent upon them for maintenance and support.

The marriage of dominion in ancient Arabia produced a situation in which a woman was subjugated by males, her father, brother or close male relatives when she was a virgin and her husband when she became a wife. As a matter of custom, she came to be regarded as little more than a piece of property. Women's low status in society is reflected in *Quranic* condemnations, especially regarding female infanticide.

When news is brought to one of them of [the birth of] a female [child], his face darkens, and he is filled with inward grief! With shame does he hide himself from his people because of the bad news he had had! Shall he retain it [on sufferance and contempt], or bury it in the dust? Ah! What an evil [choice] they decide on.

A woman had no voice in her marriage (in its initiation or in its termination). Another factor contributing to women's inferior status was men's right of unlimited polygamy, contingent solely upon the males' ability to capture or purchase women.

The prevalence of marriage agreements which led to the general denial of any rights for women in marriage, divorce and inheritance provides the social context against which the life of the Prophet and the revelation of the *Quran* must be understood in order to see the profound social changes wrought by Islam.

Islam brought a shift in the basis of the social foundation-from blood kinship to fellowship in a community (*ummah*) of believers, from loyalty to the tribe to that of the extended family as its basic unit. A strong family meant recognition not only of male rights but of female rights as well. This realization can be seen in family law reforms in the areas of marriage, divorce and inheritance. *Quranic* injunctions, intended to raise women's status and equality, represented some of the most radical departures from customary law in ancient Arabia. Classical family law as finally formulated was the product of *Quranic* reform and customary practice.

Marriage

The central role of marriage in Islam is well illustrated by the Prophet's oft-quoted expression that "There shall be no monkery in Islam." Islam considers marriage, which is an important safeguard for chastity, to be incumbent on every Muslim man and woman unless they are physically or financially unable to lead conjugal life. Through marriage, the Muslim engages in an activity that is life-affirming rather than life-denying. Marriage is central to the growth and stability of the basic unit of society, the Muslim family, the means by which the world is populated with Muslims to concretize and realize God's Will in history. Physically, the labor of men is needed to spread the faith and to fight for it.

Definition of Marriage

Marriage (*nikah*) in Islam is recognized as a highly religious sacred covenant. However, it is not religious in the sense of a sacrament, but rather in the sense of realizing the essence of Islam. In Islamic law, it is a civil contract legalizing intercourse and the procreation of children. Marriage, reflecting the practical bent of Islam, combines the nature of both *ibadat* (worship) and *muamalat* (social relations).

Essential Requirements of Marriage

The contract of marriage considerably raised the status of a woman in pre-Islamic Arabia by making her a party to the marriage agreement rather than an object for sale. A Muslim man or woman who is of sound mind and who has attained puberty (twelve years of age for boys and nine for girls) is considered to have the legal capacity to contract a valid marriage for himself or herself or as a guardian for others. Since it was customary in an agrarian society to marry at an early age, the allowance of marriage at puberty was appropriate to the social situation. Great emphasis was placed on the value of many children which a young wife with many child-bearing years ahead could more easily provide.

The law does not require any particular form or ceremony in which the contractual agreement must be made, nor does it require any evidence of the union in writing. The custom of oral contracts seems to have prevailed although the *Quran* does recommend that such an agreement be in written form: "Disdain not to reduce to writing [your contract] for a future period it is juster in the sight of God, more suitable as evidence, and more convenient to prevent doubts among yourselves".

Essential to the marriage is the offer (*ijab*) of one contracting party and the acceptance (*qabul*) of the other, occurring at the same meeting before two witnesses. In Islamic law, by *Quranic* provision, the place of one male witness may be taken by two female witnesses: "And get two witnesses, and if there are not two men, then a man and two women, such as ye choose, for witnesses, so that if one of them errs the other can remind her". The higher social regard for men as witnesses in worldly affairs is reflected in the above regulation. This higher regard for men results in granting them more extensive rights in the law. In laws governing the arrangement of marriage for minors, the rights of men and women as well as boys and girls, as will be seen in the following, differ considerably.

Guardianship in Marriage

A distinguishing feature of Islamic law is the power (*jabr*) that it bestows upon the father or grandfather who can contract a valid marriage for minors which cannot be annulled at puberty. The right of guardianship is known as *wilayat* and the guardian is a *wali*. The inability of minors to repudiate the marriage seems to rest on the jurists' assumption that fathers and grandfathers who are fond of their offspring would not have sinister motives in arranging their marriages. However, this regulation is not supported by any *Quranic* prescription or Sunnah of the Prophet. If the marriage was contracted negligently or fraudulently, or by someone other than the father or grandfather, it can be repudiated by the minor when he or she attains puberty. This is called "option of puberty" (*khiyar al-bulugh*). The option applies to all marriages contracted by those other than the father or grandfather, even the minor's mother, who, as a woman, may be "deficient in judgement."

Lack of confidence in a woman's judgement is an attitude (also reflected in Western countries for many centuries) that probably resulted from the strict division of labor and social activity in Muslim society. The woman who spent most of her life engaged in domestic duties, completely segregated from the world of legal and business agreements, came to be viewed as less competent to deal with such matters. Thus, one can see the influence of custom and traditional attitudes upon the law. Among the many illustrations found in family law are the rules governing the "option of puberty." This option is lost to the virgin female who has reached puberty if she does nothing or if she merely remains silent for what is considered a reasonable time after she has been informed of the marriage and of her option. However, the option is preserved for the boy under the same circumstances. His right continues until he actively approves the marriage or implies approval by the act of payment of dower or by actual cohabitation.

If the husband or wife does exercise the option to repudiate, it must be confirmed by the court. Until this is done, the marriage continues, and if either party should die in the interval, the other would inherit from him or her.

Classification of Marriage

Like all other contracts, marriage has certain qualifications. However, unless its most basic requirements are violated, its validity remains. Marriages are classified by the degree of their validity as (*a*) *batil*, void, completely bad in its foundations; (*b*) *fasid*, irregular, good in its foundations but unlawful in its attributes; and (*c*) *sahih*, valid and completely lawful. As will be indicated, those marriage partners who do not fulfill all legal requirements for a *sahih* marriage are, in turn, denied many important legal rights.

Batil Marriage

A *batil* (void) marriage is an unlawful union that awards no mutual rights to the partners and imposes no obligations. The death of one partner does not entitle the other to any inheritance. Since the marriage is null and void and thus not considered to exist, the offspring are illegitimate. *Batil* marriages include such situations as marriage of a Muslim woman to more than one husband at the same time, or a marriage prohibited on the grounds of consanguinity (blood relationship through a male ancestor), affinity (marital relationship), or fosterage.

Fasid Marriage

A *fasid* marriage is irregular because of (1) lack of a formality that may be rectified, as in the case of a secret marriage or a marriage contracted with less than the legal number of witnesses, or (2) an impediment that can be removed, as when a husband already has four wives. If a judge (*qadi*) is made aware of such an irregular marriage, he, as guardian of the law of God, must either legalize or terminate the relationship.

An irregular marriage has no legal effect until it is consummated, and even after consummation, the rights of the partners are limited. The wife has the right of dower but no right of maintenance. Furthermore, there are no mutual rights of inheritance. The children of this marriage are considered legitimate, however, and are entitled to a share of the inheritance. To dissolve the relationship, only a single declaration of divorce is necessary. One of the partners at any time need only say "I have relinquished you" to annul the contract.

Sahih Marriage

A *saḥih* (sound or valid) marriage conforms to every requirement of the law and is not affected by prohibitions in the *batil* marriages or in *fasid* marriages. The partners of a *sahih* marriage are entitled to all of the rights and subject to all of the obligations of a valid marriage.

Competency of the Parties in a Marriage

The various requirements which determine the classification of a marriage center around the following areas: (1) number of spouses, (2) religion, (3) family relationship, (4) *iddah*, and (5) equality.

Number of Spouses

A Muslim man may have up to four wives. This law represents another reform raising the status of women who had been subjected to unlimited polygamy practiced in pre-Islamic times. Social circumstances during this period must be kept in mind: the widely-accepted practice of polygamy and the existence of many widows and orphans left by men who had died in battle who were in need of protection through marriage. The *Quranic* verse from which the control of polygamy is derived must be understood in the context of problems resulting from the battle of Uhud (625) which had caused the deaths of a substantial percentage of Muslim men: "If ye fear that ye shall not be able to deal justly with the orphans, marry women of your choice, two or three, or four; But if ye fear that ye shall not be able to deal justly [with them] then only one".

Because of the patrilineal social structure through which children belonged to the male's family, a Muslim woman was only permitted to marry one husband at a time so that the paternity of her children could be established. If she married a second husband, this marriage was considered to be completely void. In addition, her children from the second husband were illegitimate and were therefore excluded from inheritance. They could not be legitimized by any later acknowledgement.

Religion

Under Hanafi law a Muslim man is allowed to marry a Muslim woman, or a Jewish or Christian woman (*kitabiyyah*) who believes in a heavenly or revealed religion which has a *kitab* or revealed book. He cannot, however, marry an idolatress or a fire-worshipper. A Muslim woman, again more controlled in the exercise of her options, can marry only a Muslim man.

Family Relationship

Prohibitions of marriage based on family relationship are derived from the *Quran*. Marriages are prohibited for partners who have a certain blood relationship or consanguinity. Thus, a man may not marry his ascendants h.h.s. (how high soever), or descendants h. l. s.

A man is also prohibited from marriage with relations by affinity, that is, the ascendants h. h. s. or descendants h. l. s. of his wife (provided his marriage to this wife was consummated) or the wife of an ascendant h. h. s. or descendant h. l. s. Also prohibited is a marriage where the relationship of fosterage exists, as for example, marriage with one's foster-sister, foster-mother, or her daughter.

Another barrier to marriage in the category of family relationship involved unlawful conjunction. A Muslim must not be married at the same time to women related by consanguinity, affinity, or fosterage, as for example, two sisters or an aunt and her niece. An unlawful union in Hanafi law renders a marriage irregular but not void.

Iddah

In Hanafi law, a woman is prohibited from remarrying for a specified period of time called the *iddah* (waiting period) when her previous marriage has been terminated by divorce or by the death of her husband. *Iddah* is defined as the term by the completion of which a new marriage, if contracted, would be lawful. During *iddah* a woman must remain in seclusion in order to ascertain whether she is pregnant by her husband, and thus avoid any confusion of parentage. The iddah period served a number of purposes. In addition to determining parentage, it was a period for reconciliation and required payment of maintenance. If a marriage was not consummated, *iddah* need not be observed except in the case of a husband's death, since consummation may be the subject of conflicting claims of paternity, inheritance, and maintenance.

If the marriage is consummated before it is dissolved by divorce, the duration of the *iddah* is three menstrual cycles. If the woman is pregnant, the *iddah* continues until her delivery. If the marriage is terminated by the husband's death, the *iddah* period is four months, ten days from the death of the husband. If, at the conclusion of this period, the widow is pregnant, her *iddah* continues until delivery of the child.

The prohibitions of *iddah* after divorce extend to the husband, who may not marry again during the period of his former wife's *iddah*. However, marriage before the completion of the *iddah* is not considered void, but merely irregular.

To determine consummation of the marriage, which is a key issue in the practice of *iddah*, valid retirement (*al-khalwah al-sahihah*) can be used. To prove valid retirement, the husband and wife must have privacy and there must be no reason to prevent marital intercourse. Valid retirement also has the same effect as consummation not only in determining *iddah*, but also in confirming the right to dower, in establishing paternity, and in assessing the wife's right to maintenance.

Equality

A somewhat less important doctrine regarding marriage is *kafaah*, the rule of equality which states that a marriage is a suitable union in law if the man is equal in social status to the woman. However, this obligation does not apply to the woman, since she is considered to be raised to the husband's position by marriage. In Hanafi law, equality is a necessary condition determined by (1) family, (2) Islam, (3) profession, (4) freedom, (5) good character, and (6) means: A marriage that does not favourably meet these criteria is not necessarily void. The judge (*qadi*) must carefully exercise his discretion in determining whether to annul the marriage (*faskh*) on the basis that it was a mesalliance.

Consequences of Marriage (Rights and Obligations of Partners)

Once the essential requirements for a valid marriage have been fulfilled, the marriage agreement imposes specific obligations and insures specific rights for each marriage partner. Among the most significant rights and obligations are those concerning obedience, regulation of marriage agreements, property rights, dower, maintenance, guardianship, and parentage.

Duties of the Wife

The wife's main obligation involves maintaining a home, caring for her children, and obeying her husband. He is entitled to exercise his marital authority by restraining his wife's movements and preventing her from showing herself in public. This restriction of the wife mirrors the prevailing medieval social customs of veiling and seclusion of women, practiced in order to protect their honour.

Regulations of Marriage Agreements

In many cases, the rights awarded to a woman as a legal entity contributed significantly to her rise in status in comparison to her pre-Islamic state. One important right granted in the Hanbali (but not Hanafi) school, which in modern times is recognized as a means by which women can obtain a considerable measure of independence and status in marriage, concerns the partners' ability to regulate agreements in a contract by adding clauses containing additional provisions to the marriage contract as shall be seen, this approach has been employed by modern reforms. Agreements can be formed at the time of the marriage or afterwards and are valid and enforceable provided that they are not contrary to the policy of the law. Conditions that are contrary to the object of marriage (for example, clauses saying that the wife need not live with her husband or that the husband need not maintain his wife) would be void, although the marriage would still be valid. However, clauses that extend the natural consequences of marriage, such as a husband's promise to maintain his wife in a certain life style, are valid.

This right granted by the Hanbali school can considerably mise the status of the wife in a marital relationship. Her ability to make additional conditions not automatically arising from the marriage contract, but also not contrary to the object of marriage, can solve many inequities in such areas as polygamy or divorce. For example, clauses may be added to the contract that eliminate the husband's right to take a second wife. Clauses may also grant the wife a greater amount of freedom of movement. These stipulations limit the husband's somewhat automatic and extensive legal control of his wife. And, since these conditions can be enforced by granting the wife her husband's power of divorce if they are violated, more equal rights of divorce are granted to the wife.

Property Rights

Although both parties inherit from each other, neither acquires interest in the property of a spouse because of the marriage. This principle was the result of a *Quranic* reform which gave the woman the right to own and manage property herself and to keep possession of this property even after her marriage.

Dower Rights

Another right granted to the woman as a result of *Quranic* prescription is her right to dower (*mahr*), intended to safeguard her economic position after marriage. Dower is considered to be essential in every marriage contract. It may be defined as a payment which the wife is entitled to receive from the husband in consideration of the marriage. As the *Quran* specifies: "And give the women [on marriage] their dower as a free gift". In pre-Islamic Arabia the word *sadaq* represented the husband's gift to his wife, while dower (*mahr*) was paid to the bride's father. However, Islamic law made dower payable not to the bride's father, but only to the bride herself like the contract itself this action also made the woman a party to the contract and so the marriage agreement could not be considered a sale.

Dower could also be used as a means for controlling the husband's power of divorce, since upon dissolution of the marriage he is required to pay the total amount of the dower at once. In cases where the wife is divorced before consummation of the marriage, she has the right to one-half of her agreed-upon dower or, in Hanafi law, if there is no agreed-upon dower, she is entitled to a gift of three articles of dress or their value. Such provisions are also derived from the *Quran*: "There is no blame on you if ye divorce women before consummation or the fixation of their dower; but bestow on them [a suitable gift]" and "And if ye divorce them before consummation but after fixation of a dower for them, then half of the dower [is due to them]".

Dower may be classified into several categories. The first, specified dower (*al-mahr al-musamma*), is usually fixed on the occasion of the marriage and recorded in a register by the *qadi* performing the ceremony. The amount of dower fixed by the father for his minor son binds the son for the amount, but in Hanafi law the father himself is not liable for payment.

Unspecified or proper dower (*mahr al-mithl*) refers to an amount that has not been fixed. Although it may not be specified, dower is a legal responsibility not dependent upon any contract between the parties. If dower is not determined, the amount will be decided by the social position of the bride's fathers family as well as her own qualifications, such as those cited by the *Hedaya*: age, beauty, fortune, understanding, and virtue. The amounts of dower set for other females in the bride's family will also be a determinant, but the husband's social or financial position is not a consideration.

The practice of dividing dower into two portions, prompt (*muqaddam*) and deferred (*muakhkhar*), is universal in the Hanafi school. Prompt dower is payable upon conclusion of the marriage contract and deferred dower must be paid only on termination of the marriage and thus, as mentioned above, serves as a *bona fide* protection in the event of a divorce.

The wife's claim for the unpaid portion of her dower is legally considered an unsecured debt ranking equally with other unsecured debts due from her husband or, after his death, from his estate. The wife is entitled to receive the debt herself or if she predeceases her husband, her heirs, including the husband, are entitled to the dower.

Under Muslim law a widow whose dower has not been paid is entitled to the "widow's right of retention" which enables her to retain (but not obtain) possession of her husband's estate until her debt is paid. However, her unpaid debt does not make her the owner of this property.

The guardian of a minor wife whose husband refuses to pay prompt dower may refuse to send the wife to her husband's house. In addition, before consummation, the wife may refuse conjugal rights until dower is paid. Under these circumstances if she lives outside of his house, the husband must nevertheless maintain her. However, the wife loses her right to refuse herself once consummation or co-habitation occur.

These elaborately developed laws for the husband's payment of the dower to his wife represent one part of his monetary obligations to the women in his family. In fact, this sum was often received by the bridegroom from his father or grandfather who, as the traditional head of the extended family, controlled all family wealth. In traditional times, not only payment of dower, but also the other extensive monetary obligations of the male for all his womenfolk were collectively born by the many male members of his close-knit family group, who often lived in the same household. Women in the family who were secluded, veiled, and restricted from most aspects of public life did not earn their own living. This role was traditionally reserved exclusively for the males, a role fulfilled as a point of honor. Women without an independent means of support were necessarily extensively protected through the legal maintenance obligations of their male kin.

Maintenance Rights

Maintenance (*nafaqah*), another important obligation of the husband, includes food, clothing, and lodging. Maintenance is the husband's primary obligation, regardless of his wife's private means. The wife has first preference for maintenance over her children. The husband's obligation begins when his wife reaches puberty and continues unless she refuses him conjugal rights or is otherwise disobedient since, in return for her maintenance, the wife owes the husband her faithfulness and obedience. However, if her behaviour is caused by non-payment of prompt dower or the necessity of leaving her husband's house because of his cruelty, maintenance must still be paid.

A wife is also entitled to maintenance during the period of *iddah* following a divorce, and if she ceases to menstruate before the completion of this *iddah* period, the wife is entitled to maintenance until she completes three menstrual cycles. This ruling is intended to protect women who may be pregnant. However, a widow does not receive maintenance during the *iddah* following her husband's death since maintenance is considered to be inconsistent with her position as an heir. If the husband refuses to pay maintenance, the wife has the right to sue for it. The various schools of law have defined the extent of her rights in this situation in different ways. The Hanafi school shows more preference for the male in that it does not allow the wife the right to past maintenance unless a distinct agreement was previously made. The wife who, after a period of time, sues for maintenance, has no means to obtain payment of her husband's past-due debt. In contrast, the Shafii and Hanbali schools consider maintenance arrears to be the husband's ongoing debt which can be claimed regardless of the amount of time that has elapsed. In classical Hanafi law, the wife is put at a further disadvantage economically by the fact that neither inability, refusal nor neglect to maintain are considered to be sufficient grounds for the dissolution of her marriage. This is contrary to the principles of both the Maliki and the Shafii schools. The hardships resulting from the traditional Hanafi position are numerous. For example, a wife, who in traditional society is unable to support herself and her children, is also unable to free herself from a husband who has been imprisoned for a number of years. A father is also bound to maintain those of his children who belong in the following categories:

- his infant children whether or not he had custody of them;
- the infant children of a son who is unable to do so;
- his disabled son or student son;
- his unmarried daughter of any age; and
- his widowed or divorced daughter if she is ill.

If the father is poor, the mother and then the paternal grandfather are bound to maintain the children.

Maintenance is not required of a father-in-law for a widowed daughter-in-law, and a father is also not bound to maintain his illegitimate children. The close ties between members of the larger family are reflected in the laws governing the maintenance of other relatives. Persons who are not poor are bound to maintain their poor relatives. The maintenance required should be determined in proportion to the share which they would inherit from these relatives at their death.

Parentage

Parentage is established in Islam by birth during a regular or irregular, but not a void marriage, or by the father's acknowledgement. Thus, the child's rights to legitimacy are at times dependent upon the good will of his father. A child's legitimacy determines both his rights to maintenance and to inheritance from his father.

Legitimacy is determined in classical Islamic law by the following rules: (1) A child who is born within six months of a marriage is considered illegitimate unless the father acknowledges him. (2) A child who is born after six months of marriage is considered legitimate unless the father disclaims him. (3) After the dissolution of the marriage, a child is considered legitimate if born within two years (in Hanafi law).

The father's acknowledgement of paternity (*iqrar*) is possible and effective under the following conditions: (1) when the father of a child is not known to be anyone else; (2) if the man could, at the time the child was conceived, have been the husband of the mother [this implies that it has not been provided that the child was conceived by illicit intercourse (*zina*) and that the alleged marriage has not been disproved]; (3) if the ages of the parties are appropriate for that of father and son; and (4) if the acknowledgment is not only of sonship but of legitimate sonship.

Divorce

Because marriage in Islam is the basis of society, the means by which the race is perpetuated, it has always been viewed by Sunni Muslims as a permanent institution. Contrary to pre-Islamic practtice, temporary marriages (*mutah*) are forbidden. The prophet is reported to have said that "of all the permitted things, divorce is the most abominable with God." As will be seen, many verses in the *Quran* seek to limit both the frequency and the facility of divorce in pre-Islamic Arabia.

The negative attitudes toward divorce in Islam are clearly reflected in the opinions of Hanafi jurists. As the *Hedaya* states, divorce is: "a dangerous and disapproved procedure as it dissolves marriage, an institution which involves many circumstances as well of a temporal as of a spiritual nature; nor is its propriety at all admitted, but on the ground of urgency of release from an unsuitable wife."

However, consistent with its view of marriage as a contract, freely entered by the two parties, provisions were made for legal action to protect the rights of each partner if the terms of the contract were not met. Every attempt should be made to maintain a marriage, but once the marriage becomes a failure, Muslim law allows the parties to separate from one another. Divorce in Iṣlam serves as a safety valve in cases where the spouses can no longer live in harmony and so the very purpose of marriage would be defeated if they remained together.

Definition of Divorce

Divorce is generally referred to as *talaq*, meaning "repudiation. "*Talaq* comes from the root *tallaqa* meaning to release a human being from any obligation incumbent upon him. It signifies one spouse's release of the other spouse from the marriage bond, whether by repudiation or legal process.

The attitudes of the *Quran* regarding the necessary control of divorce are reflected in the approved forms (*ahsan and hasan*) of divorce. In comparison to the completely unbridled rights of husbands to divorce their wives in pre-Islamic Arabia, these approved forms of divorce represented a significant improvement in the treatment of women.

A wife's right to divorce was virtually non-existent in pre-Islamic times. While the *Quran* granted her some judicial relief from undesirable unions, the strong influence of social customs, especially in the Hanafi school of law, succeeded in limiting that relief to very narrow grounds.

Classification of Divorce

Divorce can be classified into five major categories: (1) *talaq*, (2) *talaq al-tafwid*, (3) *khul* or *mubaraah*, (4) *lian* and *faskh*, and (5) apostasy.

Talaq Proper

The first category and the most comprehensive, *talaq* proper, is the husband's right to divorce his wife by making a pronouncement that the marriage is dissolved. The male's extensive duties in the socio-economic sphere, and thus the dominant position of the husband in the family and society is reflected in some of the consequent legal rights he enjoyed over his wife. This is most clearly illustrated in the Muslim male's rather blanket right of divorce. Many *Quranic* verses make clear the undesirability of divorce and the punishments awaiting those who exceed the limits set by Allah. The law did not translate these teachings and values of the *Quran* into specific legal restrictions on the husband's right to divorce to guard against abuses.

Conditional, contingent, or qualified pronouncements of divorce are permitted in Hanafi law. For example, a divorce may be pronounced to take place at the occurrence of some future event or at some future period of time. The husband's pronouncement of divorce must indicate an intention to divorce, as for example, in the following expressions: "Thou art divorced, " or "I have divorced thee," or "I divorce my wife forever and render her *haram* (forbidden) for me." However, regardless of the verbal meaning, actual intention to divorce is not necessary. Because Hanafi law considers the action to be one of great gravity, if the husband uses the formula of repudiation in jest, in drunkenness, or even under compulsion, it is still considered to be valid and effective.

Although it could cause hardships for wives of impetuous husbands, another consequence of this provision was that it provided wives of undesirable husbands with an unforseen opportunity to dissolve their marriages. For example, in Turkey during the rule of the Sultans a convention developed that allowed a wife to go before a *qadi* with two witnesses and claim that her husband had divorced her when he was drunk, a claim he would be unable to deny.

A husband's act of divorce in Hanafi law is unencumbered. A Muslim who has attained puberty and is of sound mind has the right to divorce his wife whenever he wishes without citing a cause. The fact that the wife has no part in the procedure is further indicated by the fact that she does not have to be present nor must she be informed. The divorce can be either revocable, which gives the man an opportunity to reconsider the decision, or irrevocable. Since the Prophet did not approve of divorce, the revocable form of *talaq* is considered to be the "approved" form. Thus, the forms of *talaq* can be classified into *talaq al-sunnah,* divorce which is in consonance with the Prophet's teachings, and *talaq al-bidah,* divorce which does not follow the Prophet's teachings. This divorce represents an innovation and is therefore unapproved.

Talaq al-sunnah can be divided into two categories. The first is *talaq al-ahsan,* the more proper and orthodox form of divorce and thus the least disapproved. This takes place during the period of *tuhr* ("purity" the time when a woman is not experiencing menstruation). If a woman is beyond the age of menstruation or if the parties have been separated for a long time, *tuhr* may be dispensed with. With the ahsan divorce, the husband utters a single pronouncement and then abstains from sexual intercourse with his wife during her *iddah.* The pronouncement is revocable (by words or conduct, as for example, resumed cohabitation) during the whole period of *iddah.* This restriction allowed considerable time for reconsideration of the husband's decision and family arbitration to bring the couple together again, and thus followed the *Quran:* "And their husbands have the better right to take them back in that period, if they wish for reconciliation". At the completion of the period, the divorce becomes irrevocable.

The *ahsan* divorce is the most approved form because of the kind and fair treatment given to the wife. The period of suspense for her is not so prolonged as in the second mode. And, since there has been only one pronouncement of divorce, there is no prohibition against re-marriage of the parties. In addition, if the husband or wife dies during the period of *iddah,* the partner still inherits.

The *talaq al-hasan* form of divorce is also approved, although to a lesser degree than the first since it follows the letter but not the spirit of the Prophet's injunctions. The *hasan* divorce is carried out by making three consecutive pronouncements (the first two having been consecutively revoked) during three successive periods of *tuhr,* with no intercourse taking place during any of the three *tuhrs.* The first pronouncement should be made during a *tuhr,* the second during the next *tuhr* and the third during the following *tuhr.* The third pronouncement serves as a final and irrevocable dissolution of the marriage, and thus with it, intercourse becomes unlawful and *iddah* is required. Now re-marriage is impossible unless the wife marries another, consummates the marriage, and is then lawfully divorced.

The third pronouncement is irrevocable to prevent the practice of divorcing a wife and then taking her back several times in order to induce her to purchase her freedom by relinquishing her dower (*mahr*) or making some other financial sacrifice: "A divorce is only permissible twice: after that, the parties should either hold together on equitable terms, or separate with kindness. It is not lawful for you [men], to take back any of your gifts [from your wives)".

Unlike the two approved forms of divorce, the following two disapproved forms (*talaq al-bidah*) do not allow for a chance to reconsider a possible capricious or hastily-made decision. These forms of divorce, similar to the husband's unfettered right of divorce in pre-Islamic Arabia, again made their way through the force of custom into common practice and were incorporated into Islamic law. They are valid but disapproved and sinful.

The first disapproved form of divorce, the *talaq al-bidah,* consists of three declarations of divorce occurring at one time. The "triple declaration" is made during a single tuhr by pronouncing one sentence, "I divorce thee thrice," or three separate sentences, "I divorce thee; I divorce thee; I divorce thee," and thus the marriage is irrevocably dissolved.

The second version of the *talaq al-bidah* consists of one irrevocable declaration. The single pronouncement can be made in oral or written form during a *tuhr* or even at another time. At the moment of pronouncement or at the writing of the divorce, the marital tie is immediately severed.

The allowance of these two forms in law directly contradicts *Quranic* prescription: "When ye divorce women, divorce them at their prescribed periods, and count (accurately) their prescribed periods,. And fear God your Lord. Those are limits set by God: and any who transgress the limits of God, does verily wrong his (own) soul" LXV. 1). However, since Islamic law permitted the *talaq al-bidah,* only the husband's conscience served as a restraint from the use of such disapproved forms of divorce.

Talaq al-Tafwid (Delegated Divorce)

The second main category of divorce is *talaq al-tafwid.* In traditional Muslim law, while a husband enjoys an almost unflateral right to divorce, a wife's ability to divorce is very limited, a restriction that mirrors women's dependent role in society. It fails to reflect verses in the *Quran* which indicate a wider range of divorce options for the wife. For example: "And women shall have rights similar to those against them, according to what is equitable".

One power of the wife to divorce, strictly controlled by her husband, is *talaq al-tafwid* (delegated divorce). Here, the power of divorce is delegated to her by her husband when he expresses such words as "choose" or 'divorce yourself."

Khul and Mubaraah (Mutual Divorce)

A *Khul* divorce comes about through the common consent of the wife and the husband: "If ye (judges) do indeed fear that they would be unable to keep the limits ordained by God, there is no blame on either of them if she give something for her freedom". This mutual consent includes the wife's giving some compensation (part or all of her dower) to her husband. However, awarding the dower is not absolutely necessary. A *khul* repudiation can also take place without payment of compensation by the wife.

Mutual divorce may take two forms: the above-mentioned *khul* if the desire to separate is expressed by the wife, or *mubaraah* when both mutually want a separation. According to Hanafi law, the correct procedure for divorce takes place at one meeting when the husband proposes dissolution and the wife accepts it. Once the offer is accepted, in both the *khul* and mabaraah divorces, it operates as a single irrevocable divorce.

Lian and Faskh (Divorce by Judicial Process)

Dissolution of marriage may also be brought about by judicial process. The first type in this category is lian (mutual oath swearing). Here the husband alleges without legal proof that his wife has committed adultery. The wife then is entitled to file suit to bring about a retraction of her husband's statement or the swearing of an oath by her husband that she is guilty of adultery. His insistence upon her guilt under oath would thus bring the wrath of God upon him if he has accused her falsely. Once the wife has filed suit, intercourse with her husband becomes unlawful unless he retracts his claim. The swearing of the oaths in *lian* are governed by regulations in the *Quran*:

And for those who launch a charge against their spouses, and have (in support) no evidence but their own their solitary evidence (can be received) if they bear witness four times (with an oath) by

God that they are solemnly telling the truth; and the fifth (oath) (should be) that they solemnly invoke the curse of God on themselves if they tell a lie. But it would avert the punishment from the wife, if she bears witness four times (with an oath) by God, that (her husband) is telling a lie; And the fifth (oath) should be that she solemnly invokes the wrath of God on herself if (her accuser) is telling the truth.

After the oaths of both husband and wife have been made, the husband can divorce his wife. If he refuses to do so if the parties have not agreed to forgive each other, the court must dissolve the marriage. This has the same effect as one irrevocable *talaq*.

A second form of divorce involving judicial process is known as *faskh*, judicial recision of a marriage contract. *Faskh* (annulment or abrogation) means "to annul" (a deed) or "to rescind" (a bargain). In family law it refers to the power of the Muslim *qadi* to annul a marriage on the petition of the wife. The grounds that are available to women seeking divorce in the Hanafi school are both limited in number and difficult to prove. In contrast, as we have seen, the husband is required by law to cite no grounds whatever to validate his repudiation of his wife.

The schools of law differ considerably in the number and kinds of grounds available to women who wish to divorce. The Maliki school, followed by the Shafii and Hanbali schools is the most liberal. The Hanafi school is the narrowest. In Hanafi law, a court may dissolve a marriage only if: (1) the marriage is irregular; (2) a person who has the option to dissolve the marriage exercises it; (3) the parties are prohibited from marriage by fosterage; (4) the marriage was contracted by non-Muslims who subsequently adopt Islam (or vice versa); (5) a husband is unable to consummate the marriage; or (6) he is missing. In the latter case, the court can declare the marriage ended after a period of time, enabling it to presume that the wife is a widow (putative widowhood). However, the wife must wait for a divorce for a period of ninety years from the date of her husband's birth.

In contrast to the Hanafi school, the more liberal Maliki school allowed a wife to divorce on the grounds of her husband's (1) cruelty; (2) refusal or inability to maintain her; (3) desertion; or (4) serious disease or ailment that would make a continuance of the marriage harmful to the wife.

Divorce by Apostasy or Conversion

In the Hanafi school, a husband's and wife's renunciation of Islam (apostasy) whether or not the marriage was consummated, dissolves the marital tie, *ipso facto*. Because this condition also provides a possible opportunity for wives to dissolve their marriage, cases can be found in which wives would claim to have committed apostasy in order to free themselves from their husbands.

Consequences of Divorce (Rights and Obligations of Partners)

Following a divorce, certain rights and obligations of both parties come into effect.

Iddah

The wife's main obligation rests in her observation of *iddah* (waiting period) so that if she is pregnant, no question will occur regarding the paternity of her child and his right to inherit from his father. In addition, her observation of *iddah* provides a period during which a reconciliation may take place.

Dower

Considering the husband's unilateral right to divorce and the potential wrong to which the wife is exposed, *Quranic* verses cite many conditions granting the wife compensation once the divorce is carried out, and these were incorporated into the law. If the marriage was not consummated, the wife is entitled to a suitable gift, if the amount of dower had not been fixed, or one-half of the agreed-upon dower. If the marriage was consummated, the total amount of dower is due immediately.

Maintenance

During the period of her *iddah* the wife is entitled to maintenance from her husband, and this right continues, if she is pregnant, until the birth of her child. Furthermore, if the divorced wife has a young child, she can nurse him for two years. During this period, the father must maintain both mother and child.

Inheritance

Spouses may inherit from each other if their divorce is revocable. However, rights of inheritance terminate in the case of an irrevocable divorce.

Custody

In Hanafi law, the divorced mother has the right to the custody (*hadanah*) of her male child until he is seven years old and of her female child until puberty, set at age nine. During this time, however, the father, who is legally considered to be the children's natural guardian and maintainer, continues in his supervision of the children and at ages seven and nine he or his paternal relatives receive custody of them.

The awarding of custody to the father is a consistent social reflection of the workings of a traditional, patriarchal, patrilocal family. The family emphasizes the paternal line of ancestry and makes the central residence the home of the paternal grandfather where many women (aunts, grandmother) are available within the family to care for them. However, such laws do not allow much consideration for the children's now-divorced mother whose roles of wife and mother, the main source of a woman's status in a traditional society, may be taken away from her even though she was given no choice in the divorce action. In addition, if she marries another man, custody of her children, regardless of age, is given to her first husband as long as he is an able and proper guardian. A woman loses custody of her child at any age if her behavior is immoral or if she gives the child poor care.

The collective responsibility of extended family members for each other can be seen in the following assignment of relatives responsible for the child. Such a list illustrates the exact assignment of duties for each relative, paralleling the exact assignments of their own maintenance and inheritance rights.

In the absence of or disqualification of the mother, female relatives in the following order receive custody: (1) mother's mother h. h. s.; (2) father's mother h. h. s.; and (3) full sister or other female relatives, including aunts. In the default of female relations, the following male relatives obtain the right of custody: (1) father; (2) nearest paternal grandfather; (3) full brother; (4) consanguine brother; and (5) full brother's son and other paternal relations (in the order of the nearest male relative determined in the same order as that of inheritance). However, no male relative may obtain custody of a female minor unless he is related within the prohibited degrees of consanguinity. If no qualified guardians exist, the court appoints a guardian for the minor.

Reconciliation and Re-marriage

The rules governing the process of reconciliation and re-marriage of the spouses reveal the *Quran*'s emphasis upon the importance of marriage and the gravity of divorce. Regulations seek to encourage reconciliation and re-marriage while at the same time discouraging the divorce which had made a re-marriage necessary in the first place.

If, after divorce, reconciliation and re-marriage are desired, the parties are subject to the following regulations. If the husband has made one or two declarations of divorce in the two approved forms (*talaq al-sunnah*) following *Quranic* prescriptions, a reconciliation either a formal revocation of the repudiation (*talaq*) or resumption of conjugal life can take place during the *iddah* (waiting) period. Therefore, formal re-marriage is not required. Every possible allowance is made after an approved divorce is carried out to rescind that divorce and quickly reestablish married life again. However, when one or two declarations in the approved forms have been made and the *iddah* period has expired, a regular re-marriage is necessary. In this situation, the gravity of divorce is emphasized by requiring a complete renewal of the marriage agreement.

When three declarations have occurred, the divorce is final and irrevocable, reconciliation and/or remarriage are prohibited. A husband who has pronounced a triple repudiation can only remarry his ex-wife if she marries another and that marriage is terminated through the death of her spouse or through divorce.

The intent of these requirements, which originate in the Quran, is aimed at curtailing such pre-Islamic practices as perpetually divorcing a wife, pretending to take her back, and then divorcing her again in order to either convince her to relinquish her dower for her final freedom, or to prevent her from re-marrying and seeking the protection of another husband. The damage to his pride which a husband in traditional society must endure in order to re-marry his wife after an irrevocable divorce was doubtless intended to serve as a strong deterrent against hastily-conceived divorces.

Inheritance

The customary laws dealing with inheritance in pre-Islamic Arabia were designed to keep property within the individual tribe in order to preserve its strength and power. Inheritance passed only to mature male (agnate) relatives who could also fight and defend their possessions. Male minors were totally excluded. Widows, who were regarded as part of the estate, and daughters, who would no longer belong to the family once they were married, were also barred from inheritance.

The inheritance provisions in the *Quran* modified this system in order to correct injustices. Islam brought a change in the social structure. Loyalty to the Islamic community (*ummah*) transcended tribal allegiance. In the Islamic community, more emphasis was placed upon family ties between husband, wife, and children. The consequent shift in allegiance from the individual tribe to the individual family unit significantly raised the status of women in the society. This Islamic reform is mirrored in the new Quranic ally stipulated rules of inheritance that were superimposed upon certain unjust customary laws. The *Quran* granted rights of inheritance to the husband and the wife, to children, and to a number of close female relatives who had previously had no rights of succession at all. These new "*Quranic* heirs" received fixed proportions from the deceased's estate before the inheritance passed to the close male relatives. Generally speaking, female heirs were awarded a share equal to one-half that of their male counterparts, whose heavy maintenance responsibilities also cited in the *Quran* justified their larger share. However, where the parents, and uterine brothers and sisters of the deceased are only entitled to a small share of inheritance, men and women share equally in the estate. In addition, no reference is made in the *Quran* to primogeniture. Thus, all sons, regardless of age, received an equal portion of inheritance.

The reforms introduced by the *Quran*, however, did not replace the existing legal scheme. Instead, the customary laws and *Quranic* reforms were fused into a comprehensive and coherent legal structure by the efforts of jurists and the force of events. The system of inheritance that resulted represents a feat of juristic achievement. The Prophet is reported to have said that the laws of inheritance comprise "half the sum of *ilm*" (true knowledge stemming from divine revelation).

Definition of Inheritance

The system of inheritance is the science of duties or obligations (*ilm al-faraid*); specifically, religious obligations. The reform of customary law through its modification by *Quranic* verses (its Islamicization) will be seen in the explanation of classical laws of inheritance that follows. The outline arranging the structure of priority in inheritance demonstrates both the structure of the traditional extended family and the Islamic concept of social values. Furthermore, it illustrates the meticulous precision with which jurists formulated this elaborate legal system of succession.

Classification of Heirs

Hanafi jurists divide the heirs into seven categories. The first three are the principal classes.

Quranic Heirs

The first class is made up of the *Quranic* heirs (*ahl alfaraid*) whose rights were established by Divine revelation. The *Quranic* heirs have been called "Sharers" because they receive a precise fractional share prescribed by the *Quran*. Although these relatives, who are mostly women, inherit first, they take only a portion of the estate. The strong influence of customary law can be seen by the fact that the residue, usually the bulk of the inheritance, reverts back to the male agnates (*asabah*).

A list of the twelve relations that make up this first class (Quranic heirs) follows. It includes a treatment of (1) the fraction of the estate which each class of heirs will receive, singly or collectively; (2) those relatives who exclude certain other heirs from inheritance; and (3) the other key circumstances affecting inheritance. The shares mentioned for each heir refer to the net estate, the amount remaining after funeral expenses and other debts have all been paid.

The first two *Quranic* heirs are heirs by "affinity," the *husband and wife*. These heirs always succeed. They do not exclude nor are they excluded by any other relative. If they exist, they reduce the residue that may be taken by the class two relatives (agnates). The husband takes one-fourth of his wife's estate. If his wife has no living children or children of a son h.l.s. (agnatic heirs), he takes one-half The wife inherits one-eighth of her husband's estate if there are children or children of a son h.l.s., and one-fourth if there are no children. However, the wife's portion is a collective one. In the case of a polygamous union, the wives share the one-eighth or one-fourth equally. The remainder of the *Quranic* heirs (blood relations) are listed below:

The *father* receives one-sixth. However, when there are children of the deceased or of the deceased's son h.l.s., the father of the deceased is made an agnatic heir. The *mother* receives one-sixth. However, if there are no children of the deceased, no children of the deceased's son h.l.s., or only one brother or one sister of the deceased, her share is increased to one-third of the whole estate. If the husband or wife as well as the father of the deceased are alive, she will receive one-third of the residue after deducting the husband's or the wife's share.

One *daughter* of the deceased is entitled to one-half of the estate and two or more daughters receive two-thirds. However, if the deceased has a son, the daughter(s) are made agnatic heirs.

The *paternal grandfather* is entirely excluded from inheritance by the father or nearer paternal grandfather of the deceased. However, if they are not living, he takes their place, receiving one-sixth of the estate, or if there are no children of the deceased or the deceased's son h.l.s., he becomes an agnatic heir.

The *maternal grandmother* is entirely excluded by the living mother of the deceased or nearer maternal or paternal grandmother. The *paternal grandmother* is excluded by the living mother or father of the deceased, a nearer maternal or paternal grandmother and a nearer paternal grandfather. However, when they are not excluded, they receive a share of one-sixth of the inheritance to be distributed to one or to two or more collectively.

The *son's daughter* receives a share of one-half for one and two-thirds for two or more collectively. However, she is excluded from inheritance by the existence of the son or more than one daughter, or a higher son's daughter. If only one daughter of the deceased exists or if only one higher son's daughter exists, her share is reduced to one-sixth. Finally, if an equal son's son exists, she is made an agnatic heir.

The *full sister* of the deceased is excluded from inheritance by the deceased's son or son h.l.s., father, and paternal grandfather. If these are not living, one sister receives one-half of the estate and two or more collectively receive two-thirds. However, if a full brother exists, the full sister is made an agnatic heir.

The *consanguine sister* is excluded from inheritance by a son h.l.s., father, paternal grandfather, full brother, or more than one full sister.

Otherwise her share is one-half for one sister and two-thirds collectively for two or more. When only one full sister exists, the consanguine sister's share is reduced to one-sixth and if a consanguine brother exists, the consanguine sister is made an agnatic heir.

The *uterine brother and uterine sister* are excluded by the child, child of a son h.l.s., father, or paternal grandfather of the deceased. If these do not exist, the uterine brother and/or sister receive one-sixth singly and one-third for two or more collectively.

Agnatic Heirs

Once the *Quranic* heirs have received their share, the estate passes on to the Class II agnatic heirs (*asabah*), or male relations on the male line. The inheritance rights of the agnates derive from pre-Islamic customary law. Class II heirs have often been referred to as "residuaries" since the residue of the estate (often the bulk of the inheritance) goes to them. Class II contains all of the male agnates, and due to *Quranic* reforms, four specific female agnates. Agnatic heirs are formally classified by the *Sirajiyyah* in the following way:

1. Males—The agnate in his own right (*asabah binafsihi*). This group, the largest and most important, includes a limitless number of blood relatives, all male agnates who were the tribal heirs of pre-Islamic law—the son, son's son, father, brother, paternal uncle and his son, and so on.
2. Females—The agnate in the right of another (*asabah bi-ghayriha*). This section specifies four female agnates *when they co-exist with male relatives of the same degree*: daughter (with son), son's daughter h.l.s. (with equal son's son h.l.s.), full sister (with full brother) and consanguine sister (with consanguine brother).
3. Females—The agnate with another (*asabah maa ghayriha*). These consist of two irregular cases of full and consanguine sisters when they co-exist with daughters and there are no nearer heirs.

Uterine Heirs

Following distribution to the *Quranic* and agnatic heirs, the inheritance that remains is distributed among the uterine heirs (*dhawu al-arham*), often referred to as "distant kinsmen." Uterine heirs include every relative who is neither a sharer nor a residuary.

On close examination, one finds that the agnatic and the uterine together include all possible blood relatives of the deceased.

Following the first three principal categories of heirs described above, the following four subsidiary classes of heirs (successors unrelated by blood) inherit only as a rare exception:

Successor by Contract

In Hanafi law, in default of all blood relations and subject to the rights of husband or wife, the estate of the deceased goes to the "successor by contract." Through a contract this person promises to pay a fine or ransom for which the deceased may become liable, and in exchange he receives this right of succession. Such an agreement is called a *mawalat*.

Universal Legatee

The universal legatee is the person to whom the deceased, through a will, has left all of his property. The deceased may leave the whole estate if he has no living heir.

Escheat

In the default of all possible heirs mentioned above, the estate escheats to the government, the ultimate heir. In early Islamic history the inheritance would go to the Public Treasury (*bayt al-mal*).

Testamentary Bequests (Wasiyyah)

As the Hanafi inheritance laws so fully reveal, a man is not free to bequeath his whole estate to whomever he chooses. He is obligated by law to give certain fixed amounts to specific heirs. These shares represent the inviolate right of such heirs to an inheritance.

However, the verses of inheritance had been preceded by earlier verses permitting testamentary bequests to relatives. The law of testamentary bequests has its source in the *Quran*: "It is prescribed when death approaches any of you, if he leave any goods, that he make a bequest to parents and next of kin, according to reasonable usage; this is due from the God-fearing". This *Quranic* "Verse of Bequests" which was of a general and discretionary nature has generally been regarded by the majority of jurists as abrogated by the later *Quranic* verses of inheritance which, as has been noted above, stipulated fixed portions for specified heirs. However, a minority of jurists continued to maintain that the "Verse of Bequests" was in force. Modern Egyptian reforms have been based on this position.

Since the *Quranic* verses of inheritance only provided for a specific group of heirs and this only "after payment of legacies and debts," some form of bequest was still presumed. Because the *Quran* was silent as to the extent of this continued power of testamentary disposition, jurists turned to the Sunnah of the Prophet for regulations which both enabled bequests and protected the rights of *Quranic* heirs. The result is a system which recognizes the right of a Muslim to bequeath up to one-third of his net estate to parties of his own choice as long as they are not his own legal heirs. The bequest can be made for any person capable of owning property, regardless of his religion, or to an institution, or for a religious or charitable object.

The provision limiting the disposition of property to the "bequeathable third" is based on a report by the Companion of the Prophet, Saad b. Abi Waqqas:

The Messenger of God visited me at Mecca since I was near death. So I said to him: "My illness has become very serious. I

have a good deal of property and my daughter is my only heir. Shall I give away all my property as alms?" He said: "No." I said: "Shall I bequeath two-thirds of my property as alms?" He said: "No." I asked: "Half?" He answered again: "No." Then he said: "Make a will for one-third and one-third is a great deal. It is better to leave your heirs rich than poor and begging from other people."

The second restriction that a bequest may not be made in favor of a legal heir stems from the *hadith* reported by Ibn Abbas: "No legacy to an heir unless the other heirs agree."

Sunni jurists, moreover, devised a further regulation to cover cases in which a testator went beyond the limits of his power and bequeathed in excess of the allowable one-third or bequeathed to an heir. In such cases, the permission of the testator's heirs is required before such provisions can take effect. In Hanafi law this consent must be obtained after the death of the testator.

Waqf (Charitable Endowment)

The legal definition of *waqf*, or endowment, in the Hanafi schools is "the detention of a specific thing in the ownership of the waqif or appropriator and the devoting or appropriating of its profits or usufruct in charity on the poor or other good objects."

The formation of "*waqfs* is consistent with the strong emphasis on charitable deeds that is stressed in Islam, but in comparison with other institutions, its support in traditions is weak. The legal scholars (*fuqaha*), in explaining *waqf*, put most emphasis on a tradition of Ibn Umar which says that Umar asked the Prophet what he should do with valuable lands he had just acquired after the partition of Khaibar. The Prophet answered: "Retain the thing itself and devote its fruits to pious purposes." Umar followed these instructions, prohibiting the land from being sold, given away, or bequeathed and giving it as charity to the poor, needy relatives, slaves, wanderers, guests, and for the propagation of the faith. In addition, the property's maintainer could also obtain sustenance for the property as long as he did not accumulate wealth from it.

Certain conditions must be met for the completion of a valid *waqf*. First of all, the founder of a *waqf (waqif)* must have reached puberty, be of sound mind and be a free man. He must also possess unrestricted ownership and full right of disposal of his property. Secondly, the object of the endowment must be of a permanent nature and it must yield a usufruct (profit). A *waqf* is generally associated with real estate although movable property has also been awarded. Thirdly, the *waqf* must be made in perpetuity (*muabbad*) so that if it is established for individuals, the proceeds are allotted after their death to the poor. Fourthly, the purpose of the *waqf* must be pleasing to God. In addition, the ultimate purpose of a *waqf* must be *qurbah* (*i.e.*, for the benefit of the poor).

Two kinds of *waqf* can be distinguished: a religious or charitable endowment (*waqf khairi*) involving mosques, hospitals, bridges, etc., or family endowments (*waqf ahli or dhurri*) for children or grandchildren as well as other relatives or other people.

Waqfs can be made for the rich and the poor alike, or the rich and thereafter for the poor, or for the poor only. Thus, when a *waqf* is given in favour of the *waqifs* descendants, the trust is in their favour as long as a single descendant exists. When they cease to exist, the usufruct will go to the poor. Some limitation is placed on the amount of the *waqif*'s estate dedicated in certain circumstances. If a *waqf* is made through a will or during death illness (*marad al-maut*), the testator cannot award more than one-third of his estate without the consent of his heirs.

Summary

The study of classical family law demonstrates the practical bent of Islam, from its earliest days, in applying the divine imperative. The comprehensiveness of the early Muslim jurists' efforts is attested to by the highly-developed and detailed regulations governing every aspect of marriage, divorce, and succession. As we have seen, these regulations embodied both *Quranic* reforms and customary legal practices.

Quranic reforms corrected many injustices in pre-Islamic society by granting women right to which they were entitled the right to contract their marriage, receive dower, retain possession and to control of wealth, and receive maintenance and shares in inheritance. At the same time, however, family laws were formulated to meet a woman's needs in a society where her largely domestic, childbearing roles rendered her sheltered and dependent upon her father, her husband, and her close male relations. Thus, family law reflected woman's dependent position as can be seen in regulations concerning witnesses, option of puberty, initiation of divorce, and rights of maintenance and inheritance.

Since men had more independence, wider social contacts, and higher status in the world, their social position was translated into greater legal responsibilities (especially in maintenance regulations), as well as more extensive legal privileges proportionate to those responsibilities. The most notable examples of such rights and duties can be found in the areas of guardianship of marriage, extensive divorce rights, wider privileges of custody, and greater shares in inheritance.

In its attempts to meet the needs of a particular social milieu, Muslim family law reflected the social mores of the time-the traditional roles of men and women and the function of the extended family in a patriarchal society. This understanding of classical family law, which demonstrates the interrelatedness of law and society, provides a valuable perspective for modern legal reform. The duties and responsibilities of men and women in classical law remained virtually unchallenged up to the twentieth century because they paralleled the socially accepted roles of individuals and the function of the family in a basically unchanging society. Profound social forces in modern times have affected the status and roles of women and the family in Muslim society. This process has been accompanied by reforms in Muslim family law which have sought to respond to as well as to foster social change.

7

MUSLIM LAW AND WOMEN

Introduction

"Extensive discrimination against women continues to exist" together with "the lack of respect for and inadequate promotion and protection of the human rights of women." This is particularly relevant for countries ranging from theocracies to secular states where laws or legal systems governing marriage and family relations derive from interpretations of religion or are legitimized by them.

Family laws, that is, laws that govern relations between men and women in marriage, divorce, inheritance, guardianship and custody of children, provoked considerable debate at the Fourth World Conference on Women in Beijing. Women from Muslim societies discussed the contradiction between the affirmation of the universality of women's rights and the principle of legal equality in the Platform for Action and the existence of contrary family laws. The failure of numerous Muslim states to adopt and implement nondiscriminatory family laws is as disturbing as are the arguments justifying their nonimplementation. This state of affairs camouflages what one feminist asserts to be a "visceral rejection of the principle of equality."

Recent feminist research reveals a tradition of male monopoly over religious (mis)interpretation in Muslim societies. Indeed, the question no longer is what Islam says or does not say but who has said what on behalf of Islam and for what purpose. Arguments justifying discrimination in family codes and laws mirror the political projects of regimes and are a reminder that law is not a neutral agent but reflects dominant power relations in society.

Given the complexity of Muslim societies and their different schools of jurisprudence and legal practice, it is necessary for women's rights activists to develop channels of communication for facilitating a cross-cultural discussion of the diverse laws and legal systems existing within the Muslim world. Such exchanges will aid in the development of practical strategies for increasing women's critical understanding of laws that influence the nature and scope of their autonomy.

The network Women Living under Muslim Laws (WLUML) seeks to achieve this goal through its ongoing Women and Law project.

WLUML and Muslim Laws

The WLUML states:

> Women living under Muslim laws invariably lack information regarding their official, legal rights, both in terms of Muslim personal laws and/or civil codes. They remain ignorant about the differences that may exist between customary laws applied to them and Muslim laws. They also have no access to information that might enable them to challenge the validity of either type of law. Furthermore this situation is reinforced by a deliberate policy of misinformation. Given the existing monopoly and control over the matters relating to Islam, we feel the need to evolve a network for information, solidarity and support amongst women living under Muslim laws.

WLUML was initiated in 1984 when ten women attending the Reproductive Rights Tribunal in Amsterdam formed the Action Committee of Women Living under Muslim Laws. This committee was established in response to situations arising out of the application of Muslim laws in India, Algeria, and Abu Dhabi that resulted in the violation of women's human rights.

In India Shehnaz Sheikh filed a petition in the Supreme Court, arguing that the application of minority religious law violated her constitutional right to equality. In Abu Dhabi a pregnant woman was sentenced to be stoned to death, and in Algeria women fought to gain custody of their children from their ex-husbands. WLUML believed that each of these situations, although geographically scattered, were "symptomatic of a much wider problem confronting women in the Muslim world."

Two years later, in 1986, WLUML drafted a Plan of Action which identified the centrality of the public-private dichotomy in arguments justifying the denial of freedom and equality to women and acknowledged the existence of laws, both written and unwritten, drawn from interpretations of the *Quran* that merge with local tradition to influence the lives of Muslim women. Sharing experiences of the manner in which this dichotomy is used to deny women's rights in different cultural settings was considered an urgent priority of the network.

In 1988 WLUML initiated an Exchange Programme, involving twenty-four women from fifteen different countries, twelve of whom went to different host countries. The Exchange Programme facilitated a deeper understanding of the varied cultural settings, the diverse political systems, and the multiple legal systems/customary laws existing in the Muslim world. The notion of a homogenous Muslim world was demystified as was the idea that laws operative in different countries are similar. The difference between what is often categorized as "Islamic" and Muslim practice was highlighted when women from India learned about the "Islamic" practice of genital mutilation in Egypt and the Sudan or when the "Islamic" practice of veiling in parts of Asia was compared with its nonexistence in parts of Muslim Africa.

The Exchange Programme generated empirical information on the legal rights of Muslim women in different cultural contexts and also highlighted the role of law as a major factor in influencing and defining the scope of women's autonomy in Muslim societies. Given the importance of law as an agent of social change and given the fact that in several countries marriage and family relations operate with reference to Islam, the documentation of such laws, legal systems, and their social practice was considered a first step toward women's empowerment. "Intended for practical use rather than academic discussion," research conducted in the ongoing WLUML Women and Law Programme analyzes "the determinants of changes impeding or promoting women's autonomy and legal rights."

WLUML and the Platform for Action

At the U.N. Conference on Human Rights in Vienna women human rights activists exposed the gendered hierarchy of the mainstream human rights movement by pointing to the exclusion of the family from the definition of human rights. The existence of discriminatory family laws symbolizes this exclusion. Subordination through family codes and personal laws operates at two levels: at the local level of social practice and on the political level of the state. At the societal level discriminatory personal laws violate women's rights to equality within the family while at the political level governments retain patriarchal family laws to maintain the gendered boundaries of their own political priorities. It is in these two contexts that the WLUML Women and Law country projects contribute locally and internationally toward advancing the aims of the Platform for Action.

The documentation of information in the Women and Law country projects highlights the gap between formal law (or civil code) and its social practice in a particular country, captures the variance in legal interpretation and schools of jurisprudence operative within a specific national context, and reveals the intermeshing of legal and cultural patriarchy in determining women's location in Muslim societies.

A flexible research methodology allows women from different cultural settings to arrive at their own definitions of self-empowerment. For example, during the implementation of the India project its national coordinator was part of a small group of women activists who worked together to formalize a preliminary version of a Muslim marriage contract that would safeguard the interests of women, thus demonstrating the practical implementation of women's legal empowerment using religious law.

The information generated in the respective country projects in collabouration with NGOs and community-based organizations ensures local participation in developing a critical understanding of Muslim laws and their implications for women's autonomy. The Women and Law India project has been successful in establishing a network of Muslim women within the country. These women met several times during the project to discuss issues of common concern. Two women from this network subsequently attended a WLUML international meeting in Lahore in 1994. The Women and Law country projects thus facilitate the formation of information and solidarity networks within a particular country that might not have existed before and link these local networks with those of another country project within the region. These networks establish and strengthen regional links among women mobilizing for change.

Furthermore, country projects highlight the existence and application of Muslim law in countries where Islam is not the state religion. A case in point is India where the issue of Muslim family law is interlinked with constructions of so-called communal identity. The term *communal* in South Asia has negative connotations. It is based on the notion that people belonging to a particular religious community also share common social, political, and economic interests. The merging of cultural identity with the issue of Muslim family law in India and its negative fallout for women's rights was shared by WLUML with South African women. In 1993 at an international seminar in Capetown women from WLUML cautioned South African women against the potential drawbacks of demands for religion-based family laws that might erode their constitutional right to equality.

Women and Law country projects also draw attention to states that are publicly committed to CEDAW yet fail to modify or to legislate against discriminatory personal laws. By highlighting the inherent contradictions between a public policy that affirms women's rights and the retention of family laws that undermine these very rights WLUML constantly alerts women within and outside the network to the implications of what Mayer appropriately terms the new world hypocrisy on women. In a statement prepared for the 1994 World Conference on Human Rights in Vienna WLUML pointed to the "retention of personal laws based on religion, tradition and custom" in violation of the fundamental rights of women and, in some cases, of their constitutional right to equality with men.

On national and international levels the WLUML projects operate on a reciprocal basis and feed into each other. The information generated by country projects strengthens local and regional networks of women working in human rights advocacy while the international dimension of the WLUML Women and Law project facilitates a cross-cultural and international network of information, support, and solidarity among women from Muslim societies.

An international comparison of regressive laws in certain countries to relatively liberal laws in others dislodges the myth of a homogeneous Muslim world. This awareness allows women to resist imposed identities and to develop their own definitions of self-empowerment.

By 1994 twenty-five countries were associated with WLUML either as Women and Law country projects or as inputs. Shaheed writes that "with the development of the WLUML Women and Law Programme, the network appears to have entered a new phase in which a common project has merged with solidarity action and networking."

The Women and Law project unveils the violation of women's rights in the Muslim world, it also reclaims the centrality of women within the discourse on Islam and women's rights. As Mernissi observes, "Muslim history, from the first century to the present, has had to struggle with women's refusal to conform to such models," (of sexual segregation). WLUML acknowledges this history of resistance-through documentation, affiliation, and joint action and by doing so, ensures that it will continue.

The presence and participation of women from WLUML at the Beijing conference reflected the specificity of Muslim women's struggles within the larger women's movement. The Beijing conference reaffirmed the universality of humanhood as being independent of racial, cultural, or religious identity. It also underscored the importance of cross-cultural networks of solidarity among women from Muslim societies for working toward the realization of women's human rights in the face of the rising challenge from forces opposed to women's self-determination.

8

Legal Methodology for Reform in Islam

Introduction

In the name of social progress, reform legislation has been enacted to more equitably meet the changing social and economic needs of women and the family in modern Muslim society. However, salutary as substantive legal change may be, and noble as reformers' motives may have seemed, their solutions have been of an *ad hoc* and piecemeal nature and their legal methodology has been deficient.

The true effectiveness of existing reforms is dependent upòn their acceptance not simply by those who legislate but by the entire Muslim community. Thus reforms must be rooted in a consistent Islamic rationale, one which would demonstrate a link of continuity between change and past tradition. Jurisprudence, the legal principles and methods underlying the reforms, must play a key role since it alone can insure both inner consistency and historical continuity with the Islamic tradition.

Tradition and Change

While tradition plays an important role in most cultures, in Islam it has been elevated to an almost sacrosanct status. The reasons for the eventual "sacralization" of tradition are not difficult to identify. The progressive idealization of the history of Islamic law tended to separate the ideal from the real, the immutable from the mutable. The customary practice (*sunnah*) of Arabia, which was incorporated into Islamic law, came to be equated with the *Sunnah* (practice) of the Prophet and thus it was given an unwarranted, elevated religious status. The acceptance of al-Shafii's formulation of the sources of Islamic law also meant a down-playing of the role of reason in the development of law. In classical jurisprudence, the restriction of reasoning (*ijtihad*) to analogy (*qiyas*) created a sense that law was simply the product of specific *Quranic* and *Sunnah* teachings plus those doctrines clearly derived from the *Quran* and *Sunnah* through the application of *qiyas*. Thus, much of substantive law (*fiqh*), which was actually based upon human understanding and interpretation, was given a more sacrosanct character. *Ijma* (consensus) also contributed to the process of absolutizing tradition. Although ijma served as a check on individual interpretation (*ijtihad*), the ongoing dynamic, dialectical *ijtihad-ijma* relationship tended to be forgotten. This is reflected in the saying attributed to the Prophet: "My community will never agree on an error." A mechanism created to arrive at authoritative interpretations took on the aura of infallibility. Thus, the substantive law (*fiqh*) found in the manuals of the law schools, much of which was conditioned by historical and social circumstances as well as the use of reason, came to be "enshrined" as a detailed immutable blueprint for society. The doctrine of *taqlid* (imitation or following) was the natural conclusion to this process of the sacralization of tradition.

Ijtihad *vs.* Taqlid

At the center of the struggle for reform is the doctrine of *taqlid*. According to this teaching, with the end of the period of the great *imams* (end of the tenth century), Islamic law has reached its completion. No longer were jurists considered capable of or permitted to exercise independent reasoning. The doors of *ijtihad* were closed and the creative activity during the golden age of Islamic jurisprudence came to an end. It was followed by what a noted Muslim jurist has called "the era of sterility," which has lasted to the present time.

This state of affairs continued for an extended period of time mainly because Islamic society remained relatively stable. Few social forces or individuals challenged the authority of *taqlid* or the medieval legal manuals. Among the noteworthy exceptions, however, was Ibn Taymiyah, the distinguished Hanbali jurist who claimed his own right of ijtihad. Others did not follow his lead until the advent of pre-modernist movements in the eighteenth century. Muhammad ibn Abd al-Wahhab in Arabia and Shah Wali Allah of Delhi rejected the blind following of medieval jurists and asserted their right to *ijtihad*. Their general plan was to renew the Muslim community by going back to the primary sources, the *Quran* and *Sunnah* of the Prophet. Their efforts provided a principal legacy to Muslim modernism in the late nineteenth and twentieth centuries.

The great Egyptian modernist Muhammad Abduh wrote in the late 1900's of the disease of *taqlid* which afflicted many Muslims. Abduh often argued that Islam had freed Muslims from blind imitation and enjoined the reasoning of *ijtihad*:

> The *Quran* directs us, enjoining rational procedure and intellectual inquiry. It forbids us to be slavishly credulous and for our stimulus points to the moral of peoples who simply followed their fathers with complacent satisfaction and were finally involved in an utter collapse of their beliefs and their own disappearance as a community. It (*taqlid*) is a deceptive thing, and though it may be pardoned in an animal is scarcely seemly in man.

A similar attitude toward the continued right to *ijtihad* was voiced by the Indian modernist Sayyid Ahmad Khan, and in the twentieth century by the most celebrated Muslim modernist of Pakistan, Muhammad Iqbal when he wrote: "The closing of the door of *Ijtihad* is pure fiction suggested partly by the crystallization of legal thought in Islam, and partly by that intellectual laziness which, especially in the period of spiritual decay, turns great thinkers into idols."

The influence of the doctrine of *taqlid* in legislative reform can be seen in the indirect and often inconsistent legal techniques employed by modern Egyptian jurists to provide a *taqlid* façade and thus avoid the charge of practicing *ijtihad*. In Pakistan, the direct assertion by the *Marriage and Family Laws Commission of* 1955 of its right to *ijtihad* resulted in a swift and strong reaction from the majority of the *ulama* and other conservative forces which contributed to the delay until 1961 of family law legislation.

Distinction between *Shariah* and *Fiqh*

Modern legislators' dependence upon taqlid is directly related to an important distinction, often blurred in modern times, between *Shariah* and *fiqh*. *Shariah* is the Divine Law while *fiqh* is the product of human understanding that has sought to interpret and apply the Divine Law in space and time. It is the confusion of this distinction between *Shariah* and *fiqh*, reinforced by the doctrine of *taqlid*, that has led to the overly sacrosanct attitude toward the *fiqh* of the ancestors. Early jurists acknowledged this distinction. An awareness of the profound difference between the perfection of the *Shariah* and the imperfection of man's comprehension of it was well-illustrated by the reluctance of many early jurists to accept the office of *qadi*, a judicial office that would make them responsible before God not only for the interpretation but also for the application of law.

Usul Al-fiqh (Sources of Law) and Islamic Reform

The primary textual sources of the law are the *Quran* and *Sunnah* and it is to these that reformers address themselves. As the very word of God, the *Quran* is the fundamental textual source of the *Shariah*. Not a comprehensive legal manual but rather an ethico-religious revelation, its primary legal value is as the sourcebook of Islamic values: The *Holy Quran* is the Godmade, sublime statement of the ought-to-be the *Holy Quran* contains a complete and perfect world-and-life view." It is the source from which the specific regulations of substantive law (*furu al-fiqh*) are derived through human effort.

The primary area of concern in the relationship between the *Quran* and legal reform is exegesis. A distinctive emphasis which emerges in modernist writings is the necessity to get at the motive, intent, or purpose behind *Quranic* passages. This approach reasserts the original influence of *Quranic* values in the early development of law and, as such, seeks to renew the process by which *Quranic* values were applied to newly-encountered social situations in the first centuries of Islamic legal history. The demands of a rapidly-changing society require once more, as in the formative period, substantive legal reforms to meet the needs of the Muslim family. Therefore, a clear grasp of the content of the Divine Will as expressed in the

Quran and as applicable today is imperative. The fundamental questions facing Muslims today are those that confronted the early jurists: "What is the moral imperative which the *Holy Quran* had brought from God? How does it read when translated into the language of obligation pertinent to the concrete situations of real life?"

The possibility of *Quranic* norms providing a complete basis of legal reform has also been recognized by a Western authority on Islamic law: "The *Quranic* precepts are in the nature of ethical norms broad enough to support modern legal structures and capable of varying interpretations to meet the particular needs of time and place."

The task of Muslim exegetes is a systematic study of the value system of the *Quran* and the hierarchization of its ethico-religious values. This method would resolve the problem of *naskh* ("abrogation", the suppression of one *Shariah* rule by a later one where divergent regulations exist) as well as supply a reasonable explanation for the claim of the comprehensiveness of the *Quran*. Most importantly, it would provide a context within which one could understand the value of specific *Quranic* regulations.

Emphasis would be shifted beyond the specific regulations to its intent, to the value it sought to uphold. Thus a *Quranic* prescription has two levels of importance the specific injunction or command, whose details may be relative to its space and time context, and the ideal or *Quranic* value, whose realization the specific regulation intends to fulfill. Since the task of the Muslim community is the realization of these *Quranic* values, the goal of jurists is to insure that *fiqh* regulations embody these *Shariah* values as fully and perfectly as possible.

This approach could, for example, be applied to a particularly timely problem in family law reform, namely, the equality of the sexes. Verses from the *Quran* have been used by different factions to both support a woman's subservience to a man and to defend her rights of equality. This seeming contradiction can be resolved by an analysis of the relevant *Quranic* verses. One can reduce the concerns of these verses to two basic categories: the ethico-religious and the socioeconomic. On the ethico-religious level, the positions of men and women are on an equal standing, both as to their religious obligations toward God and their peers as well as their consequent reward or punishment: "The Believers, men and women, are protectors one of another: they enjoin what is just, and forbid what is evil; they observe regular prayers, practice regular charity, and obey God and His Apostle. On them will God pour His mercy. God hath promised to believers men and women, gardens under which rivers flow, to dwell therein, and beautiful mansions to dwell in gardens of everlasting bliss".

In the socioeconomic sphere, scholars of Islam agree that a major concern of the *Quran* was the betterment of woman's position by establishing her legal capacity, granting her economic rights (dower, inheritance, etc.), and thus raising her social status. However, some also cite *Quranic* verses whose traditional interpretations support what today would be an inequitable position for women. Perhaps the most commonly cited verse is *Quran IV*:34, which some interpret as indicating men's priority over women: Men are in charge of women, because Allah hath made one to excel the other, and because they spend their property [for the support of women]."

However, the "priority" attributed to men over women is best understood as originating from their greater responsibility as protectors and maintainers within the socioeconomic context of Arabian society during the Prophet's time. Men, by virtue of their duty to defend and support their extended family members, enjoyed more rights and subsequently a different status in Muslim society. This understanding of man's role is illustrated by another possible translation of the same *Quranic* verse: "Men are the guardians [*i.e.* protectors and maintainers] over women because God made some of them [to excel] over others and because they [men] provide support from their wealth."

The resolution of the dilemma caused by this verse in modern times can be found by applying the principle of the hierarchization of *Quranic* values. The moral and religious equality of the sexes before God represents the highest expression of the value of equality. Furthermore, the ethico-religious equality of women is independent of, and not subject to, change of social situation. This value, then, enjoys a higher degree of priority over any value that is dependent upon a changing social context. The religious obligations incumbent upon man and woman equally belong to the *ibadat* (religious duties due God) regulations which are not subject to change. In contrast, matters of the socioeconomic sphere belong to *muamalat* (social relations, transactions) which are subject to change.

The assertion of man's "priority," in the sense of "responsibility" for woman, reflects his superiority over her by virtue of her socio-economic dependence upon him in a particular form of society. The traditional interpretation of man's priority mirrored the influence of customary practice upon some exegetes. However, when the social situation of women changes, as it has for increasing numbers of women in the twentieth century, they will no longer necessarily be dependent upon their husbands for maintenance and protection. Consequently, the concept of "priority" of husband over wife in the socioeconomic sphere is subject to change.

The two prime areas of family law affecting women's equal rights today are divorce and polygamy. Both provide excellent illustrations of the use of *Quranic* values in justifying legal reform.

The *Quran* recognized the necessity of divorce, it did so reluctantly, viewing divorce as a last resort where the marriage contract has been strained to its limits. The existence of these values in early Muslim society was further reflected in the traditions of the Prophet Muhammad, such as: "Get married, and do not divorce; indeed, divorce causes the Throne of God to shake!"

The religious and social equality of women with men is a theme well-documented in the *Quran*. Equality is specifically affirmed in the area of divorce: "And women shall have rights similar to the rights against them, according to what is equitable". While this verse recognizes equal rights of divorce for women, no *Quranic* verse supports the license of divorce presently awarded to males.

Equality of divorce rights is further exemplified in *hadith* literature. The *Sunnah* of the Prophet embodied in these *hadiths* provides a record of the Muslim community's lived experience of *Quranic* values. Where possible, then, while grounding legal changes in *Quranic* values, reformers can also utilize the traditions of the Prophet to ascertain how these values were understood and thus exemplified through the actions of the Prophet. One noteworthy tradition dealing with women's rights to dissolution is that of Aishah, the wife of the Prophet, who reported:

A girl came and stated that her father had given her in marriage and told her to wait till the Prophet arrived. When the Prophet came, I told him the full story of the girl. He at once sent for the father of the girl and inquired of him whether the facts stated were true, after which he told the girl that she was at liberty to choose or repudiate her husband. The girl replied saying that she chose to retain her marriage, and that she wanted only to know whether women had any rights in the matter.

The very form of this *hadith* reveals its didactic intent -that of affirming women's right of divorce. Another illustration of women's right to a dissolution of an unfavorable marriage is cited in a report from Imam Malik and Abu Daud. "The wife of Thabit bin Qais, Habibah bint Sahil told the Prophet 'I and Thabit cannot pull together.' When Thabit came the Prophet said to him: 'This is what your wife says about you, so leave her.'"

These hadiths, if coupled with the previously quoted *Quranic* teaching regarding women's right to divorce, provide an Islamic rationale for legal reform in divorce that will enjoy the twofold support of the traditionally-acknowledged material sources of Islamic law, the *Quran* and the *Sunnah* of the Prophet.

To implement this legal reform, citing the inequitable situation that has resulted from the male's abuse of *talaq* and basing oneself on *Quranic* values, a strong case can be made for establishing equal divorce rights by taking away the male's extrajudicial rights of repudiation and equalizing the option to exercise divorce by requiring that all divorce suits be subject to the courts as has been done in a number of Muslim countries.

In addition, based on *Quranic* values, arguments for the restriction and even the prohibition of polygamy are also possible. The *Quran* had introduced reforms in pre-Islamic Arabian practice by restricting the prevalent practice and limiting the number of wives permitted a man to four. But even this permission was contingent upon the just treatment of each wife: "Marry women of your choice, two, three or four. But if ye fear ye shall not be able to deal justly (with them) then only one". Taking into consideration the unrestricted polygamy of pre-Islamic Arabia as well as the social situation in which this verse was written, namely the battle of Uhud and the death of many warriors and consequent problem of numerous widows and children, an argument could be made that the social context of these *Quranic* times made it difficult to go beyond the limitation of four wives. Yet one could conclude with Muhammad Abduh and Ahmad Khan that the ideal of the *Quran*, as seen in the *Quranic* value of impartiality, is monogamy. Thus, the *Quranic* value of "equal justice" for each wife can be used as the criterion for restricting polygamy today. A similar approach has been used in drafting legal regulations which require a married man who wishes to take another wife to demonstrate to the courts his ability to treat his wives equally in terms of finances as well as love and affection.

Moving even further, the absolute prohibition of polygamy may be based on the requirement of impartiality and the impossibility of its full realization today. *Quranic* support for this contention is available. In addition to *Quran IV*:3, a corollary verse states: "Ye are never able to be fair and just as between women, even if it is your ardent desire". Therefore, an Islamic defense of the above legal changes in divorce and polygamy could be based upon the argument that a necessary continuation of the ongoing task of Muslim jurisprudence is to insure that the laws of *fiqh* for each age express *Quranic* values as fully as possible. Subhi Mahmasani in discussing the reasons for the decline of Muslims underscores the failure of some early jurists to incorporate *Quranic* values in law as fully as possible: "However some jurists were influenced by dominant pre-Islamic customs. and declined to apply in such cases the rulings imposed by the teachings of religion. If they had done so, giving religious and ethical principles more consideration, along with as much implementation in law as had been possible, their attitude would have been closer to the spirit of Islamic jurisprudence and teaching." In effect, then, these reforms may be viewed as taking those *Quranic* values which traditionally had been regarded as moral exhortations for Muslims' personal conscience and incorporating them as legal conditions.

Sunnah of the Prophet

As has already been indicated in examples of *hadiths* regarding marriage and divorce, an axiological approach can validly be applied to the second material source of law the *Sunnah* of the Prophet. The *Sunnah* also provided those Islamic values which permeated the development of classical legal theory. To focus once more on these ideals, freeing them where necessary from the limitations of specific details which reflect the space and time context of early Islamic society, would enable the reapplication of these *Sunnah* values in contemporary Muslim society.

The validity of this method is justified by an appreciation of the historical development of *Sunnah* and *Hadith*. Twentieth century scholarship has, in fact, demonstrated that the development of Islamic jurisprudence in general and *Sunnah* in particular was a much more dynamic and creative process than classical theory would suggest. Indeed, at the center of the creation of Muslim law by jurists and *qadis* was the application of Islamic values to the concrete social situations facing the community on a wider scale than had even been imagined. Thus, a more accurate historical view provides a corrective for misconceptions regarding the formation and nature of Islamic law. This results, as will be seen, in a rationale or methodology more conducive to Muslim family law reform, as well as Islamic reform in general.

Although the classical theory of *Sunnah* and *Hadith* has predominated until modern times, twentieth century Orientalist scholarship has rejected the authenticity of much of the Prophetic *Sunnah*. Drawing on the investigations of I. Goldziher, D. S. Margoliouth and C. S. Hurgronje, Joseph Schacht in his *Origins of Muhammadan Jurisprudence* concluded that the bulk of the Prophetic *Sunnah* could not be considered authentic in the classical sense. Schacht believed that very little information about the Prophet, outside of the *Quran*, was handed down from the past. He maintained that what is called *Sunnah* of the Prophet is not the words and deeds of the Prophet, but apocryphal material originating from customary practice that was back-projected in the eighth century to a more authoritative source: first the Successors, then the Companions, and finally to the Prophet himself.

Schacht's thesis, then, is that the term *Sunnah* of the Prophet actually developed for the first time in the eighth century under the influence of the Traditionalist Movement and the aegis of al-Shafii was the first major jurist to limit the term *sunnah* (custom or practice) to the verified *Sunnah* of the Prophet, *i.e.*, his model behavior. Schacht maintains that the use of this term actually gave legal authority to later customary practices and traditions. Therefore, he claims, what is called *Sunnah* of the Prophet is not a reliable source of Prophetic norms.

Schacht further held that because al-Shafii had won special status for the *Sunnah* of the Prophet as a material source of law, he had essentially excluded those traditions of the early schools that many believed were true manifestations of the Prophetic *Sunnah*. As a result, many jurists recognized the need to justify and authenticate those traditions they favored. Thus, the fifty-year period following Shafii's death witnessed a sudden burgeoning of narratives (*hadith*) about the Prophet's actions which came about in one of two ways: first, by the original creation of new *hadiths* which were actually contemporary interpretations of what the Prophet would have said or done about some problem, or, second, by the projection of *sunnahs* originating from the Companions or Successors back to the most authoritative source, the Prophet himself. On the basis of his research, Schacht found no evidence of legal traditions before 722 or one hundred years after the death of the Prophet.

Although Schacht's findings are helpful for more fully understanding the creative role of the community in the development of Islamic law, his conclusions seem excessive. To state that no tradition goes back prior to 722 creates an unwarranted vacuum in Islamic history. To consider all *hadith* apocryphal until they are proven otherwise is to reverse the burden of proof. Rather, a *hadith* accepted for over ten centuries should stand until proven otherwise. This sifting process, while more laborious than Schacht's approach, seems sounder. Secondly, the "first century vacuum" theory does violence to the deeply ingrained sense of tradition in Arab culture which all scholars, both Muslim and Orientalist, have acknowledged. As Fazlur Rahman notes: "The Arabs, who memorized and handed down poetry of their poets, sayings of their soothsayers and statements of their judges and tribal leaders, cannot be expected to fail to notice and narrate deeds and sayings of one whom they acknowledged as the Prophet of God."

And finally, what of the science of *hadith* verification with its specific and detailed criteria for establishing authority? While it was not foolproof and forgeries certainly existed, the wholesale inaccuracy that Schacht and those who follow him in this matter attribute to this Muslim science is unjustified.

The central problem that Schacht's thesis seems to have created for Islamic jurisprudence involves the normativeness of the *Sunnah*. Many Western scholars, on the basis of Schacht's findings, have maintained that the so-called "Prophetic *Sunnah*" are merely the attitudes of early generations of Muslims (actual customary practices) that developed normativeness only after two centuries when they were idealized as "*Sunnah* of the Prophet." Rather than constituting a stumbling block, the findings of Schacht, if correctly understood, present a dynamic picture of the development of Islamic law which demonstrates the viability of the sources of Muslim jurisprudence as a methodology for change.

Much of the misunderstanding about *Sunnah* results from its long and various usage in history. The original meaning of the base root of the word, *sanna*, is "to open or pave a road, to introduce, or set an example." The secondary meaning is "to follow." *Sunnah* in the sense of first introducing a precedent and second following that precedent was used even in pre-Islamic times.

With the advent of Islam, while some pre-Islamic customs were rejected, most continued some reformed, some supplemented, and others approved either expressly or tacitly. They could never again be merely the customs of pre-Islamic days because tribal practices and beliefs (*i.e.* customs) had been accepted or modified by the *Quran* and by the example of the Prophet. Muhammad's judgments, attitudes, and conduct revealed *Quranic* values in concrete form as he lived daily in the community. This concrete revelation set new precedents to be followed the Prophetic *Sunnah*. These precedents were acted upon as future generations set their own examples or *sunnahs*. It is in this sense that Abu Yusuf in his *Kitab al-Kharaj* asks the Caliph Harun al-Rashid "to introduce some good *sunnahs*." The values of the Prophetic *Sunnah* permeated early Muslim society both in themselves (*i.e.* Muslim works and deeds) and as ideals in light of which new practices were judged and either accepted or rejected.

But just how the reality of the *Sunnah* of the Prophet had been operating through the early generations must yet be described. As has been indicated, the term "*sunnah*" has been used throughout history to describe a number of phenomena. We have discussed the meanings or usages of the term *sunnah* as precedents established by the ancestors in pre-Islamic Arabia as well as the Prophetic *Sunnah* or Muhammad's ideal conduct that superseded and modified the pre-Islamic customs. This led to the *sunnah* or exemplary behavior of the earliest generations (the Companions) in the Islamic community, the behavior that grew out of the precedents set by the Prophet. To this list we must add the *sunnah* of the next generation, the Successors, which consisted of their interpretations of law based on the living tradition of the earlier generations and the *hadith*. The interpretations of early jurists in this period who reasoned on the basis of *Sunnah* varied. Disagreement about which incidents in the Prophet's life were more significant to a certain problem and their application naturally led to differing regional interpretations, and so regional *sunnah* developed. All, however, were ultimately based on Prophetic *Sunnah*.

A significant point to remember is that in early Islamic thought *Sunnah* of the Prophet was far from being differentiated from the *sunnahs* that followed: *sunnahs* of the Companions or of the Successors. People who believed that they were following the Islamic norm would naturally equate the Prophet's *Sunnah* with their own. For example, the early Medinese community viewed itself as the community of the Prophet, having lived directly under the Prophet and his Companions. Quite naturally, they would equate their way of life with the *Sunnah* of the Prophet and would never have occasion to draw distinctions.

Prophetic *Sunnah* served as the point of reference for Companions, and through their example, for the Successors who followed. The admissability of an action was judged in the light of the Prophetic ideal, *Sunnah* values. This understanding of Prophetic *Sunnah*, while it adds a more dynamic and creative dimension to the theory developed by medieval Muslim scholars, comes to the same conclusion in its emphasis on the importance of *Sunnah* as a material source of law. The normativeness of *Sunnah* as a source of Islamic values remains, while a more historical and developmental understanding emerges. The classical idea of *Hadith* literature as bonafide narrative reports that convey the Prophet's *Sunnah* has been the subject of considerable controversy. Much of modern scholarship, following Schacht's theory regarding the development of *Sunnah*, has maintained that most, if not all, of the traditions ascribed to the Prophet were actually written much later, and therefore lack authenticity. But were the *hadith* always regarded as strictly historical? Many *hadiths* themselves seem to admit the formulation of new traditions. Consider, for example, the tradition in which the Prophet says: "Sayings attributed to me which agree with the *Quran* go back to me whether I actually said them or not," or the *hadith* in which the Prophet says, "Whatever of good saying there be, I can be taken to have said it.

These *hadiths* and many others evidence concern not for strict historicity, but rather for sound interpretation of *Quranic* norms. In keeping with this line of thought, Fazlur Rahman calls the *hadith* "the *Sunnah-Ijtihad* of the first generations of Muslims," a "gigantic and monumental commentary of the Prophet by the early community" which "constitutes an epitome of the wisdom of Classical Muslims."

Thus, despite the lack of historicity of some *hadiths*, they still represent the Prophet-directed vehicle for the interpretation and elaboration of *Quranic* norms. As such, they provide a rich source of Islamic values as lived and realized by the early community. As H. A. R. Gibb has observed: "Study of the *hadith* is not confined to determining how far it represents the authentic teaching and practice of Muhammad and the primitive Madinan community. It serves also as a mirror in which the growth and development of Islam as a way of life and of the larger Islamic community are most truly reflected.

In conclusion, while the result of twentieth century critical studies does render an interpretation of the historical development of *Sunnah* which differs from the classical theory, this does not constitute a threat to Islam. Rather, a reinterpretation of the formation and nature of Islamic jurisprudence emerges. The result is a dynamic picture of the ongoing process of Islamization which is reflected in the *hadith* collections of the *Sunnah* of the Prophet. This same traditional methodology (as newly understood or rediscovered), contributes to a viable method for contemporary legal reform. That process which was essentially formulated to meet the needs of the classical period and was unfortunately "frozen" by the "closing of the door of *ijtihad*" and the ascendancy of *taqlid* (blind imitation), can now be continued once more.

Ray and Qiyas

In addition to the two material sources of Islamic law, the *Quran* and *Sunnah*, the classical sources (*usul al-fiqh*) included *qiyas* (analogy) and *ijma* (consensus). As with the textual sources, the fuller historical perspective of *qiyas* and *ijma* available today enhances their viability as mechanisms for contemporary legal reform by showing their original dynamic nature.

Study of the development and usage of *qiyas* must be placed within the general context of the development of *ijtihad*, of which it is a part. *Ijtihad* means "self-exertion," to exert oneself in understanding and interpreting the Shariah. During the period of the early development of Islamic Law, the *ijtihad* was *ijtihad al-ray*, the exercise of "opinion or personal judgement" by the early *qadis* (judges). The history of Islamic law shows that ray played an important role in the decisions of the early *qadis* and the functioning of the ancient schools of law. The task of the early *qadis* was the application of local law. Basing themselves on the customs of their locale as well as *Quranic* norms and available *Sunnah*, the *qadis* would render their opinion via legal decisions. The legal decisions of the courts were almost totally dependent upon the personal discretion of each *qadi* both as to his understanding of local law as well as the extent of his application of *Quranic* norms.

Ray also played an important role in the early development of the ancient schools of law during the eighth century; it was especially associated with the schools of Iraq. The jurists of the early law schools employed ray in the formulation of new rules. Finding themselves a century after the Prophet in a socio-economic situation quite different from that of seventh century Arabia, the task of the Iraqis often involved the formulation of Islamic solutions for new problems. Reason was employed to extend divine prescriptions to novel situations. The use of personal judgment became progressively more systematic and disciplined by the use of *qiyas*, analogical reasoning.

Throughout the dynamic processes described above, the major activity which emerges is the use of reason to apply Shariah values derived from the *Quran* and *Sunnah*. These were a determining factor in qadi decisions, and most importantly, constituted the ultimate standard for the process of Islamization undertaken by the ancient schools of law. Furthermore, *Shariah* values continued to occupy a central role in the drafting of Islamic solutions for newly encountered problems: first, in the use of ray and even more consistently and systematically, with the development of qiyas (*ijtihad al-qiyas*) (reasoning by analogy). The role of Shariah values in the process of qiyas has aptly been described as: "The deduction, from a shariah principle, of the hukm, or shariah value, applicable to a new problem.

Istislah

The use of reason, in fact, stretched beyond the *ijtihad at-qiyas*, which came to be the only form recognized by classical theory. For Islamic jurisprudence was concerned with insuring the *Quranic* concern for human welfare, justice, and equity. This concern to guarantee that should the letter of the law as arrived at through qiyas result in a harsh or rigid conclusion, a means be available to restore its spirit, resulted in the principles of istishab (presumption of continuity), istihsan (juristic preference), and *istislah* (public interest). It is this last principle, *istislah*, which seems best suited for contemporary legal reforms for it provides a greater scope for the exercise of *ijtihad* and clearly puts into perspective the ends of law, namely, justice and equity, and human welfare or public interest (*maslahah*).

The employment of the Maliki principle of *maslahah* as a source of contemporary legal reform was championed by Muhammad Abduh and his follower, Muhammad Rashid Rida and the Salafiyyah movement, a reform movement initiated by Jamal al-Din al-Afghani and carried on by Abduh and his disciple Rida.

The traditional Maliki position was that the muamalat (social transactions) regulations of the *Quran* and *Sunnah* had rational connotations and that God's purpose in revealing them was the promotion of human welfare. Thus, a jurist should select an interpretation which best accorded with the public interest (*maslahah*).

Abduh and Rida extended this concept so that where social needs were not covered by specific *Shariah* texts, a jurist using his reason might interpret the law in light of the public interest. The result was a method (*istislah*) by which Islamic law might continuously and comprehensively be adapted to changing societal needs.

Istislah can function today in two instances: first, when conclusions arrived at through reasoning by analogy (*qiyas*) seem contrary to public interest; second, where a social need exists and the interest involved has not been covered by any specific *Shariah* texts. This latter usage is relevant in modern Muslim law reform. The introduction of legislation becomes possible provided such legislation is in the public interest and in harmony with the spirit of the *Shariah*, *i.e.*, Shariah values. The result is a comprehensive methodology for reform which provides the recognition of the social welfare dimension of law as well as its Islamic character. While this approach differs somewhat from the classical formulation (law as the product of the *Quran* and *Sunnah* texts, analogical deductions, and consensus), it is, in fact, more in accord with the actual history of Islamic law in which historical and social influences and needs played important roles.

This use of *istislah* places greater emphasis on the probability of law rather than its infallibility. The greater recognition of the use of reason, in determining a more equitable solution in light of public interest and its concordance with *Shariah* values, underscores the human character and limitations of the substantive law of *fiqh*.

The employment of *iststah* as outlined above would resolve a juristic difficulty caused by the position advocated by the majority report of Pakistan's Marriage and Family Laws Commission in 1956. The majority advocated a right to *ijtihad* provided the desired social change was not prohibited by the *Quran*. Such a methodology appeared to lack a positive Islamic rationale and thus seemed simply utilitarian and un-Islamic. However, the same results could be achieved by the advocacy of the principle of *istislah*. Its use would result in the more positive emphasis on looking to the revealed texts for *Shariah* values to support the legislation rather than the negative criterion of lack of *Quranic* injunction. A continuity between reform legislation and the Islamic tradition would be more clearly established. In addition, acceptance of the criterion of public welfare (*maslahah*) means recognition that should the interests of the community necessitate change, the law can adapt itself. This would assure the Islamic character of a dynamic and comprehensive law.

The Egyptian reform that sought to protect the rights of orphaned grandchildren of the deceased provides a good illustration of the use of ististah. In drafting their reform legislation, Egyptian reformers took a circuitous route and avoided a direct change in the law of inheritance since they could find no traditional authority to ostensibly follow. Instead, they took an indirect route and provided for orphaned grandchildren by introducing the concept of "obligatory bequest" in the law of testamentary disposition.

However, a more direct reform in the law of inheritance itself could have been achieved by a twofold argument which satisfied the two criteria for the exercise of *istislah, i.e.,* public welfare and consonance with the spirit of the *Quran*. First, the general welfare of Muslim society requires the rectification of this deficiency in the law of inheritance so that the rights of orphaned grandchildren are protected. Second, such a change is in harmony with the spirit of the *Quran* in which the welfare of orphans is a prominent theme. In addition, the general intent of the *Quran* regarding inheritance is to protect inheritance rights, as witnessed by the "inheritance verses," and not to deprive someone of his share.

This same argument (*i.e.,* the general welfare of Muslim society plus *Quranic* concern to protect inheritance rights) applies to the Egyptian reform regarding collaterals of the deceased. Through this reform, collaterals were protected by giving them a right of succession equivalent to that of the grandfather of the deceased. As has been discussed, this was done to prevent their exclusion from inheritance in their brother's or sister's estate by their uncle.

Ijma

Because of its role in closing the door of *ijtihad, ijma* (consensus) has often been associated with the stagnation of *taqlid* (blind imitation). Such an understanding can be deceptive if *ijma* is understood as an unchanging Islamic institution from earliest times. In fact, the concept of *ijma* enjoyed a complex history of formulation, best characterized as a living creative process.

The earliest stage of *ijma* was that of the period immediately after the Prophet when almost every Muslim had been a "Companion" of the Prophet. During this time, *ijma* functioned not as a conscious concept but rather as the agreed-upon practice of the Muslim community living in accordance with the *Quran* and the example (*Sunnah*) of the Prophet. This same situation held true for the next two generations, that of the "Successors", *i.e.,* the

Companions' children (*tabiin*) and the Companions' children's children (*tabii al-tabiin*).

With the passage of time, the community grew and spread geographically. Muslims increasingly found themselves in differing social situations faced with many new problems. It was during this period that the early law schools developed and that *ijma* as a formal legal principle emerged.

Political and juristic leaders of the early communities in Medina, Iraq, Syria, etc., exercised *ijtihad* (interpretation) to determine new modes of action. The agreed-upon practice of these leaders constituted the *ijma al-aimmah, i.e.*, the consensus of the leaders.

Early *ijma*, then, provided the Muslim community with a living instrument for revision and growth in the creation of fresh law to fit changing times. In the ancient schools of law, the relationship between *ijtihad* (interpretation) and *ijma* (consensus) was an ongoing process, moving from individual opinion to community approval to accepted practice to difference of opinion if conditions changed, and therefore to the reinterpretation of *ijtihad* and *ijma* again.

Moreover, this process of thinking and re-thinking was itself subject to differing views as to its nature. Early in its development, *ijma* was more a regional interpretation by the jurists of a particular province. The Maliki School, for example, gave great emphasis to the *ijma* of Medina. Since it was the home of the Prophet, they felt that their *ijma* was a continuation of the Prophet's *Sunnah*. The Hanbalis stressed the *ijma* of the Companions. The Shafii and Hanafi Schools believed that *ijma* should be applied not only to the earliest generations but to all times and to all geographical areas.

Ijma contributed to the great diversity of interpretation and doctrine in the Muslim community, a diversity which, as we have seen, clashed with the strong Traditionist Movement (*Ahl al-Hadith*) in the eighth century, with its successful drive for uniformity both in the sources of law and therefore, in substantive law itself. The *ijma* practiced by the early schools was strongly condemned by al-Shafii for its diversity. He recognized only the consensus of the entire Muslim community as valid and thus insistently told the differing schools, "You do not have agreement (*ijma*) but disagreement (*iftiraq*). " Al-Shafii's conception of *ijma* was radically different from that of the early schools. For them, *ijma* was not al-Shafii's theoretical and, practically speaking, unworkable source of law which required a total agreement of all Muslims. The *ijma* of the early schools, linked as it was with *ijtihad* in a dynamic dialectical process, provided a powerful means for the adaptation of law to changing circumstances. But with the increasing power of the *Ahl al-Hadith* and the consequent rejection of original interpretations of the law through *ijtihad*, the organic interrelationship between *ijtihad* and *ijma* was severed. *Ijma* was isolated – no longer in dynamic tension with fresh *ijtihad*, it became a principle of rigid approval which, once made, was considered forever binding.

In the final classical theory of Islamic law, established in the tenth century, the agreed-upon doctrines of the schools were considered fixed, unchangeable. Henceforth, jurists were to practice *taqlid*, to follow the established principles of their individual schools. Thus the "closing of the door of *ijtihad*" in the medieval period, which had its authoritative basis in the consensus of the scholars of the time, became the prime cause for the general loss of dynamism.

Al-Ghazzali was among the noteworthy exceptions in this process of legal stagnation. He recognized the consensus of the religious scholar (*ijma al-ulama*) of a generation as a source of law and thus continued to acknowledge the possibility of a living consensus. However, the process of legal stagnation was not to be reversed.

Modernist Muslim thought has sought to restore *ijma* to its rightful place and thus re-establish the dynamic dialectic of the *ijtihad-ijma* relationship. Muhammad Abduh, the "Father of Muslim Modernism, who was a strong advocate of the role of reason, the right of *ijtihad*, viewed *ijma* as a consensus of reason which can reasonably be presumed free from error. However, Abduh's concept of *ijma* is less dogmatic than the traditional notion. His idea of freedom from error is more the presumption of a reasonable possibility, where the agreement of a generation's most learned interpreters (*mujtahidun*) is obtained, than the affirmation of an absolute infallibility. Abduh recognized the right of future generations, in view of changed circumstances, to reinterpret the law (*fiqh*). In this way, the dynamic relationship between reason (*ijtihad*) and collective reason or a consensus of reason (*ijma*) is restored.

Muslim modernists follow Abduh's position *vis-a-vis ijma* and the question of its infallibility. In essence, no denial of the value and binding power of *ijma* occurs relative to the period in which it occurred. For indeed, the function of *ijma* is to serve as a brake and safeguard on individual subjective *ijtihad,* which by itself is no more than fallible conjecture (*zann*), and either to reject it as erroneous or to approve it as applicable for Muslim society. What modernists reject is an unlimited or absolute infallibility which denies that such as *ijma* is open to question and change in future generations as societal circumstances change.

Among reformers in the Indian subcontinent, a progressive reinterpretation of *ijma* has occurred in an attempt to adapt it to the needs of contemporary Muslim society. Ameer Ali advocated the broadening of the notion of *ijma* and its incorporation within the constitutional government of a modern state. This general notion has become progressively more developed in the writings of Muslim reformers such as Muhammad Iqbal, considered by many to be the outstanding twentieth century modernist of India-Pakistan, and Fazlur Rahman.

Iqbal described *ijma* as "perhaps the most important legal notion in Islam." He recommended the transferral of *ijtihad* "from individual representatives of schools to a Muslim legislative assembly." The *ijma* of the community would be equated with the consensus of the legislatures of modern Muslim states.

Fazlur Rahman, former director of Pakistan's Islamic Research Institute and a member of the Islamic Ideology Council, has pursued a similar line of argument. For Rahman, the *Quran* is not a law book, but rather a guide. Within the framework of its general moral principles the Islamic community is free to develop its legal system. Even those "quasi-laws as do occur in the *Quran* are not meant to be literally applied in all times and climes; the principles on which these legal or quasi-legal pronouncements rest have to be given fresh embodiments in legislative terms." As with most Muslim modernists, Rahman's methodology rests on the dual principles of *ijtihad* and *ijma* which provide both the dynamism and permanence required to meet the needs of a changing society. *Ijtihad* is that means by which individuals "think out new solutions of problems on the basis of Islamic principles." The Islamic community will then have a spectrum of interpretations to weigh, discuss, and debate. The consensus which emerges from this process is its *ijma*, that consensus which will inform new laws passed by the legislature. Should public opinion change, the law is repealed and replaced by one which embodies the new consensus of the community (*ijma*).

What emerges from the equation of *ijma* with the consensus of a modern legislative assembly is a reinterpretation which is significantly different from traditional usage. In the past, the consensus of the community as a whole (*ummah*) or of the major figures in the law schools (*imams*) or of the religious scholars (*ulama*) occurred over a protracted period of time as certain interpretations (*ijtihad*) became more accepted than others and eventually became the agreed-upon practice. This traditional view of consensus is quite different from that obtained through the process of legislation in a national assembly.

Effective change need not necessitate the reorientation of *ijma* advocated by Iqbal and Rahman. Their suggestions regarding the transfer of *ijtihad* to a legislature can be used productively for dynamic legal changes to meet societal needs. At the same time, the difficulties which their method raises can be circumvented by equating the resulting social legislation with *ijtihad* alone and not *ijma*.

It is at this point that the dynamic relationship of *ijtihad* and *ijma* can be restored. *Ijma* provides the test of time and community experience which a new interpretation (*ijtihad*) must undergo in order that its long-range value be accepted by the community. If the new legislation (*ijtihad*) does not survive the questioning and debate within the community, it will be repealed and replaced. In contrast, should it remain unchanged, then its community acceptance (*ijma*) and authority will be established. However, it is important to note that even this fresh *ijma* may in future generations be subject to renewed *ijtihad* as the dialectical process continues.

It will serve to clarify this process and its importance. The question of polygamy has been a major issue in twentieth century Muslim family law reform. Reformers in most Muslim countries have attempted to restrict the exercise of polygamy through legislation based on their interpretation of *Quranic* values which concludes that monogamy is the *Quranic* ideal and thus should be the community's legal norm. The reform called for would constitute a significant departure from traditional Muslim social and legal practice. Furthermore, it means serious change affecting husbands, wives, and children. Therefore, the acceptance of monogamy as a long-range religious norm must be approached cautiously. To equate a legislative change enacted at a particular point in history by a single act of a legislative group with the *ijma* of the community is a drastic step. The passage of such legislation may be due to fortuitous circumstances in which a strong minority legislates a position repugnant to the majority. Such reform legislation may be repealed soon afterwards, or simply ignored by the majority of the population. Equating such an activity with *ijma* would reduce it to a meaningless concept.

Historically, it is possible to view the question of polygamy vis-a-vis monogamy in the contemporary Muslim world as a juncture in the *ijtihad-ijma* dialectic. Throughout the twentieth century, reformers have called for change. Initial draft legislation such as that submitted to and approved by the Egyptian Cabinet in 1927 was vetoed by King Fuad. However, in 1953 *Article* 17 of the *Syrian Law of Personal Status* enacted the first law restricting polygamy. Since then other countries such as Pakistan have passed similar legislation. The most sweeping legislation occurred in 1957 when *Article* 18 of the *Tunisian Law of Personal Status* decreed that polygamy was prohibited.

The debate regarding polygamy in the Muslim world today continues. Personal as well as collective (legislative) *ijtihad* has offered two basic reform positions restriction of polygamy or prohibition of polygamy. These are juxtaposed against the traditional *ijma* supporting the right of polygamy. Out of this protracted debate, a new *ijma* will emerge.

The use of *ijtihad* and *ijma* to provide a rationale for drafting Islamic law raises two controversial issues: (1) Who possesses the power to make laws? and (2) What is the role of the *ulama* (religious scholars)? Many conservative Muslims would agree that only Allah (God) can make laws and, thus, no individual or elected body can legislate. Most of the *ulama* and their followers would claim that only the *ulama* possess the traditionally accepted qualifications and expertise required to be a *mujtahid* (one who exercises the right of *ijtihad*).

The dispute regarding the power to make laws is again rooted in a failure to distinguish between the immutable *Shariah* (the divinely revealed principles and values) and *fiqh* (that body of law worked out by jurists and therefore the product of human understanding, interpretation, and application) which is historically conditioned and subject to change. Due to the predominance of the doctrine of *taqlid*, the law enshrined in the legal manuals has been viewed in practice if not in theory as divinely mandated. Thus, even where conservative religious leaders speak of the possibility of changing certain *fiqh* regulations, in practice they are often loath to do so.

The second issue who is qualified to interpret Islamic law is rooted in the *ulama*'s assertion of their traditional role as guardians of the law. They claim that they alone possess the traditionally accepted qualifications of a *mujtahid* (interpreter). Muslim reformers respond that the term *atim* (pl. *ulama*) simply means a learned person. Since there is no ordained clergy in Islam, all Muslims may qualify for this designation. As to the areas of knowledge which a *mujtahid* must possess, reformers maintain that knowledge of the traditional religious disciplines (*Quran, Hadith, Shariah*) is not restricted to the *ulama*. More importantly, the demands of modernity are such that expertise in many modern disciplines, such as economics, psychology, and sociology are also required today. This expertise falls beyond the competence of most *ulama*. Indeed the *ulama* are looked upon by many reformers as obstacles to change men whose limited training and world view, as well as a tendency to protect their own vested interests, prevent them from fully appreciating the demands of modernity and providing the leadership necessary for Islamic reform. The Iranian reformer Ali Shariati noted that the traditional religious leaders "suppressed true knowledge of religion, and hindered the true understanding of Shii beliefs."

Custom

In seeking an Islamic rationale for contemporary legal reforms, besides the official sources of Islamic jurisprudence, there are "extraneous sources" (from the classical viewpoint) which contributed significantly to substantive law. By far the most important of these is customary practice. A study of the role of custom provides a fuller picture of the sources of the material content of law and helps to explain the existence of certain attitudes and mores evident in classical family law.

Although not officially and theoretically recognized, customary law played a key role in the development of Islamic law. Custom (*adah, urf*) in pre-Islamic Arabia, as in many early traditional societies, served as law. For the majority of the Arabs, custom, the body of unwritten rules which had been developed and passed down through the generations, provided the positive laws of their society. Normative legal custom constituted the *Sunnah* (path or way) of the tribe.

The advent of Islam signalled a profound and radical change in Arabian society. Yet, while recognizing the introduction of new beliefs, regulations, and institutions, a good deal of the Islamic way consisted of a reform of existing customs and a continuance of that which was not in need of specific reform.

There are numerous ways in which custom became incorporated into Islamic law, among them, the procedures of the *qadis* (judges), the content of traditions (*hadith*), the Malikite regard for the *ijma* of Medina, and the *fatwas* of the *muftis*.

In the early courts of the Umayyad and early Abbasid periods, *qadis* in rendering a decision would look to the *Quran* and *Sunnah* for guidance, but where no relevant texts were found, they would then resort to the custom of their community. An example from the sphere of family law is the division of dower (*mahr*). The practice was to separate the dower into two parts, the first paid immediately, and the other deferred usually until the ending of the marriage. In situations in which the proportionate amounts had not been stipulated in the contract, the allotment was usually determined on the basis of local custom. This approach continued to be followed in modern times. The *Majallah* (Ottoman Civil Code) states: "A thing acknowledged by custom is regarded as an agreed upon stipulation".

A second avenue for the entrance of custom into Islamic law was the tradition (*hadith*) literature. The usual classification of the *Sunnah is al-sunnah al-qawliyah* (words), al-sunnah al-filiyah (deeds), and *al-sunnah al-taqririyah* (what Muhammad permitted). It is this last category, comprising actions performed in the presence of the Prophet without his disapproval, which represents that body of pre-Islamic Arabian customary practice which continued to be followed.

The *ijma* (consensus) of the Maliki law school, which was restricted to that of the Medinan community, is indicative of another historical source for custom. Where no explict text existed, the customs of the Medinese were regarded as a legal source. Besides the importance of the Prophet's community, this Maliki concept reflects the early tendency for the *ijma* to be a local geographical consensus (for example, the *ijma* of Kufa, Basra, Medina) which became its *sunnah*, or ideal pattern of behaviour of each local school. For example, the Hanafi doctrine of marriage equality (*kafaah*) which required that the husband be the equal of his wife in a number of respects, among them lineage, financial standing, and profession, is peculiar to the Hanafi school and reflects the practice of a more socially-stratified, class conscious society than Medina.

A final source for the incorporation of custom in law was the *fatwas* (opinions) of *muftis* (legal consultants). A *fatwa* is an opinion on a point of law rendered by a *mufti* in response to a question submitted to him by a private individual or by a *qadi*. The need for the office of *mufti* existed from the earliest period of legal development. Due to the vast expansion of Islam, the Islamic community found itself mingling with new cultures, novel ideas, and new problems. There were myriad occasions necessitating reference to competent legal scholars. As law developed and became increasingly complex, these legal specialists became increasingly important. Where a specific revealed text did not provide an answer to the legal problem before them, *muftis* adopted or modified customs of the day in light of *Shariah* values. As the times and their customs changed, so too might the substance of the *fatwa*.

Although the function of the *mufti* was essentially private and consultative, and so a *fatwa* was not legally binding, it could be utilized by a *qadi* and incorporated in his decision. More importantly, when a *fatwa* issued by a *mufti* on a new problem became recognized by the *ijma* of the scholars of a school, it was incorporated in the legal handbooks of the school. Finally, compilations of the responses of noted *muftis*, such as the *Fatawa Alamgiriyya*, came to be reckoned among the important authoritative legal references complimenting the standard *Shariah* manuals.

Although not officially recognized by classical theory, customary practice, then, came to form a substantial part of Islamic law. This realization should assist reformers in three ways. First, it underscores the extent to which custom did contribute to the body of substantive law, and so the inclusion of modern social standards or customs can be viewed as consistent with the manner in which law had been formulated to meet particular social needs in the past. Second, it demonstrates the process of Islamization of this customary law and therefore lays the foundation and provides the method for the replacing of old customs with newly Islamized customs appropriate to changed social situations. Third, it emphasizes the extent to which *fiqh* was influenced by fallible and mutable human understanding both in its content (since custom is the non-revelational product of a human society) and method (the reason of the *qadis*, *muftis*, and jurists of the law schools whose decisions incorporated custom in law). This makes the distinction between *Shariah* and *fiqh* that much clearer to all who still do not distinguish the immutable and the sacrosanct in Islamic law from the fallible, the particular and the human.

Summary

The twentieth century represents a period in Islamic history as critical as any yet encountered. The central problem is modernization and the key question, change. Muslim family law reform provides the major arena for Islamic reform. Muslims have grappled with the two major issues of reform: (1) the relationship of tradition and change, and (2) the means or methodology for reinterpretation and reform.

The classical theory of law presented a definitive picture of the formation of law, both its jurisprudential method (*usul al-fiqh*) and the branches of substantive law themselves (*furu al-fiqh*). The four sources of law (*Quran*, *Sunnah*, *qiyas*, and *ijma*) produced a body of law consisting of religious observances (*ibadat*) and social transactions (*muamalat*) of which family law is a major part. By the end of the tenth century the consensus (*ijma*) of scholars concluded that the basic rules of law had been discerned. The task of future jurists was to follow the teachings of the great *Imams* of the past. Thus, the gate of *ijtihad*, of independent interpretation, was closed, and *taqlid* or imitation reigned. Down through the ages, with few exceptions, the consensus of medieval jurists affirmed the completeness and authoritativeness for all times of law (*fiqh*) as found in the law books of the four Sunni schools. The law was complete; there was no need for substantive change.

As long as the structure of Muslim society remained essentially unchanged, Islamic law could generally meet the needs of the times. This is especially evident in the field of family law which remained operative until contemporary times. Muslim family law was a well-developed comprehensive approach to the major aspects of family life marriage, divorce, inheritance, etc., basically in tune with medieval Muslim society. Thus, during the long span of ten centuries, the classical view of law reigned throughout Muslim society.

However, this situation has been abruptly challenged in the modern period as Muslim societies have sought to respond to the challenges of modernization. The results of these new developments have led to social changes, among them changes in family structure and most especially in woman's status and role in society. While these changes have not affected all of society to the same degree, reforms in Muslim family law have occurred in most Muslim countries.

Despite the changes thus far, the conflict between the forces of conservatism and modernism has continued. Resistance to change often resulted in indirect, ad hoc legal methods of reform as well as the shelving of draft legislation. The problem which has emerged is still very much that of *taqlid* (following tradition) versus *ijtihad* (reinterpretation), the infallibility of classical law versus legal change. The task is not an easy one, namely, to provide an Islamic rationale for change, one clearly rooted in Islamic history.

The importance of providing an Islamic methodology for Islamic reform is especially evident today. As noted at the outset of this study, one aspect of the Islamic renewal or resurgence is a call for more Islamically oriented societies. Given the totality of Islam and the comprehensiveness of its world view as reflected in Islamic law, this has meant a call for more *Shariah* law. Potentially, such change could affect every area of life, from the nature and institutions of the state to family relations. Debates on the advisability of such attempts, as well as the nature of a return to *Shariah* rule, have occurred from

Egypt and the Sudan to Pakistan and Malaysia. Does a return to *Shariah* law mean simply going back to those laws which developed during the first centuries of Islam and reflect the society of those times, or will it be a law which is the product of reinterpretation (*ijtihad*) and reform? As Muslims seek to root their personal and national identity in an Islamic past, the importance of reinterpretation (*ijtihad*) and community consensus (*ijma*) is evident. Providing an Islamic methodology for reform is an essential part of this process. Lack of such a methodology undermines any sense of the Islamic character of reforms and consequently the acceptance of such reforms by the vast majority of Muslims. While passage of reforms may be effected through an autocratic leader of a legislature comprised of a small elite, their ultimate acceptance by the vast majority of the Islamic community will not be assured. Thus, for example, the Islamic Republic of Iran has repealed the *Family Protection Act*. Pakistan is reviewing provisions of the *Muslim Family Laws Ordinance of 1961* which rests on a weak Islamic methodology. In Egypt, among the major criticisms levelled against the family law reforms of 1979 by conservatives was its questionable Islamic methodology which included the use of *talfiq*. Therefore, care in the mechanisms employed in rendering reforms is of the utmost importance. Islamic jurisprudence provides the resources for such an undertaking.

Contemporary scholarship has begun to provide the historical perspective and materials for such a project. The complex origins of Islamic law, long forgotten by the idealized traditional picture of classical theory, have resurfaced and, if properly interpreted, provide a historical justification for Muslim family law reform. More importantly, a new understanding of law's development demonstrates that Islamic jurisprudence is fully capable of again providing the methods for reform.

To once more realize the divine imperative in history, the Muslim community possesses its immutable source the *Quran*. Constant and firm belief that this sourcebook of Islamic values is the very revealed word of provides Muslims with the principles and values upon which to base legal reform. If *Quranic* values are applied correctly, Muslim society can accommodate social change in the twentieth century while preserving its link with the history of the Islamic tradition. Furthermore, the task of reassessing the role of the *Sunnah* and its utilization in legal reform will not be a novel endeavor. Voices calling for a historical critique and re-evaluation of the *hadith* have existed throughout Islamic history from the early movement which led to the development of the science of hadith criticism to pre-modern reformers like Muhammad ibn Abd al-Wahhab and Shah Wali Allah and finally to the Muslim modernists of the twentieth century.

However, the successful implementation of the last two sources of legal reform (*ijtihad* and *ijma*) constitutes the greatest challenge for contemporary Muslim society. Education continues to be the most important ingredient for change, for Islamic reform in general and women's status in particular. The basic fight against illiteracy as well as the struggle to reform the educational systems of both secular and religious institutions is essential. An important task in educational reform is the implementation of measures which insure that the educational system incorporates the best of both scientific knowledge and religious values.

Part of the legacy of modernity is the bifurcation of education in most Muslim countries through the creation of modern (national) schools alongside traditional (Islamic) schools each with a curriculum reflecting differing and competing world views. The situation has been further compounded in those Muslim countries where the government has sharply curtailed direct financial support for Islamic schools as well as reduced their revenue through the reform or repeal of religious endowments (*waqfs*). The result of such a bifurcated educational system may be seen in its products. Western educated elites possess modern scientific and technological skills, but have little intellectual knowledge of or appreciation for their tradition. Therefore, they lack the vision to draft reforms which take into account the history and values of their culture. Traditionally educated individuals are the products not only of a limited curriculum which provides a deficient appreciation of modern problems, but one whose intellectual outlook does not incorporate a sense of the creative, dynamic process which characterized the formative period of Islam. Thus, they are less open to substantive reinterpretation and reform. As Fazlur Rahman has observed regarding the traditional Islamic schools (*madrasa*): "The *madrasas* have aimed at merely imparting a system of ideas not at creating newer systems; and therefore they have not been interested in inculcating the spirit of inquiry and independent thought."

Education is a key factor in assuring the expertise necessary for a wise reinterpretation (*ijtihad*) and an enlightened community consensus (*ijma*) which keeps pace with social change.

The Islamic revival has highlighted not only the strength of traditional religious leaders and the force of the classical Islamic world view, but also the existence of a growing generation of Islamic reformers. In general, these reformers are not members of the *ulama;* many are Western educated but Islamically oriented. Alongside the Ayatullah Khumayni and the majority of Iranian religious leaders, the Islamic movement in Iran has included others like the sociologist Ali Shariati, and the economist and former Iranian President Abol Hasan Bani Sadr, both Sorbonne educated. The more vibrant leaders of the Islamic movement in Malaysia are Western-educated professors and students Likewise, among the leaders of the Islamic movement in the Sudan are the Oxford-educated former Prime Minister, Sadiq al-Mahdi, and the London-Sorbonne educated Hassan Turabi, currently Attorney General of the Sudan as well as the President of the Muslim Brotherhood Party.

While differences abound, these Islamic reformers do share certain common attitudes. First, there is an acceptance of modernization, but a rejection of an uncritical adoption of westernization and secularization. Second, there is general agreement that more indigenously (Islamically) oriented models of political, economic, and social change need to be implemented. Third, reformers claim the right to *ijtihad* and thus reject a blind following of the past. Fourth, their methodology includes a return to fundamentals (in this sense they may truly be termed fundamentalists!), *i.e.*, to the *Quran* and the example of the Prophet. While reverencing past tradition, they do not feel bound to it, since they view the traditional world view embodied in Islamic law as the product of past *ijtihad* to meet historically conditioned needs. Therefore, they see themselves as undertaking once again the process of Islamization which characterized the early formative period of Islam—a process during which Muslims borrowed freely from other cultures, adopted and adapted the best that was available, and added their own distinctive contributions. Once again, reformers seek to interpret and apply Islamic principles and values to the exigencies of modern life and thus develop appropriate Islamically acceptable responses for modern Muslim societies.

The challenges facing the developing nations of the Islamic world are formidable. What path(s) Muslim countries will ultimately choose is an open ended question. For many a present and future which embodies some continuity with their Islamic past will continue to be an important concern. Given the traditional role of Islamic law as the ideal, comprehensive statement of the Islamic way of life, calls for more *Shariah* reform are inevitable. Moreover, as Muslim women's status changes due to increasing educational and employment opportunities, pressures for continued family law reform will intensify.

Islamic history, if correctly understood, has a lesson for both conservatives and reformers. It offers a picture of a dynamic, changing, adaptive religious tradition. A fuller appreciation of the real as well idealized Islamic past can provide the understanding and means or methodology for Islamic responses to the challenge of modernity as Muslims once more repeat the process of Islamization to develop a viable political, legal, and economic model for society and to draw on all available data and practices, but to do so in light of *Quranic* principles and values.

9

Primitive Marriage Laws

Introduction

The Arabic word for marriage is *nikah*, which, according to many *Quranic* commentators and Muslim jurists, means "*unity*." This word, which occurs frequently in the *Quran*, is an old Semitic term that also means *sexual intercourse*.

The Quran uses many "*anatomical*" words, derived from the names of the body parts of both animals and humans, the true meaning of which would surely offend a person of modest sensibilities. It was very common among pre-Islamic Arab poets to use phrases praising the reproductive organs: "It was not unusual in poems for a woman to extol the charms of her vagina, nor for a man to sing the praises of his penis." Gradually, these words spread and developed new meanings.It is therefore not surprising to find out that the word used in the *Quran* for marriage means sexual intercourse, not wedlock, as interpreted by various jurists.

The women of the pre-Islamic era were much freer in their movements than they were subsequently allowed to be.They showed hospitality to their husband's friends. They were regarded as equals to their men and their companionship was sought by men of all ranks. Women attended public gatherings, took part in the armed campaigns against the enemy, nursed the wounded, encouraged the warriors by reciting verses of songs and lyric poems, and held high offices.

The great majority of Arab women were nomads, and this group enjoyed more freedom than urban females, who, under certain circumstances, were made to observe some rules.Nomadic women were free to mingle with men, work with them, milk and graze the cattle, receive men in their tents, and dismiss them when they pleased. Pre-Islamic women could even choose their own mates. In case of need, they could rely on their tribes for help. They were indeed an asset to the tribes and valuable members of their clans.

As for other, neighbouring countries which were later overrun by the Muslims, it is certain that the women of these countries enjoyed a much happier life than what was imposed upon them by Islam later on.The following pages will show, very briefly, the position held by women in some of these countries prior to the advent of Islam.

Women in Ancient Egypt

The position of women in the Nile Valley before the Muslim raids was very favourable. A woman could initiate a courtship freely with a man, and if she wanted to, propose to the man of her choice. If the conjugal life proved impossible, she had the right to divorce her husband. She also had the right to draw up the terms of the marriage contract.

The Egyptian woman was unveiled and could move about freely at public gatherings without fear of prosecution. She attended to her own business affairs and was free to make trips or stay out of her home town visiting her relatives, a fact easily verified by the many letters that exist in the early Egyptian histories.

Some researchers maintain that women in pre-Islamic Egypt were in a much better position than many contemporary females in the advanced world. "The position of women," wrote Will Durant, "was more advanced than in most countries today. No people, ancient or modern, has given woman so high a legal status as did inhabitants of the Nile Valley."

Many Egyptian women attained the highest political status some became queens of that vast empire. Hatshepsut and Cleopatra are but two shining examples that illustrate the level of political achievement attained by Egyptian women in antiquity.These women ruled their country as well as many other male rulers before them, if not more efficiently and firmly, and they went to war or maintained the peace with the same zeal and willpower as their male counterparts.

The powerful pharaohs were very careful not to offend their wives. They respected them and admonished their sons to treat their wives as nicely. "Make glad her heart," instructed a pharaoh to his son, "during the time thou hast her, for she is a field profitable to its owner. If thou oppose her it will mean thy ruin." The pharaoh's instruction directly contrasts with Allah's ordinance that says, "Your women are (like) a tilled field for you, so go into your tilled field as you will." According to the *Quran*, the wife's consent is not important.

In fact, ancient Egyptian women enjoyed so much freedom that travellers to Egypt were often astonished at such liberty. In marriage contracts, the obedience of the husband was explicitly required. Diodorus Siculus, a Greek writer, told exactly how the obedience of the husband was specified in marriage bonds. A wife managed her husband's property and supervised his estate. In fact, she was the lord of the house. The servants and slaves took their orders from her. "The woman in ancient Egypt was the full mistress of the house. She could manage her husband's property and earnings, and moreover; the estate descended in a female line." The surviving papyri show no divorce in ancient Egypt.

Women in Babylonia

The position of the woman in ancient Babylonia, though not as high as in Egypt, was far superior to what Islam has provided in the last fourteen centuries. Babylonian women enjoyed a special independence that was unique and unparalleled. Protection of women's rights in Babylonia was one of the most outstanding achievements of the ancient world. According to the Code of Hammurabi, the man was responsible for the maintenance of his wife. He could not dismiss her even if she were incapable of carrying out the household duties. If her husband abandoned her willfully and left the town, a Babylonian woman had the right to marry another man of her choice; if her first husband returned, he had no right over her any more.

The guardianship of the children resided with the mother, and if she separated from her husband, he had to provide for their livelihood and subsistence. Upon her husband's death, she acquired a portion of his estates. "The married woman had a right to do business independently and most of the transactions were done by the women."

Women in Elam

On the basis of many archaeological discoveries obtained from the ancient city of Susa, we are certain that women in Elam had acquired a very high position in their society and were treated equally with men, some two thousand years before our era.

Ancient cuneiform tablets reveal that the women of Elam could go to the courts, give their testimonies free of any formalities or restrictions, and they could file claims or defend their rights. In signing a contract, the nail print of the woman was placed next to that of her male counterpart. In one of these documents, we see that a man left all of his estates and properties to his only married daughter. In another, a father left his field to his daughter, and she, too, transferred the entire estate to her own daughter. In another document, a mother with two sons and a daughter bequeathed all of her estates solely to her daughter, and her two sons had to swear before the king that they would not file any claim against their mother's will.

Men in Elam had a great respect toward women and in many fields women enjoyed special privileges. According to one of the tablets, a man had stated that as long as he lived, his daughter would nurse him and after he was gone, she would be in charge of the preparation of sacrifices, alms giving, and the temple services. If any of his sons raised "any objections to the validity or contents of the will, his tongue and hand must be cut, and he ought to pay a fine equal to four minah" (one minah equalled sixty shekels). Of the sixteen witnesses who signed the testament, four were women. One of the Elamite women became the ruler and absolute monarch of Susa.She was the sister of Shilkhakha, the grandmother of the great dynasty of Elam.

Women of India

One of the Indian codes states: "The mother exceedeth a thousand fathers in the right of reverence." The ancient people of India respected women and never dreamed of irritating a female. "The women are not to be struck even with a flower."

From the different texts of ancient Indian literature, one can clearly infer that the women of India enjoyed much freedom in choosing their own husbands or in attending social gatherings. In religious rites or ceremonies, they were on equal standing with men. "She had more to say in choice of her mate than the forms of marriage might suggest. She appeared freely at feasts and dances, and joined with men in religious sacrifices."

In part of India that fell under Muslim domination, the marriage laws were changed and Islamic rites replaced all of the previous social and religious customs. Women were barred from social gatherings. Singing, dancing, and mingling of the sexes were totally prohibited. Women were confined to their quarters and gradually lost their identities and privileges. They had to accept the veil, a practice that had been totally unknown previously. These changes and the loss of freedom for women echo what happened in each of the countries that has been discussed.

Types of Marriage

In pre-Islamic Arabia, there were four kinds of marriage prevalent among the nomads of the peninsula.

1. Marriage by Capture: Woman was considered an asset, the mother of a future swordsman, the cook, the master of the dwelling, and the companion of the man. Women were considered so valuable that tribes attacked their enemies to capture as many as they could. This slavery, arising from the capture of women, is evident in the early days of Islam. Muhammad himself frequently pursued and conquered other tribes' wives and children.

There were four main reasons for capturing women. First, the captive women were held as hostages and only released after ransom money was paid. In this way the victorious tribe was able to strengthen its financial standing or, at least, avert the dangers of destitution and famine. Sometimes the women were sold to other tribes for profit, as Muhammad did when he destroyed the Jewish tribe of Banu Qurayza.Second, it was often cheaper to acquire a woman by fighting than to purchase her in the customary marriage contract. At least two of Muhammad's wives were procured in this way (Safiyya and Juwayriyya). Third, the hostile tribes wanted to have more women in order to produce more fighting men. Many of the Islamic swordsmen in the third generation after Muhammad were the offspring of women captured in different raids by the founder of Islam and his close associates and successors. Fourth, the tribes who experienced a shortage in their female population found it easier, and probably more economical, to capture others' wives and daughters. This practice is vividly seen in the early days of Muhammad's flight to Medina, when the number of his male followers was many times that of the females. To procure women for his followers, he used the same method as his primitive ancestors, violent forays.

2. Marriage by Friendship: In this kind of marriage, the male approached the woman and offered her his friendship. The Arabic word for this sort of marriage was *sadiqa,* which means "girlfriend." The would-be husband approached the woman with the word "*khitb,*" which means, "I am a suitor," and to accept him the lady uttered the word "*nikah,*" which is interpreted as "I wed." There were no witnesses and no wedding ceremony in this type of marriage. The man gave a gift to the bride, a sort of price or gift reflecting the woman's value. This nuptial present was called "*sadaq.*"

The children of this type of marriage remained with the mother and the woman's tribe protected her as much after her marriage as before it. The woman could dismiss her husband by merely showing him the door of her tent. In some cases, the woman would offer some nuptial gift, in cash or kind, to have the man of her choice. It is reported that once a rich woman offered herself to Abdullah (Muhammad 's father) and said, "If you will take me you can have as many camels as were sacrificed in your stead" (*i.e.,* 100 camels).

3. Marriage by Contract. In this kind of marriage, the intended husband drew up a contract with the girl's parents to buy his future wife from them. The purchase price (mahr) was paid by the suitor, and the parents, after accepting the offer, delivered their daughter to the bidder. As the selling of the daughter would procure additional income, the father was congratulated on the occasion of the birth of a female child.

The marriage was based on an equal match. One of the conditions of this sort of marriage was that the children born in the union were to be returned to the girl's tribe. This condition was always challenged by the husband, who would argue that because he had paid for his wife the children belonged to him, and eventually a law (*al-walad li l-frash*) was introduced by which the child was reckoned to the bed on which he was born. (Muhammad adopted the same primitive law and added that to Allah's commandments.) For example, if a captive woman was pregnant when taken, the child she bore was considered that of the captor or his tribe. The outcome of such a law was that the husband could without shame send his wife to sleep with another man and get pregnant, so that she might bear him a "goodly seed."

4. Temporary Marriage: By this arrangement a man paid a woman for a specified length of time for cohabitation. This type of marriage, *mut'a* ("enjoying a thing"), continued well into Muhammad's time and was eventually abolished by 'Umar, the second caliph. *Mut'a* was similar to *sadiqa*, or friendship marriage, in that the woman stayed with her own family and any children belonged to her tribe. The wife could easily dispose of her temporary husband.

Temporary marriage was basically devised for those men who were away from their homes on business trips or military expeditions. They wanted to enjoy the companionship of a young woman for the period that they would be in her neighbourhood and away from their legal wives. Thus, they would hire a woman for a certain period of time for a specific amount of money for mutual living and sexual pleasure. It is generally believed that temporary marriage is the heritage of ancient Arabia and was a sort of national custom, especially among the nomads of the Arabian Peninsula. "It was considered permissible for men and women to form unlicensed unions (trial marriages) terminable at the will of either party."

This early Arab custom, which in reality amounts to harlotry, survived in Islam. It is true that all of the Islamic schools believe it unlawful, but, as will be shown later, the Shiites continue the practice of *mut'a.* According to Falari, the renowned exegete, Muhammad engaged in temporary marriage himself. Based on this view, the Prophet of Allah enjoyed this form of marriage after he started his new religion, possibly as late as his flight to Medina.

Another Muslim historian affirms that in the early days of Islam the Muslim soldier, when he left his town, might enter a temporary marriage and secure a wife for the period of his stay in the assigned place. Al-Bukhari has quoted Abdullah as saying, "We used to participate in the holy battle, led by Allah's apostle, and we had nothing (no wives) with us. So, we said, 'Shall we get ourselves castrated?' He forbade us that and then allowed us to marry women with a temporary contract."

This, however, contradicts the view of the Muslim doctors who maintain that temporary marriage is unlawful in Islam. Muhammad permitted it himself, and by reciting from the Quran—"O you who believe! Make not unlawful the good things which Allah has made lawful for you but commit no transgressing" (5: 87)—he actually made it divine law. The Orthodox Islamic schools, to counter both the Quranic verse and criticism from the protagonists of *mut'a,* created another story that clearly specifies the unlawfulness of temporary marriage. They claim, "The prophet permitted mut'a... for three days in the year of Awtal, after which he forbade it."

Another group of Muslim teachers maintains that the Prophet permitted *mut'a* for three nights and then he made it unlawful. It is reported that 'Umar, the second caliph and Muhammad's father-in-law, proclaimed that it was definitely unlawful to marry a woman for a temporary period of time. Since that time, the Sunni school does not practice *mut'a.* It is dear from the different traditions that *mut'a* was permitted by Muhammad and he sanctioned it in the Quran.Later, perhaps after the Muslims invaded Egypt, Persia, and Syria, as they confronted the monotheistic religions of Judaism, Christianity, and Zoroastrianism, they then forbade it. Even Ibn 'Abbas, Muhammad's cousin and one of the verse exegetes, is reported to have advocated temporary marriage and only dismissed his views and considered it unlawful just before his death.

Temporary marriage was as lawful as the regular wedding during the first century of Islam. According to al-Tabari, many commentators on the Quran, as late as the second century after the Hegira, maintained that the fixed-period marriage against a specified sum of money was lawful. Al-Suddi, for instance, who died about 129 after the Hegira, held that mut'a was a marriage that could be contracted with the permission of the guardian of the girl in the presence of two witnesses. According to him, the two parties should separate after the expiration of the contract term and neither had a claim on the other, nor could they inherit from one another.

During the two hundred years after Muhammad's death Muslim doctors gradually forbade mut'a. *The* Sunnis, however, devised a new trick to make temporary marriages lawful. They held that if the period of the marriage is not mentioned in the contract, but the man has the intention to dissolve the marriage after a certain period of time, then *mut'a* is valid.

The Shiite school, apparently, has remained faithful to the deeds of the Prophet and consider the *mut'a* an irrevocable contract just like regular marriage with the exception that the period of legal obligation must be stipulated in the contract. No witness is necessary, and no notary public or other official need be present. No clergy is needed to conclude the contract or to supervise the ceremony. For the contract to be valid, the words, "I enjoy you," must be definitely mentioned and the man must pay the wage or "hiring price" in advance.

Upon the expiration of the period, the temporary marriage is ended automatically, and if the couple want to continue being with each other, a new contract with a new bed-wage must be drawn up for the new period of time. There is no divorce in such a marriage, which is based on sexual relations alone, and repudiation is impossible. In fact, the man is not even obliged to provide food or shelter for the woman. At the expiration date, the woman has to wait forty-five days before she enters into another in-bed agreement with someone else. But since there is usually no witness to the marriage and separation, the woman could enter into another contract immediately after the previous contract had expired.

As was mentioned, the temporary marriage is practiced today only by Shiite Muslims.These people are the followers of Muhammad's cousin and son-in-law, 'Ali, who is reported to have said: "Verily, the prophet prohibited the *mut'a* marriage of woman on the day (of the conquest) of Khaybar [see chapter 1] and he prohibited the eating of the domestic ass." If this quotation is valid, then'Ali opposed temporary marriage, but his followers don't seem to agree with him.

The Shiite clergy hold that temporary marriage is definitely sanctioned by Allah in the *Quran*: "but those of whom you seek enjoyment (*istamt'atum*) give unto them their pay (reward) as a duty and there is no sin for you by mutual agreement after such lawful due." (*Quran* 4: 24) According to this school, the words "wage" or "reward" in the above verse is the proof of its permissibility.

We do not intend to enter here into the discussion, or the dispute, between the opponents and proponents of temporary marriage. Rather, we shall continue by explaining permanent marriage, or the union by contract, that is accepted by all the Islamic schools and is considered by the Muslim as one of the most progressive laws in the world.

Conditions for Marriage

Contract

Islamic law necessitates a contract for each and every marriage without which the union is not valid. This requirement is not without precedent. The Babylonian code, for instance, had stipulated long before Muhammad that if the marriage contract is not drawn up the marriage is not legal. The Code of Hammurabi, which was promulgated during his empire (Hammurabi died in about 1750 B.C.E.), states: "If a man takes a wife, but did not draw up her contract, that woman is no wife." This law, too, is rooted among the customs of the ancient people living in that part of the world.The Law of Eshnunna, for example, which is almost two hundred years older than the Code of Hammurabi and dates back as far as 2000 B.C.E., states: "If a man marries another man's daughter without approval of her parents, even if she lives one year with him, she is not his wife."

The Sumerian laws, such as the Law of Ur-Nammu and the Law of Lipit-Ishtar, which go back twenty-two centuries before our era, stipulate the requirement of the marriage contract very clearly. Thus, Muhammad's law regarding the marriage contract is not unprecedented. There are two features in the Law of Eshnunna that should be noted, however.

1. The Law of Eshnunna stipulated the approval of the girl's parents in order for the marriage to be legal; in this the ancient Semitic law is superior to that of Muhammad, because the latter required only the approval of the father or a male guardian and not the approval of both parents. In other words, Islamic law is more patriarchal and male oriented.
2. According to the Law of Eshnunna, in the absence of the marriage contract the union is not legally recognized, but the man and woman could live together if they pleased. In Islam, a woman who lives with a man without a marriage contract is committing fornication and is liable to receive a penalty of not less than one hundred lashes if discovered.

Religion

A Muslim girl may not marry any man she chooses because the basic condition for marriage is that her husband must be a Muslim. "And do not give (a Muslim woman) in marriage to idolaters until they have accepted Islam, and certainly a believing slave is better than an idolater even though he should please you."

The word "idolater" in the above verse is defined to mean a nonbeliever whether a Jew, Christian, Buddhist, or Zoroastrian anyone but a Muslim.Thus, according to the *Quran*, no Muslim girl may marry a man whose religion differs from hers.

Does the same law apply to men as well? Not exactly, since a Muslim man can marry any woman who is not an atheist. In other words, a man may have a Christian, a Jewish, or even a Zoroastrian woman as his wife, because Muhammad's scripture explicitly allows such a marriage: "And the chaste from among the believing women and the chaste from among those who have been given the book before you (are lawful for you) when you have given them their marriage portion taking them in marriage." The phrase "those who have been given the book before you" refers to Jews and Christians, who have their own Bibles.

In comparing the status of men and women in the Quran, we find out that the two are not treated equally. Although a man is allowed to marry a non-Muslim woman, the woman is totally prohibited from marrying any non-Muslim man.

Muslims believe that the new order proposed by Muhammad as a religion is based on justice and equality. They maintain that no other religion has ever treated women more fairly than Islam, and yet we see that in the very first condition laid out for marriage the male gets the better share. The divine law is made in the man's favour; the woman is disadvantaged.

Is Allah biased against women? Does Allah, the Supreme Being, like an ordinary pre-Islamic man, favour the man over the women? Or, is it Muhammad, the lawgiver, who wants to ensure the supremacy of the male under the name of a new religion? It is surely the Prophet, and not Allah, who debases the woman and deprives her from the right to choose her mate.

Legal Age for Marriage

There is no specific age for marriage stated in the *Quran*, but the tradition of Muhammad and his close associates reveals that a man, no matter how old he is, may contract and consummate a marriage with a girl as young as nine years old. In fact, Muhammad himself married Aisha, the daughter of Abu Bakr, when she was six years of age, and took her to his bed three years later. Thus, child-marriage, which was a remnant of primitive Arab rites (pagan Semitic tribes used to draw up contracts in which the guardians chose mates for their underage children), was perpetuated by Muhammad and made a divine law. "It is usual," writes Jones, "for orthodox Muslims to claim that a child-marriage, though not enjoined either in the *Quran* or traditions, is part of the very fabric of Islam.They contend that the custom is sanctioned by the practice of Muhammad, who himself married a child wife and gave in marriage a child-wife."

Today, in the civilized world, the cohabitation of a fully grown man with a female child of nine or ten would be considered child molestation, not marriage, and the offender would be prosecuted under the law. Nonetheless, some Islamic jurists try to justify Muhammad's action in marrying Aisha when she was still a child. One Muslim doctor had this to say: "Aisha's Nikah [marriage] was performed in Mecca long before the details of the Islamic laws were revealed to the holy prophet, and therefore, her marriage at nine can be no agreement [justification] for the marriage of a minor." This poor excuse is not only contrary to the fact, but also falls short of justification for Muhammad's behaviour because:

1. According to all reliable Islamic history books, only three years passed from the day Muhammad married Aisha to the day he took her to his bed. During this period, no law regarding the marriage age of the girl was enjoined. In fact, during the entire life of Muhammad no specific rule was set down determining the minimum age of a girl for marriage.
2. If the details of Islamic law were revealed to the Prophet after his marriage to Aisha, then he should have amended his marriage in a lawful manner to evade any criticism. On the contrary, Muhammad seemed to have enjoyed his union with his child-wife, as he spent most of his harem time with her and she was his favourite.
3. From the beginning of Islam to the present time, a great many Muslim males have followed Muhammad's example and married minors. For instance, 'Umar, who was one of Muhammad's closest friends, his immediate successor, and is believed to have been very orthodox in trying to carry out the Quranic law to the letter, married 'Ali's daughter, Umm Kulthum (Muhammad's granddaughter) when she was barely ten years old. 'Umar was then in his late fifties.

   Islamic chronology is full of such examples of child marriage. This demonstrates that taking a minor as a wife did not end with Muhammad's death on the contrary, it became a law. Almost all of the caliphs of the Umayyad, 'Abbasid, and Fatimid dynasties practiced child-marriage.
4. The very author who tries to justify Muhammad's marriage to a child-wife contradicts himself a few lines later, when he says: "*Fiqh* [Islamic jurisprudence], however, recognizes the legality of the minor marriage when contracted by a lawful guardian."

If the legality of child-marriage is accepted by Islamic jurisprudence, the apologists cannot justify Muhammad's marriage to a nine-year-old by saying it was performed "long before the details of Islamic law were revealed to the holy prophet." The phrase "details of Islamic law" is synonymous with jurisprudence, and jurisprudence recognizes such marriages. In other words, this attempt at justification nullifies itself because it simultaneously condemns and redeems Muhammad's action.

According to Islamic law, the guardian of the girl (her father or grandfather) could negotiate the terms of marriage with either the suitor or his parents, just as Abu Bakr (Aisha's father) discussed his daughter's terms of marriage with Muhammad when Aisha was but six years old. 'Ali did the same with 'Umar, when 'Ali's daughter, Umm Kulthum, was a mere child.

Marriage is a contract and is simply based on the mutual consent and agreement, oral or written, of the two parties involved. Marriage, therefore, is a secular contract and not a religious rite. If the bride or suitor is a minor, his or her guardian can enter into the terms of marriage even without the child's consent.

Those concluding a marriage contract must be sane and have reached the age of legal majority. "Among the Shafais [school], a woman cannot personally consent to marriage. The presence of the guardian (*wali*) is essentially necessary to give validity to the contract. The guardian's intervention is required by the Shafais and Malikis to supplement the presumed incapacity of the woman to understand the nature of the contract." Thus, in Muhammad's law, the woman has no capacity to conclude her own marriage, even if she were of the legal age to do so.

Some Islamic schools of thought, however, such as the Hanafi and Shiite, may allow a woman to decide her own marriage. In contrast, other schools do not believe that a woman ever has a right to conclude her own marriage. In such Muslim communities, if an adult woman marries the man of her choice without the approval of her guardian, that marriage is completely invalid. Aisha is reported to have said: "Every woman who marries without consent of her guardian, her marriage is null and void," and she repeated herself three times to emphasize the statement.

It is noteworthy that Aisha, who outlived Muhammad by many years, is considered to be one of the best sources of her husband's words and deeds, and some two hundred narrations from Muhammad believed by all schools to be authentic are attributed to her. Her narrations are taken seriously by some schools because it is argued that she is merely reflecting her husband's ideas.

It is indisputable that child-marriage was practiced during Muhammad's time. He perpetuated it, and ever since his death this sort of marriage has tantalized a great number of Muslim clergies, jurists, and theologians. One such example is Imam Ja'far as-Sadiq, one of the main sources of the Shiite school and the great-grandson of Muhammad. Ja'far as-Sadiq is considered to be one of the foremost scholars in the field of Shiite jurisprudence. This man, the direct descendent of the apostle of Allah, is reported to have said: "Virtuous is the one whose daughter does not start menses at her father's house." By this he means that a girl must be given away in marriage before she begins her menstrual cycles or monthly periods, and any father who does so is a true Muslim and virtuous believer.

In some schools, the ward, "on attaining puberty," may repudiate the marriage contracted by her guardian. The marriage, however, is perfectly valid up to that time. Sometimes infants may be contracted in marriage by their guardians. Thus, the marriage of an infant or an underage boy or girl is lawful if it is contracted by the nearest male kindred. What happens when such infants attain majority? Could they themselves sanction the marriages that had been contracted in their infancies? Apparently the male can give his consent without approval of a guardian, but there is a difference of opinion with regard to the woman on whether she can give her consent without the approval of her guardian.

Bride-price in Marriage

According to the Quran, any Muslim male who wishes to get married must stipulate a certain amount of money in his marriage contract as a bride-price. The specific sum should be paid to his future wife or her immediate male kinfolk (*i.e.*, her father or grandfather). One of the Muslim authorities in jurisprudence said: "A dowry (*mahr*) must also be settled on the woman according to the holy Quran."

This word, *mahr,* which is used by all Muslim jurists as well as the layman in the street, is not, curiously enough, mentioned in the Quran at all, not even once! Jones said, "It is a curious fact, however, that the term, *mahr,* is nowhere used in the Quran, though it is common in the tradition." There are, however, other terminologies used instead of *mahr,* which are derived from the pre-Islamic period when the Arabs worshiped different deities. The word mahr is apparently the Arabic pronunciation of the old Hebrew word *mohr*.

Instead, the word *ajr* is used, which actually means wage or reward. For instance, if you hire someone to work for you, at the end of the day or week you pay his wages (*ajr*). The plural of ajr is ujur, meaning the wages for the hired one.

The other terminology used in the *Quran* for dowry is *fariza,* meaning what is obligatory for the man to pay to his wife before or after the marriage, for having her in wedlock. Ajr, as used in the Quran, may be translated to mean the hired-wage, bride-price, bed-wage, or reward for cohabitation.

The Friendship Gift (Sadaq)

The Quran states: "And give unto the women (whom ye marry) free gift of their marriage portions." (Quran 4: 4) The "free gift" is the translation of sadaq, which, as was explained earlier, is the gift or money exchanged in the friendship-type of marriage. In pre-Islamic days, a friendly union of a man and woman necessitated the payment of money or other kind of property, which the suitor would usually hand over to his prospective wife. She could regain her freedom by returning the sadaq to her man. Sadaq, according to some authors, was a gift besides a bride-price. The bride-price was usually paid to the girl's parents, whereas, the friendship gift (sadaq) was given exclusively to the wife herself. Under Muhammad, this custom was changed and now only mahr (dowry) is paid either to the father of the girl or to her nearest male kin.

The Bride-Price for Slave Girls

In Islamic communities, men have traditionally been permitted to take as mates two classes of women: free women and concubines (captured women or slave girls).

If a slave girl was to be married to a free man, *i.e.*, her master, she was then freed and given a bride-price, unless her master agreed to give her freedom as the bride price. Muhammad himself kept some captive girls as concubines, and instead of a bride-price, he freed them and added them to his harem.

On the other hand, if a slave girl was married to another slave, a wage or reward had to be stipulated in the marriage contract. It should be noted that although slavery was abolished in most countries quite a long time ago, it is not prohibited in Islam, and prominent Muslim jurists have thus far not denounced this institution. Muslims believe that the *Quran* is the indisputable word of Allah; therefore, no true Muslim faithful would ever dare to defy the text of this holy book. Thus, slavery is an accepted precept in Muhammad's law. The *Quran* also states that if a Muslim army conquers a town of nonbelievers or defeats enemy soldiers, they may make the vanquished people their slaves and sell or dispose of them any way they please. Because the institution of slavery is fully recognized by the *Quran*, many of the laws regarding the taking and handling of slaves are being taught in Muslim religious schools and universities even in modern times.

The wages due for cohabitation with a slave girl are specified in the *Quran*: "So marry them [slave girls] with the permission of their masters and give them their bed wages justly." Thus, a bride-price must be paid for slaves as well as free women.

In accordance with the text of the *Quran* and the tradition of Muhammad, the two main sources of Islamic laws, the payment of the bride-price must be made at the time of marriage, whether the bride is a free woman or a slave. If the bride-price is not explicitly specified in the marriage contract, it has to be determined and paid later on. If for some reason or other, the payments were not made soon after the marriage and the husband died, this deferred payment would be charged against his property and deducted from what he left as his legacy to be paid to his widow.

Amount of the Bride-Price

The minimum amount of the bride-price is not mentioned in the *Quran* or in later Islamic jurisprudence, just as the minimum age for marriage is not clearly specified; it all depends on the husband's wealth and the position of the woman. This is clearly stipulated in the Muslim scripture: "the wealthy according to his means, and the poor according to his means." Thus, Islam considers the woman as a commodity, and her price is determined by her position. If she is rich, from an affluent family with higher standing, or beautiful and well-bred, her bride-price would be higher. On the other hand, if the prospective bride belongs to a lower stratum of the community and is from a poor family without influential background, her price would be much lower, no matter how rich her suitor may be.

A woman is bought according to her position and her bride-price is paid on that basis. The marriage price for Muhammad's daughter, Fatima, who was given to ' Ali, when Muhammad did not have much money and ' Ali was equally poor, amounted to only 400 dirhams (some writers argue that it was equivalent to the price of ' Ali's armour). The bride-price for Muhammad's granddaughter, Umm Kulthum, however, when she was handed over as a wife to ' Umar, the second caliph, is recorded by most Muslim historians to be 10,000 gold dinars, because at that time ' Ali, the bride's father, was a rich man, thanks to his share of the booty received from plundering other communities. He possessed many orchards, cultivated lands, date-palm trees, houses, horses, camels, sheep, goats, cash money, and many male and female slaves. Thus, Umm Kulthum's status was much higher than that of her mother.

Ancient Origin of the Bride-Price (*Mahr* and *Ajr*)

It was mentioned previously that the Arabic word *mahr* (dowry) is derived from a Hebrew word, *mohr.*

> Zimmerman maintains that the two may have originated from the ancient Assyrian word mahiru, meaning "price." This suggests that the man actually buys his wife from her father. Koschner supports this theory by arguing that marriage in ancient Babylonia was merely the purchasing of the woman, and the price the husband would pay for his wife was called mahiru. The girl's father would receive money or its equivalent from the bridegroom or his father.
>
> Koschner goes on to define tirhatum, a word from Middle Assyrian law (ca. 1400 B.C.E), as "bride-price." Kohler, another linguist, translated it as "woman-price" (frauen-preis).

Tirhatum, in Assyrian, is derived from the word which means sexual intercourse. The *mahr,* therefore, is the price paid by a man to cohabit with a woman. As was noted previously, the word *ajr* used in the *Quran* is the price of acquiring a woman in wedlock, the price of a woman practically hired to live with her husband as long as he wants her around. So we observe that the *Quran*, by using the word ajr, is directly taking after the Assyrian law prevalent in Northern Arabia and Assyria in pre-Islamic days. Consequently, Muhammad requires his faithful followers to pay a price to a woman for her sexual services.

The bride-price is much more ancient than even the Assyrian law, let alone Islamic jurisprudence. The Code of Hammurabi (the set of laws promulgated by the ancient king of Babylonia) in many sections refers to the bride-price. The following is quoted to demonstrate how the ancient Babylonians legalized the bride-price: "If a man, who had the betrothal gift brought to the house of his father-in-law and paid the marriage price, has then looked upon another woman, and says to his prospective father-in-law, 'I shall not marry your daughter,' the father of the daughter shall keep whatever was brought to him." One can easily infer from this law why the different schools in Islam require that the bride's guardian should draw up the marriage contract for his daughter, as he is usually the one who received the ajr for consenting to the wedding.

Another law stipulates, "If a man has had the betrothal gift brought to the house of his prospective father in-law and paid the marriage-price, and the father of the girl then says, 'I shall not give you my daughter,' he shall pay back double whatever had been brought to him."

There are more laws concerning the marriage price in Hammurabi's Code, but two examples suffice to show the ancient origin of ajr (bride-price) in Islamic jurisprudence.

Bride-Price: Dívíne Revelatíon?

Muhammad himself paid the bride-price to his first wife, Khadija, almost fifteen years before he declared himself to be the Prophet of Allah and began revealing the verses of the *Quran*.Hence, the bride-price could not have been a divinely inspired tenet of Muhammad's new faith, as orthodox Muslims insist, because this custom, like so many of the Quranic laws, had been in practice some two thousand years prior to Muhammad and his revelations. Most of the marriage laws that appear in the *Quran* were originated by the tyrant-despots of the ancient world.

The question, therefore, that believers in the *Koran*'s inerrant truth must answer is why Allah's revealed laws are so similar to the laws of ancient pagan monarchs. Why would Allah who is explicitly described in the *Quran* as the "Knower," the "Sovereign Lord," the "Majestic," the "Superb," and the "Compeller"enjoin all his faithful to marry according to non believers' rules?

Could not Allah the Creator, the Shaper-out-of naught, and the Fashioner have devised marriage laws that did not debase women and reduce their position to that of a mere commodity, which could be sold and handed over after "its" price was paid? Couldn't Allah have made a more equitable law?

In comparing Hammurabi's law to the Quranic tenets with respect to the bride-price, we find that Muhammad's law is in no way an improvement over that of the king of Babylonia, and in modern Islam marriage is still the act of purchasing a wife, just as it was two thousand years before the time of Muhammad. According to the tenets of Islam, if no bride-price is mentioned in the contract, the wife is entitled to an appropriate payment. The real meaning of bride-price as a form of hiring or payment for services is well understood when we consider the fact that a woman may refuse to let her husband enjoy sexual intercourse until she receives the bride-price. She has the right to do so. As long as she is not paid the specified price, she may stay away from her husband's bed. As soon as he pays, however, he obtains full authority over his wife.

If a woman dies after the marriage is consummated, her right to a bride-price is not transferred to her family. But if her husband dies at the same time, the wife's heirs can take the dower (*mahr*) out of the husband's estate. If a minor girl who had been given away in marriage by her guardian dies before she reaches legal maturity, her husband inherits her dowry, not her parents.

If consummation does not occur after the girl is married, she receives one half of her bride-price. Also, it is customary for the parents to give to the bride a trousseau. In such cases, if she is divorced, she must receive back whatever was originally given to her by her parents, plus the bride-price. These laws further demonstrate that marriage in Islam is merely a sales transaction.

Summary

Muslim theologians and clerics maintain that the position of woman has improved under Islam, and Muhammad is hailed by them as the greatest emancipator of women from the cruelty and oppression of the Dark Ages of Arabia, the pre-Islamic days.

This, however, is not true. As was discussed earlier in the chapter, pre-Islamic women enjoyed much more freedom than Muslim females do. They could choose their own mates, were free to move around at will, conducted their own business affairs, and shared the same privileges as their male counterparts. Lyall notes:

The place of women in the society of pagan Arabia was appreciably higher than that which they hold under Al-Islam.They had much liberty which was afterwards denied them. They were much freer in their movements than they became after the ordinance of the veil had been prescribed. In many cases, they selected their mates for themselves, instead of having to accept the choice for them by their guardians.

Nicholson agrees: "On the whole, their position was high and their influence great. They were regarded not as slaves and chattels, but as equals and companions."

Islam, on the other hand, treats women as inferior beings and women have lost their independence through the advent of this religion. For example, the lot of Indian women changed when Islam was forcefully imposed upon them. The inferior position of women in Pakistan and part of India today is undoubtedly the result of the influx of Muhammad's religion in the subcontinent, which started as early as eleventh century of our era.

It is clear, then, that pre-Islamic women enjoyed some sort of independence and liberty before they were forced to accept the religion of the Muslim war-wagers, who would stop at nothing short of surrender and submission. Literally, *Islam* means "submission" to the will of Allah, but this religion came with force, changed the ideology of the ancient world by force, and reduced women to the status of slaves and chattel through an iron fist and the sword.

Widespread movements composed of educated and liberal-minded Muslim writers have become prevalent, calling for reform with regard to the status of women. For example, in Turkey and Tunisia, new regulations were passed which instituted a number of legal reforms especially affecting women. A minimum legal age for marriage was established. It stipulated that the marriages that were contracted and licensed by Muslim clerics were only valid if registered with the government agencies.

Reform in women's education has also occurred. In 1893, for instance, Turkish women were permitted to attend classes in the medical colleges of Istanbul University for the first time. Six years later, women were allowed to take part in regular medical studies.

Courses for women in other sectors of the university began as early as February 1914. This was a dramatic change in a country that was the official seat of the Muslim caliphate for four hundred years.

Iraq (the modern name of ancient Babylonia), which was under the rule of the Ottoman Empire for centuries, enjoyed almost the same liberty given to Turkish women in Istanbul.In 1899, the first regular girls' school was opened, which began the coeducation system in Baghdad University.

Regular classes for girls in primary school began in 1917 in Iran. Tehran University, a latecomer to Middle Eastern higher education, accepted women as full-time students shortly after World War II. In the meantime, as of 1935, women were allowed to get jobs in different government offices, something that even a decade earlier had been unthinkable.

The age of marriage for both Iranian girls and boys was raised, and all of the marriage contracts had to be registered. Child-marriage was prohibited by the law, and severe punishment was prescribed for those who concluded any wedding contract for minors.

In Tunisia, the minimum age for marriage was also raised-eighteen years for boys and sixteen for girls. This was raised once more a little later to twenty and eighteen, respectively.

In Turkey, Tunisia, and Iran, the right of the guardians who could enter into a marriage contract on behalf of minors was rescinded and anyone who committed such a felony was liable to prosecution. All of these reforms were possible in places in which a strong centralized government defied the Islamic laws of marriage and curbed the authority of the Muslim fundamentalist clergies in the *Shariat* (religious procedure). Islamic jurisprudence came under severe criticism by liberal minded intellectuals who believed child-marriage to be inhuman.

Despite these changes, Muslim jurisprudence concerning marriage is still incomplete and sometimes inefficient. Although Muhammad claimed the laws to be those ordered by Allah, in reality they are based on nomadic rites and traditions, and the inequality of the sexes prevalent in them merely reflects the ancient culture with which Muhammad was familiar.

10

Punishments for Sexual Misconduct in Islam

Introduction

In Islam woman is considered to be the property first of her guardian (usually her father) and then ownership over her is transferred to her husband. This view of woman as belonging at all times to some man reflects a heavily male-dominant, patriarchal social system with ancient roots. Such a social system can be found all over the world and was especially prevalent at the earliest stages of history. In fact, according to Darwin, the same attitude is seen in many animal species. For example, a male ape who has several females in his possession will not permit any other male to approach them, even if the males are the offspring of his own females.

Even among peoples where women have more influence than they do in Islam, any outside interference with female sexuality is usually seen as an infringement of a man's rights and arouses his jealousy.By the same token, adultery on the part of the woman is avenged by the man, who by this system of reasoning believes that his proprietary rights have been violated.

The jealousy of the man naturally increases when he is permitted, as he is in Islam, to have more than one wife under contract, because he therefore has acquired more property to be defended against infringements from other men. Obviously women were kept in a state of subjugation under this social system and as a result any punishments meted out were always more severe for women than they were for men.

In this chapter we will look at the verses in the *Quran* dealing with sexual misconduct and discuss the punishments stipulated for each violation.

First Injunction: Confine Lewd Women

As for those of your women who are guilty of lewdness, call to witness four of you against them. And if they testify (to the truth of the allegation) then confine them to the houses until death take them or Allah appoint for them a way.

This is the first Quranic law revealed on the subject of adultery, which is presumably what the term "lewdness" refers to. According to the above ordinance, any woman who is proven to be unfaithful is to be confined to her house for the rest of her life. This life confinement, severe as it may seem, was perhaps considered light punishment for fornication in the opinion of Muhammad. Many Muslim women are not free to leave their quarters anyway. In some orthodox Muslim communities, women stay home all their lives and seldom venture out of the house except on very special occasions.

The law seems incomplete, however, because it does not provide any punishment for the man involved. Presumably in a male-dominant society he would be the aggressor, and yet he is permitted to live as before without even being questioned.

Muhammad's companions and close friends probably hinted at the incompleteness of the law to him and thus prompted him to change, or rather abrogate, it. Thus the second commandment given by Allah in this connection is much more strict and provides a prescribed punishment for both the man and the woman who have committed adultery.

Scourge the Adulterer and Adulteress

The adulterer and adulteress, scourge ye each one of them (with) a hundred stripes. And let no pity for the twain withhold you from obedience to Allah, if you believe in Allah and the Last Day.And let a party of believers witness their punishment.

Depending on the physical strength of the executioner and his zeal for inflicting punishment, a flogging of one hundred lashes would sometimes result in the death of the condemned. More often than not, this sort of savage punishment caused both culprits, especially the woman, to be crippled forever. Flogging can also result in severe internal injuries.

In the Islamic courts, which are supervised by a member of the clergy, the Mullah, there is no right of the accused to defend themselves. As soon as the four witnesses render their testimonies, the judge will give the predetermined verdict and the executioner then carries out the sentence to the letter. There is no defence counsel.

There is also no minimum or maximum punishment or any option in between. Even the judge is not free to decide between the maximum or minimum sentence, nor is he free to pronounce the sentence in a way that he thinks is appropriate as a human being. In other words, the judge is not free to render a judgement. The law is made by Allah and no one dares to defy or change it. When the court accepts the testimonies of the four witnesses, the verdict is already known, and it stands at one hundred stripes, no more and no less.

This law by itself reflects the barbarity of an ancient patriarchal system, which probably dates back to pre-Islamic days. The woman is brutally treated and her paramour is savagely flogged. Someone has trespassed upon a man's private property and so his rights must be satisfied through punishment of the offenders.

Note the second line. If you are a true believer in Allah and faithful to Islam, you should not show any sign of compassion or mercy. Although Allah is repeatedly described in the *Quran* as "the compassionate and merciful," by modern standards his justice is very cruel. In fact, many passages of the *Quran* describe him in quite a different light. He is the avenger: "Allah is mighty, able to requite"; Allah plots against his own creation, against his people: "And they [the disbelievers] plotted, and Allah plotted [against them]: Allah is the best of the plotters"; Allah punishes very severely, his revenge proves fatal: "Lo! Thy Lord is owner of dire punishment"; "Thy Lord is swift in prosecution"; "He is powerful to revenge: He is omnipotent over His slaves."

Following these Quranic depictions of the Almighty, no Islamic judge would dare to have mercy on the accused. Allah's law is rigid and the sentence is inflexible. There is no appeal from the sentence either. A judgment rendered in the seventh century for the desert nomads must be rendered in the same way at the end of the twentieth century without any improvement or alteration.

The final line of this second injunction stipulates that the flogging must be carried out in public and in the presence of the faithful: "And let a party of believers witness their punishment." The intent is obviously to deter others from wrongdoing. A public flogging is a most humiliating punishment not only for those under sentence, but for their kinfolk, friends, and relatives, who had no part in the "crime." All of their kin share in the anguish of the punishment. Apparently, this barbaric law aims to destroy the root of love that binds family and friends together.

Muslim jurisprudents and apologists hold that only through such laws, "handed over to" Muhammad by Allah, can Muslim communities, or any other community for that matter, be cleaned of evils. They argue that if the Quranic law is carried out to the letter in each Muslim country, there would be no more crime.

A little research will reveal the hypocrisy of this contention. A good deal of lewdness goes on in Muslim countries with orthodox laws, but it is never uncovered. As long as lovers keep a low profile and conceal their love affairs, they are safe when there is no witness, there is no trial, therefore no conviction. Extramarital affairs have not stopped altogether among even very orthodox Muslim people.

Stoning

It was pointed out in the preceding sections that according to separate verses of the *Quran* adultery should be punished either by house confinement or by a hundred lashes administered in public. Adding to this confusion is a tradition that maintains the punishment for adultery was later changed to stoning of both the adulterer and the adulteress. It is said that Muhammad replaced the punishments specified in the *Quran* with stoning, which is believed to have been derived from Judaism.

After Muhammad died, a difference of opinion emerged among the believers. Most of them maintained that the *Quran* plainly and explicitly abrogates the sentence of stoning. But 'Umar, whose personality was very dominating among the faithful, argued that the Prophet had ordained stoning of adulterers. Being Muhammad's father-in-law, close associate, and the second caliph, he eventually silenced the dispute and favoured the traditional accounts of the deeds of the Prophet (sunna) against the text of the *Quran*.

Another theory holds that the injunction of stoning had been originally a part of chapter thirty-three, but this is doubtful. One can clearly see that there was some confusion of mind on the part of Muhammad regarding the seriousness of this transgression. At first he decides to enjoin house confinement of the woman alone. Then he changes his mind and commands flogging of both parties involved. If we are to believe traditions outside of the *Quran*, he later changed the punishment to stoning. Such confusion makes it next to impossible for the objective reader to accept the *Quran* as the inerrant word of God.

In any case, Muslim jurisprudence applies both punishments. It draws a distinction between two types of adultery, the latter being more serious:

1. An extramarital affair of a man with a woman who is not married to someone else. Scourging is administered for this lesser transgression.
2. An extramarital affair of a man with a married woman. Death by stoning is the penalty in this case.

The transgression is established in two different ways in the Islamic court: either the accused admits the crime personally and makes a confession or proof of the deed is presented to the court.

In the first instance, the court procedure is simply an automatic decision-making process. The judge, after hearing the confession, establishes the fact that the accused is a legal adult and of sound mind, and asks the accused if he (she) really considers himself (herself) to be a violator of the Quranic law. If the answer is affirmative each time it is asked, the crime is established as a fact in the eyes of the law and the sentence is pronounced accordingly.

In the second instance, when the accused is brought before the court, Islamic law calls for four eyewitnesses "who are able to confirm the truth of the accusation in detail." They must swear that they have seen the actual penetration. The requirement of four male witnesses is enjoined in the *Quran*: "Produce four witnesses from among you against them." Although it may seem improbable that four witnesses could prove that they actually saw the penetration of the woman by the man, if they swear to it, their evidence must be credited, and the judge cannot reject it. This act of infringing upon someone else's privacy and spying on the bedroom of a neighbor or friend is thus compatible with and in some ways encouraged by Islamic laws.

Usually these four witnesses are required to be male, but if it is not possible to produce four male witnesses, then three male and two female testimonies are considered just as valid, *i.e.*, two women witnesses in lieu of one man. This is the only combination acceptable in Islamic court. This does not, however, mean that for every male, two females could testify. The law accepts a total of only two women witnesses, no more. This is another patent example of the way in which woman in Islam is treated as the inferior sex.

The mode of execution for those found guilty of adultery, according to tradition and Islamic law, is unbelievably cruel and barbaric.

After the sentence for stoning to death is issued by the judge, the woman is taken out of the court to a public place to give the curious the opportunity to view the execution. A hole is dug for her and she is placed in it in a standing position. The hole is then filled in with dirt so that she won't be able to move.

The four eyewitnesses come forward and approaching her in this helpless position, each throws a stone at her. Next the judge takes part in this savage act, hurling a stone at her from the prepared "ammunition of death." Finally, every one of the Muslim bystanders joins in the show, pelting the miserable creature with stones.

It is indeed a show of savagery. A helpless, panicked woman, buried in a grave in an upright position, is murdered by a frenzied crowd of zealots, some of whom joyfully compete to inflict the most terrible injuries upon the wretched soul. And all of this is fully sanctioned by law. In the last seven years, at least four cases of this barbaric punishment have been implemented in the Islamic Republic of Iran alone.

This method of stoning reportedly goes back to Muhammad himself, as once he ordered a hole to be dug for an Arab woman named Ghamdiya who was accused of adultery. 'Ali, his cousin and son-in-law, who succeeded him as the fourth caliph, tried another woman accused of fornication and condemned the girl, Shuraha Hamdiani, to be stoned to death exactly in the same manner as the Prophet had done some thirty years before. Since accounts of Muhammad's deeds are the main source of jurisprudence next to the *Quran*, 'Umar, 'Ali, and all the other Muslim jurists and rulers had no other alternative but to follow the example of the Prophet.

There is no specific rule for stoning a man. Apparently, based on a tradition of Muhammad, when he sentenced a man named Maiz to be stoned, he did not clarify the mode of execution. We quote from a reliable and authentic Muslim jurisprudence text on the subject of execution by stoning:

It is necessary, when a whoremonger is to be stoned to death, that he should be carried to some barren place void of houses and cultivation, and it is requisite that the stoning be executed first by witnesses and after them by the Imam or Qadi [religious leader or judge], and after those by the rest of the bystanders, because it is so recorded from 'Ali [Muhammad 's cousin], and also because in the circumstances of the execution, begun by the witnesses, there is a precaution, since a person may be very bold in delivering his evidence against a criminal, but afterwards, when directed himself to commence the infliction of the punishment which is a consequence of it, [he] may from compunction retract his testimony; thus, causing the witness to begin the punishment may be a means of entirely preventing it. [The Muslim apologists do not explain, however, that if the witnesses who accuse a man are his antagonists and through perjury maliciously conspire to convict him, then there is no one who could stop the execution.]

When a woman is to be stoned, a hole or excavation should be dug to receive her, as deep as her waist, because the Prophet ordered such a hole to be dug for Ghamdiyah before mentioned, and 'Ali also ordered a hole to be dug for Shuraha Hamdiani. It is laudable to dig a hole for her, as decency is thus most effectually preserved. There is no manner of necessity to dig a hole for a man, because the Prophet did not do so in the case of Maiz.

According to the above report, it was Muhammad himself who enjoined the savage law of stoning in Islam, and it was also he who devised the barbaric way of carrying out the sentence.

Discrimination against Women in Penal Laws

The inequality of man and woman in Islam is seen even in the mode of their punishment. In regard to stoning, the woman is buried in a standing position up to her waist (really her breasts) under the pretext of preserving public decency and cannot move at all, much less cover her head and face to avoid the barrage of deadly stones. But the convicted man is free to move around, cover his head and face with both arms, and even run for his life, as anyone in that situation would do. She experiences a more bitter and horrible death.

Islamic law enjoins that even a condemned sick woman must be put to death immediately. There is no moratorium in such cases. Muslim theologians maintain that since the adulteress must be destroyed anyway, as Muhammad ordained, there is no justification for delay.

In certain Islamic schools, a woman convicted of fornication receives a double punishment: first, she is scourged with a hundred lashes as specified in *Quran* 24: 2, and then she is stoned to death in the manner explained before. Many scholastic minutiae are presented by different sects. The Shiites, one of the fanatical Muslim sects, advocate this double punishment for fornication. They also maintain that if a married woman (*muhsan*) has sexual intercourse with a minor boy, she should receive a hundred lashes only; but if she cohabits with an adult man who is mentally imbalanced and is not her husband, then she should be stoned to death without scourging. Discrimination against woman is manifested here also. If a man has sexual intercourse with a teenaged girl or an insane woman, he is sentenced to one hundred lashes only and not stoning.

If a man has divorced his wife by means of the irrevocable repudiation of triplicate divorce (*Talak, Talak, Talak*), and then is caught with the divorced wife in bed, both of them will be stoned to death.

If a man commits the act of sodomy with a woman other than his wife, according to the Hanafi school (which comprises the largest number of believers), he is to be corrected by scourging. But sodomizing one's own wife, even without her consent, is permitted in Islam, because the *Quran* enjoins: "Your women are (like) a tilled field for you, so enter into your tilled field any way you please."

Obviously there is very little systematic consistency to these penal laws. A man who sodomizes a woman who is not his wife gets away with a lesser punishment than a man who sleeps with his divorced wife. The former is scourged while the latter is stoned to death!

There are many other examples of such inconsistencies and inequalities: If a Muslim man commits adultery with a nonbeliever's wife in a non-Muslim land or in the territory of Islam where the populace revolted against their government, he is not to be stoned.

If a man who had confessed to adultery is able to run to safety during the execution process, the process must stop. This opportunity to escape not only can save his life, but his former confession is considered thereby nullified. A woman, on the other hand, could never escape her punishment because she is buried up to her waist in a hole and unable to run to safety. Even if she decides to deny her confession of adultery, there is no reprieve from the execution sentence.

If a man cohabits with a slave girl of his son or grandson, there is no punishment for him. However, if a woman has sexual relations with a male slave of her daughter or granddaughter, she will be punished accordingly.

Strangely, under certain penal laws, slaves are better off than free persons. For example, slaves are not stoned for adultery or fornication. They are flogged, but with only fifty lashes. This too follows the *Quran*: " then if they [the slave girls] are guilty of adultery when they are taken in marriage, they shall suffer half the punishment (prescribed) for free women."

Having sexual relations with an unmarried woman calls for chastising both parties by flogging. In order to implement the punishment, the man's clothing is taken off except for his underwear (slip), his hands are tied to a pole or a tree, and he is then flogged in a standing position. The woman, on the other hand, is scourged in a sitting position with her veil wrapped around her body. This mode of scourging for the man and the woman is attributed to 'Ali, Muhammad's cousin, who reportedly said: "Correction is to be inflicted upon a man standing and upon a woman sitting." In Islamic jurisprudence "correction" means scourging, of course. Scourging is practiced today in Muslim countries with orthodox governments: Saudi Arabia, Pakistan, Sudan, and Iran.

Caliphs are Above the Law

Of course, for the supreme ruler there was no punishment and no accountability to the law. When the caliph or his standing jurisprudent committed a felony, such as bribery, theft, fornication, or even rape and murder, no one could prosecute him. With the exception of a handful of caliphs a great number of Muslim rulers indulged in sexual intercourse outside of their overfilled harems, and they even had incestuous and unlawful sexual relations with their blood relatives.

Drunkenness was also a frequent weakness of many caliphs. Most of the Umayyid caliphs were often drunk, even during prayer time. Regarding sexual transgressions, there are some notorious examples. Harun al-Rashid, the great 'Abbasid caliph, slept with his own sister. Ma'mun, his son, who ruled the western part of the vast Muslim empire, cohabited with his aunt. Khalid Walid, the commander of the Muslim army under the first caliph, Abu Bakr, killed a chieftain in a most treacherous way in order to possess the man's wife for himself. She was very pretty and the commander had developed a strong sexual desire for her. When Abu Bakr was told what his army commander had done, the caliph would not prosecute Khalid because, he said, he was nicknamed the "sword of Allah" (*saif Allah*) by the Prophet and he could do nothing against Allah's sword!

But the wives of these high-ranking Muslim officials were not exempted from punishment like their mates. For according to *Quran* 4: 34: "Men are in charge of women, because Allah hath made the one of them to excel the other."

False Allegations and Oath

Sometimes the husband may accuse his wife of infidelity based solely on jealousy. If he cannot prove that his wife was unfaithful by providing four just witnesses, his punishment is eighty lashes for slander. In order to avoid the prescribed punishment of flogging, he must repeat his allegation four times and each time take an oath to Allah that he is telling the truth.

As for those who accuse their wives but have no witnesses except themselves; let the testimony of one of them be four testimonies, (swearing) by Allah that he is of those who speak the truth; and yet a fifth, invoking the curse of Allah on him if he speaketh not the truth.

Against this allegation there is only one avenue open to the wife to defend herself. She, in turn, can also swear that she is innocent and her husband is not telling the truth. In other words, when a man, filled with jealousy or malevolence, accuses his wife of adultery without producing four witnesses, she can defy his allegation by taking an oath and swearing four times that the accusation is false. In this connection, the *Quran* states:

> And it shall avert the punishment from her if she bear witness before Allah four times that the thing he said is indeed false. And a fifth (time) that the wrath of Allah be upon her, if he speaketh the truth.

Swearing by a deity to back up one's statement was an old custom among the nomadic Arabs.It did not start with the Arabs and was a prevalent technique among many ancient peoples thousands of years before Muhammad.In this particular case, when a man accuses his wife of sexual relations with another, there are some very striking similarities between the injunction of the *Quran* and the Code of Hammurabi from ancient Babylon, which we mentioned previously. Hammurabi's law was copied and sent to different parts of his empire and was later translated into different languages, becoming the basis of many civil laws of the ancient world.The Arabian peninsula, especially its northern section, could not have been out of the influence of the code; so it is not unreasonable to assume that it influenced Arab legal tradition, which was later adapted by Muhammad.When we compare the *Quran* with the Code of Hammurabi regarding the allegation of infidelity, we find that, according to the Babylonian law, any husband who suspects his wife of infidelity could not have punished her without proof: "If a man's wife has been accused by her husband, but she has not been caught lying with another male, she shall swear by a god and return to her home."

Despite a time difference of about twenty-three centuries, the two laws regarding the slandering of a wife are almost identical. It therefore stands to reason that Muhammad perpetuated an old established law, which can be traced all the way back to Babylon.

Nonetheless, in spite of the similarities of the two laws, there are some good points in the Code of Hammurabi, which make it much more liberal to an open- minded student.Let us compare the law of allegation in both documents and look at the merits and shortcomings of each.

1. Quranic law 24: 8 requires the wife who is accused of infidelity by her husband to "bear witness before Allah four times" in order to avert the danger of harsh punishment, whereas the Code of Hammurabi requires the wife to swear only one oath.
2. Quranic law stipulates that the accused wife must swear by Allah, god of Islam.But if the wife is a nonbeliever or non-Muslim, swearing to Allah does not have a real meaning and the oath is useless. In Hammurabi's law, the wife could take an oath by "a god," any god she respects, not necessarily her husband's god. Apparently, the Babylonian law establishes a mode of freedom in beliefs.
3. In accordance with the Quranic injunction, after the wife takes the oath by Allah four times, she is required to call on Allah a fifth time to curse her if she is a liar. However, there is no such sanction for her husband, who may have mistakenly or maliciously accused his wife of infidelity.

   Here the woman is humiliated because it is she who has to apologize indirectly by imploring Allah to curse her if she is not telling the truth. Her defense is questioned even though the accusation remains unproven. In Hammurabi's law, the accused wife does not have to go through the mental agony of begging the god to curse her. She does not have to prove anything. Obviously, neither of these laws would meet modern Western standards. But if a woman of any civilized society today were compelled to choose one of them, she would probably prefer the Babylonian law to that of the *Quran*.

False Accusation and the Controversy Surrounding

And those who accuse honorable women but bring not four witnesses, scourge them (with) eighty stripes and never (afterwards) accept their testimony. They indeed are evil doers.

Commentators on the *Quran* tell us that the above passage was revealed in response to those people who doubted the chastity of one of Muhammad's youngest and prettiest wives, Aisha. In a incident that related the circumstances that led to Aisha being left behind Muhammad's caravan one night. The next day she rejoined her husband with the help of a young man named Safwan ibn al-Mu'attal. Her disappearance and then reappearance with the young man gave rise to malicious rumours about infidelity and much consternation on Muhammad's part. The episode took place in the fifth year of the Hegira when Aisha was only thirteen and Muhammad was returning from the campaign against the tribe of Banu al-Mustaliq.

This is how Aisha told her side of the story:

> When Safwan passed me, he had fallen behind the main body for some purpose and had not spent the night with the troops. He saw my form and came and stood over me. He used to see me before the veil was prescribed for us, so when he saw me, he exclaimed in astonishment, "The apostle's wife!" He asked what had kept me behind, but I did not speak to him. Then, he brought up his camel and told me to ride it while he kept behind. So, I rode it and he took the camel's head going forward quickly in search of the army, and by Allah, we did not overtake them and I was not missed until the next morning.

Then the army halted and while they were resting, the man came up leading me. Then the liars said what they do say, and the army was in a state of turmoil.

The people who saw the young camel driver, Safwan, with Muhammad's youngest wife were at first astonished and later started to gossip, accusing Aisha of infidelity.

The scandal loving Arabs were not slow in drawing sinister conclusions from the inopportune situation and spread the word abroad. The estrangement of Muhammad from his favourite wife strengthened the grounds of defamation.

Muhammad, in his distress, did not know what to do. Although he was burning with anger and jealousy, he was very attached to his child-wife and did not want to part with her after all, she was his favourite.

Muhammad apparently questioned his wife's fidelity as well because she was sent to her parents' house. As he could not and did not want to lose her, and he could not stop the tattling tongues of his followers, he asked the advice of some of his close associates. A variety of opinions were presented. His cousin, 'Ali, told him to divorce her and get rid of the scandal. Some Islamic writers maintain that Muhammad's youngest daughter, Fatima, who was married to 'Ali and very jealous of Aisha because she had attracted the affection of her father and taken her deceased mother's place, encouraged her husband, 'Ali, to present the harshest solution: "Divorce her! There are plenty of young and beautiful girls who would be more than willing to marry you."

As always, he referred the matter to Allah, who came to his aid by giving him the following verse:

> Lo! They who spread the slander are a gang among you. Deem it not a bad thing for you; nay, it is good for you. Unto every man of them (will be paid) that which he hath earned of the sin; and as for him among them who had the greater share therein, his will be anawful doom. Why did not the believers, men and women, when ye heard it, think good of their own folk, and say: it is a manifest untruth? Why did they not produce four witnesses?

Since they produce not witnesses, they verily are liars in the sight of Allah.

It is said by most historians and biographers of Muhammad that there were especially two men in Medina, named Hassan and Mistah, who were responsible for spreading rumors of Aisha's infidelity. Basing his actions on the *Quran*, Muhammad ordered his soldiers to seize the two men and inflicted on them the Quranic punishment eighty lashes each.A woman named Hamma also received the same punishment.She was the sister of Zaynab (Muhammad's wife) who, perhaps out of pure jealousy, was Aisha's ardent antagonist and adversary. After such a severe punishment, the slanderers were quieted and the gossip died down.

Aisha once more resumed her role as the Prophet's favourite wife and she kept that position in his harem for the next five years until he died. There is, however, another side to this story which throws a shadow of doubt over the whole episode, especially Aisha's chastity. According to a great many Islamic historians, the above incident occurred when Muhammad was triumphantly returning from a campaign against the Banu Mustaliq tribe. It was after this expedition that Muhammad acquired a new wife named Juwayriyya, to whom Aisha took an instant dislike because of her beauty.

During the honeymoon Muhammad apparently must have neglected Aisha, who was accompanying him on the expedition. Polygamy always has its ill effects. Perhaps Aisha, feeling forsaken, tried to have a little fun for herself with a young, good-looking man who was in the same expedition. There are a number of factors that make this interpretation of the events probable:

1. At the time of the episode, Muhammad was in his late fifties and Aisha, at thirteen, was on the crest of teenage passion and feelings. The Prophet's attention was divided among his various military expeditions, social activities, and cohabitation with a dozen wives. It would not be unnatural for a young girl like her under these circumstances to search for a paramour as her husband did so often.
2. According to Aisha herself, she knew the young camel driver before the order of the veil was imposed; therefore, they were not meeting for the first time.
3. The history writers tell us that because Aisha was very small and thin, the man in charge of her litter did not notice, or rather did not feel, her absence when he lifted the litter onto the camel's back. It is difficult to accept this childish reasoning. The man in charge of the litter could easily have detected that it was empty from the lack of sounds from within. It is true that the order of the veil would have prevented his seeing his mistress's face, but he was not barred from talking to her to know if she felt comfortable or needed anything. In fact, the *Quran* specifically allows such conversation: "When you ask of them [the wives of the Prophet] anything, ask it of them from behind a curtain." How is it possible that Aisha's

attendant did not become aware that his mistress was missing the entire night?

4. It is reported that Aisha arrived at Muhammad's headquarters the next day with the young camel driver leading the camel. How could her husband not have known that she was missing that night and even part of the next day until she arrived? Muhammad had taken Aisha with him on this expedition so that he might have the pleasure of her company during the journey. Perhaps Aisha disappeared when Muhammad was preoccupied with Juwayriyya.
5. When a camel bearing a litter is brought up to the door of a tent or house, it is made to kneel down until the passenger enters the litter. During this time, the curtain of the litter is drawn to one side to allow the rider in. As soon as the traveller is inside the litter, she herself or her attendants draw the curtain, the sign that she is ready to move along. Then the camel stands up and proceeds. The man in charge of Aisha's litter could not have failed to notice that the curtain was not drawn and that she was not inside.
6. According to the biographers, after this incident, Muhammad quarreled with his wife. He was angry with her and afterwards would not talk to her. She fell ill from sorrow and his indifference. Later, she was sent to her parents. Her father, Abu Bakr (literally: "father of the virgin"), spoke with his son-in-law about the divorce of his daughter. Aisha stayed one month in her parent's home and Muhammad refused to sleep with her for that time.
7. By Aisha's own account, Safwan recognized her without difficulty because he had seen her before Muhammad's wives were forced to wear the veil. She also says she did not talk to him. If she was wearing her veil, how could he have known her in the middle of the night in the Arabian desert without any light? Does not this part of the story seem a bit strange?
8. It is curious that of all the followers of Muhammad the man who was assigned to follow the caravan and pick up the strays or missing items was a young, handsome camel driver of twenty-four who had known Aisha before the order of the veil was imposed.

9. The allegation of the infidelity of Aisha was mainly made by close relatives of Muhammad himself: his daughter, Fatima; his cousin, 'Ali; and his sister-in- law, Hammam.They should have had his interests at heart.
10. It is reported by some writers that because of this episode, Safwan did not receive the same attention from Muhammad any more. Some even believe that he was mysteriously killed in one skirmish. Thus, the man on whose account fifteen verses of the *Quran* were revealed disappeared quietly from the scene of Islamic history without further trace.

Based on the aforementioned points, it is not unreasonable to conclude that there may have been some truth to the rumor of Aisha's infidelity. Muhammad himself probably suspected as much, but he was also aware that he could not stay away from his beloved child-wife, the only woman who had offered her virginity to him. Let us not forget that virginity of the woman was a very important factor in marriage among the Arabs.

In any case, with the Quranic law stipulating that four eyewitnesses were necessary to prove an adulterous love affair, Muhammad was able to put an end to the rumours of his wife's infidelity. Clearly, no one could furnish four men who would testify that they had seen the act of sexual intercourse between Safwan and Aisha, especially since their encounter took place in the middle of the night and in the vast, isolated space of the desert. Thus Aisha's status in the harem was restored and her accusers were punished with eighty lashes, as the law also commands.

11

Islamic Higher Learning in Muslim Women

Introduction

Muslim women within the context of the historical interaction between western secular and missionary systems of education and contemporary Muslim dogmatic ones, this understanding may shed fight on the process that was responsible for Muslim women's inability to reflect on their beliefs and their actions and, hence, may lead to positive changes.

My earlier research findings suggest a more serious problem than merely women's limited access to secular or religious educational institutions. They suggest that deeper knowledge of the sacred may pave the road to reversing the historical process of disenfranchisement or, at least, to finding new and better ways to conceptualize and study Muslim women.

One of the primary tenets of the Islamic revelation is justice (*'adl*) as the basis of human interaction. Justice is established when an individual makes a conscious, informed choice to reject or to realize the divine will as expressed in the words of the Quran and to make it the basis of action. According to the Quran (2:30), God has entrusted (*i.e.*, given *al-khilafah*, viceregency, trusteeship) all humans with the divine will (shari'a, moral guidelines) to act in a moral, just manner based on freedom of choice. Will is not moral unless it is exerted freely and acted upon by a free, informed agent. Justice in Islam is based on this ethical moment of choice that encompasses all human thought and actions. The belief in One God, trusteeship, and justice must be realized in action. But before this can happen, the listener to or reader of the Quran must avoid preconceptions and see "in Islam the unfolding of something unique, which has to be understood in its own terms."

As human rights advocacy means to realize women's "active participation in all spheres of public and private life," human rights among Muslims are established by recognizing that Muslim women, regardless of how they are defined or define themselves, can actually participate only within a particular ideological context of choice. For Muslims the unique authority of the Quran, the position of the Prophet as the greatest man, and the strength of the Muslim family constitute the enduring frame for the constancy and flexibility of Islam over time. Two prerequisites, therefore, are needed to fulfil the human rights declaration within the Islamic concept of justice. First, Muslim women's self-identity must be acknowledged by both Muslims and nonMuslims before one can expect women to be agents of change instead of receivers of change. Second, Muslim women must formulate their own choice before one can claim that a free identification with Islam is actualized.

To move the Beijing platform from a plan into strategies of action for Muslim women, every woman needs to understand the platform's ramifications within the context of her chosen identity before one can claim a "people-centred sustainable development" that will alleviate the present conditions of injustice. Here is where I argue that full access to Islamic higher learning, that is, deeper knowledge of the Islamic primary sources beyond the ritual religious acts, is the basis for Muslim women to effect a change. The fact that many Muslim women rely solely on others' interpretations of the scriptures to guide their basic spiritual, intellectual, and physical needs is evidence that a Muslim woman's right to understand, to choose, and to act on her choice is being compromised. Full access means that women take part in the interpretation of Islamic teachings and in the interpretation of the Platform for Action to maintain the dynamics of Islam rather than being limited to procreation and maintaining the Muslim family structure or individual human rights as suggested by others. Human rights and Islamic identity are not given but are gained by the individual's conscious efforts toward self-realization.

To realize herself as a Muslim a woman first must understand that her basic human right is to reject or accept Islam in its fundamental combination of faith and action, both rooted in divine will. To know the divine will human beings are given two things: revelation a direct disclosure of what God, the source of all values and knowledge, wants them to realize on earth (the law of nature, *al-minha/al-nizam*) and rational ability necessary to discover the divine will unaided. Humans must exercise moral sense to discover God's will. A human being begins his or her life with *fitṛa*, "natural endowment", but individual destiny is what each person makes of it. If one relates fitra to the most frequently recited verses in the Quran (1:12: "In the name of Allah, Guardian of the World, the Merciful, the Magnificent; thanks be to Allah"), the method of objectifying the Quranic principles becomes clear without the need of others' interpretations. Such a strategy can be applied by any woman regardless of her level of education. For example, it was employed by early Muslim women who realized that by accepting the Oneness of God they were able to question the social constraints that surrounded them, including some of the Prophet Muhammad's own earlier injunctions. This is expressed in Sura *al-mujadalah* and in Asma Bint Yazid's and Hind Bint 'Utbah's questioning of the Prophet on the respective roles and rewards of men and women at the time when they were giving their own vote to the Prophet and accepted Islam. These women had not been taught critical thinking by anybody. It was their conscious choice to relate to the meaning of the Oneness of God as the core of values that made them critical even of the Prophet's interpretation of the verse about women's voting.

My findings among both North American and Syrian women and their families are illustrations of this point. They indicate that a higher level of formal, secular, or religious education does not correlate with Islamic higher learning as explained above. Instead, it correlates with a widening gap between males' and females' understanding of Islam. Men tend to see Islam as something that gives them superior power and knowledge over others despite their definition of Islam as "submission to the will of God," whereas women see Islam as a protective power that requires of them total submission to the win of God as interpreted mainly by men. In addition, higher education (both religious and secular) has not changed the problematic attitude toward the proper place of women in Muslim societies. Muslim women are still viewed and view themselves as mothers, daughters, sisters, and as wives but rarely as having an autonomous trusteeship in line with the Quranic intention of al-khilafah.

In the Islamic worldview deciphering the signs, (*ayat*) of the Quran is, as Schimmel and Rahman assert, endowed in human existence: "And we should show them our signs in the horizons and in themselves". What prevented women from deciphering the Quran in the last few centuries is the introduction of the perception that the act of deciphering the sacred requires special preparation and is limited only to elite males. For example, when I was trying to derive the meaning of *taqwa* (consciousness of Allah, usually translated as piety) from my interviewees both in North America and Syria, I asked them to tell me how they could be both pious to God and to other humans at the same time. A twenty-one-year-old female college student said: "As women, our first role is to attend to the family and, hence, our piety to God is only possible when we pray and fast while our piety to others is shown by accepting and fulfilling our role." Clearly, she had accepted a view of piety that showed a heavy male bias and resulted in a gendered meaning of the term. This biased meaning, it seems, has led to the injustice of denying women trusteeship and full moral responsibility. Taqwa in Islam is the only distinction between individuals. This is the divine criterion by which every individual is judged: how well balanced he or she has discharged the responsibilities toward God and those toward people.

Muslim women's emancipation needs to be approached from another direction besides education, namely, perceptual and attitudinal change. The implications of this statement are more far-reaching than a critique of a misleading interpretation of the Arabic word *taqwa*. They imply that this college student assumes that one can only be pious or conscious of God's presence when performing the religious rituals, whereas Islam intends the conscious realization that "the standard whereby [human] action is to be judged, lies outside of [the human]"; that to be pious is to be silent, whereas Islam affirms that to be silent when injustice is taking place means to be impious; and that to be silent is a woman's sign of consent to a marriage or any other matter that a male in her household may insist on, whereas Islam explicitly affirms that a marriage contract is a condition for the consummation of the marriage. Such a realization makes conscience as central to Islamic identity as love is to Christian identity.

Educational, historical, anthropological, and sociological studies of Muslim women rarely show interest in women's spiritual and intellectual development that has more far-reaching meaning in Muslim women's struggles for justice than has mere "gender equality." Even recent studies in human rights among Muslim women pay little attention to the women's own realization of their part in understanding Islam. Before introducing women to concepts from outside the sphere of Islamic beliefs, such a realization is critical to effecting real and participatory change. Without realizing that her own perception of her role is in contradiction with the system that she has come to know as "Islam," a Muslim woman's changes of her role will only be temporary.

Content of Islamic Higher Learning

The Quran, as Rahman suggests, is a document that is squarely aimed at the human being. Originally, it was intended as a "guidance for humankind" for proper action. To fulfill the purpose of human existence as the trustee that Muslims see as a Quranic mandate, a Muslim woman must at least be acquainted with the Islamic system and its methodologies before she can turn the article of faith into action. This acquaintance is not limited to women who are literate nor to those who read Arabic nor to those who acquire higher degrees in secular or religious institutions. To the contrary, by relying mainly on the oral traditions transmitted in local languages understanding Islamic guidance and the Islamic worldview is as simple as the ability to recite and know the meaning of the article of faith stripped of the many layers of translations and meanings that over time have added class, ethnic, or other biases. This does not imply being cut off from previous knowledge and tradition but keeping that knowledge and the traditions in their correct place as secondary sources. Nor does it imply a denial of the centrality of Arabic to spiritual immersion in Islam; Arabic is the only language of prayer, even when the praying individual does not understand the Arabic text. The language of the scripture itself is not only a tool of expression but a means of uniting the individual with God, once the basic message of the scriptures was communicated in the individual's own language. The issue in Islamic higher learning, therefore, is not access to secular or religious higher education but allowing the Quran to speak for itself to the individual, to be a person's guide. Schimmel asserts that by listening to the primordial sounds, one understands why sound can be regarded as creative power. This deep significance in the recitation of the divine words even if the listener does not know Arabic has become almost unavailable to Muslim women in the last few centuries because women were largely deprived of attending and participating in recitations. This deprivation is the result of many layers of restrictive interpretation that have accumulated to the point where some contemporary extreme Muslim groups even consider a woman's voice in public an 'awra (lack of chastity). Once Islam took on an institutional structure in which women were viewed as dependent on men, a Muslim woman's experience of God became a vague belief mediated through her male household, an Imam, or saint. Without direct access to what the Quran has to say so that her belief in God's existence will become clear in her mind and in her heart, the proxy structure will remain standing in the way of her trusteeship, and the "functional existence of God" that calls on every individual to reflect on the meaning of Allah in her own life will be denied.

Islam as a belief system and a worldview ought to permeate individuals' thoughts and actions. Higher learning in Islam is the direct, deep contact with Islam's basic principles, primarily in their oral form, and in interactions of the sacred word and text with daily life. A Muslim woman who, for example, recites the verses "In the name of Allah, Guardian of the World, the Merciful, the Magnificent" tens of times in daily prayers without relating to their significance as defining the human relationship to God and to others may not be able to realize herself as a Muslim. This phenomenon, it seems, is one of the main reasons that Muslims in the last three centuries have been missing the meaning of three main points of 'hese verses: (1) that everything except God is contingent upon God; (2) that God's might is essentially a mercy; and (3) that both these aspects entail a proper relationship between God and humans and, consequently, also a proper relationship among humans. I argue that because women were prevented from direct involvement in Quranic studies, beginning with the art of listening and recitation and ending with the science of interpretation, they in effect are not practicing Islam as a pedagogical system of the trusteeship. As a result, women do not realize themselves nor are they being realized as Muslims in the full meaning of the word.

The belief in the Prophet Muhammad is troubled by the fact that the Prophet is a man. The result of the difficulty in separating Muhammad the Prophet from Muhammad the man may result in cognitive dissonance. Although the confusion seems to exist in the minds of most contemporary Muslims because of the idealization of the Prophet over the centuries, it is a more acute problem for women because the suppression of their Muslim identity is the result of the claim of male superiority and guardianship. Idealization of male authority prevents living one's trusteeship fully.

The Quran itself in effect became marginalized by interpretations and by being recited only during certain rituals. It lost its purpose of being God's guidance of human behaviour through direct contact. As this aim receded in importance behind rituals, women's identification with Islam became particularly ritualistic, atomized, confusing, and ineffective. In addition, the interaction between European missionary systems of knowledge and the view of some Muslim philosophers resulted in "preaching orthodox religion to the masses and a kind of rationalist, natural law deism to the elite." This historic change in teaching the Quran affected women's Islamic higher learning negatively. Such learning deteriorated further with the introduction of universal schooling with its separate curricula for males and females: home economics and child care were the core for females' education in the Third World even beyond the 1960s. Islamic education is referred to in the Quran as the process of shaping character within the Islamic worldview, that is, to learn and to act as guided by the Book. Over time, Islamic education deteriorated from comprehensive training in the first Islamic community in Medina to a mere course of study on religion or its inculcation in social mores.

Education and Islamic Higher Learning

The introduction of secular and missionary educational systems in the Muslim world, women were largely prevented from participating in either of the educational systems because Muslims, largely men, feared cultural hegemony. Later, the curriculum in the few girls' schools was limited to memorization of some verses and *figh*, rules of jurisprudence of purity and prayer, and to home economics, whereas for males it included the study of *usul al-figh*, the foundations of jurisprudence, the art of recitation, and other Quranic and related sciences.

The introduction of universal schooling to Muslim societies could not change the attitudes about women's education nor about women's Islamic higher learning. Women in Western societies may have partially benefited from secular universal education because their minds had already been "sharpened" by medieval Christian theology. Yet even where contemporary Western feminists have taken the interpretation of the scriptures in their hands, they could not change the concept that Eve was created of Adam's rib nor the perception of female morality resulting from Eve's fall as proclamations by the "new religious right" attest. Now, even when Western feminists discuss these spiritual and religious factors from within their own faith and with new conceptual tools, with very few exceptions (such as Fiorenza Schussler) they do not contribute to the religious debate much because, in Rahman's words, secularism has destroyed the sanctity and universality of all moral values. Any reconstruction of these universal values within the secular framework will demand a grounding in a particular perspective and, consequently, relativism will continue to haunt any human rights standards no matter how just they may be. Muslim women, by contrast, may still benefit from the prevalent acceptance of Quranic moral values as the standards no matter how neglected they might be in practice at the moment. These standards may help Muslim women to interpret the specifics of the Islamic worldview without trapping the latter in secularism. Western feminists ignored the marginalization of women's "religious" higher learning early on in their own movements, and despite many failures they still largely do not recognize it as fundamental to social change when they reach out to women in societies where religio-moral worldviews prevail.

For example, in Muslim societies, universal secular schooling did not enable Muslim women to overcome any biased social construct of womanhood. Thus, contemporary female graduates of Shari'a schools such as al-Azhar, the oldest Islamic university in the world, are not members of Muslim councils (*Majalis al-Shura*) and other similar religious bodies. After two hundred years of secular education and about fifty years of UNESCO's war on Hhteracy, most Muslim women still could not change the misconceptions surrounding their social roles. Had Western feminism been equipped to discuss Muslim values as part of the general paradigm of Islamic studies, of Muslim women's studies, and of area studies, women might have had more success in facilitating change, might have less-polarized views, and might have a paradigm for the study of Islam and of Muslim women different from the present static, dogmatic Muslim and the atomized, secular-based Western ones.

Without placing the Beijing Platform for Action within the framework of women's Islamic higher learning, I argue that women may be able to translate some of its articles into realistic gains for some Muslim women but may not be able to objectify the Islamic concepts as intended in the Quran away from their social and narrow ritualistic meanings nor enact the sustainable and effective participation that the platform recommendations suggest. Formal education and universal, secular schooling alone will not help bring about a profound change in the self-understanding of women. The recent reports on Syrian women's gains in third-level education support my argument. The *U.N. World's Women 1995* reports that the number of Syrian females per one hundred males enrolled in third-level education was sixty-eight in 1990. The Syrian Arab Republic *National Report* to the Fourth World Conference on Women, September 1995, also indicates that female enrollment in Syrian universities in 1980 was 26.12 per cent, increasing to 39.08 percent by 1993. Female university graduates rose from 27.33 per cent in 1980 to 35.97 per cent in 1993. Although the statistics indicate a significant increase, when I probed deeply into the actual impact of these and other gains, my findings, confirmed by other studies conducted by Syrian women, suggest that the same old hypocritical attitude toward women's liberation still exists at the individual, religious, and political levels, locally, nationally, and internationally: a woman's first role is to be a wife and mother.

This attitude becomes more consequential when the Syrian government, like other governments that claim secular administration, gives male graduates of Sharia schools and other men prominent public exposure to preach a religious rhetoric against women's public participation under the disguise of protecting the social fabric. At the same time the state, claiming gender sensitivity, feminizes the teaching profession, and this reinforces traditional gender attitudes. Meanwhile, none of the female graduates of the religious schools fill public preaching positions or serve in the Muslim councils that produce different *fatwas* (injunctions) against a woman's right to self-realization. This situation became worse when some of the extremist women's religious groups were allowed to develop their own study groups, preaching gender differences and segregation. Although some may argue that these extremist groups show increasing women's participation, their gender politics are endangering the real gains in women's human rights issues, nevertheless. The issue is not merely to let women participate in interpreting the divine will but to ask whose interest the interpretation serves and by what methodology, paradigm, and framework it was formulated.

What complicates the matter further among Muslims in Syria and in other places, including North America, is that Muslim and nonMuslim polarized groups continue to speak for essentialized Muslim women, reinforcing the misconception that a Muslim woman cannot self-identify her needs and course of action. As these groups speak at each other, the majority of Muslim women are caught in-between with no voice of their own and no solution of their problems in sight. Only a few of the universally schooled women, so far, are able to speak in their own voices, but fewer yet realize the prerequisite for identifying with Islam: self-identity through active participation in the interpretation process.

The Quranic chapter, al-Nisa, (the women) opens with the verse: "Oh, humankind, be conscious of Allah (your guardian) who created you of a single soul, *nafs wahidah*, and created of it her mate, *zawjaha*." About the understanding of the Islamic stance on women, this verse says that a Muslim woman who identifies with Islam is an essential part of the interpretation process of Islam. Human nature is distinguished by its soul, *nafs*, which realizes the existence of God through its relation with itself and nature. The compelling ridness of these meanings in the Quran, as Abd al-Rahman wrote, is what has allowed generations of Muslims to find yet new interpretations. Yet, once a non-Quranic framework of interpretation was introduced and/ or once a particular interpretation was enforced as the ultimate one, such as al-Ghazali's acceptance of the Greek, Christian, and Hindu concept of separating human nature into the mental and the physical, the ability of Muslims to realize their direct relation to these meanings was lost. One sees, for example, how the concept of Adam and Eve from the Judeo-Christian tradition has influenced the prevailing translations of Quranic verse 4:1 quoted above. The feminine marker of the word *nafs* was changed to imply both sexes and was translated as "Person." The feminine pronoun attached to *zawjahah* (her mate) was changed to a masculine one and translated as "his mate." Eventually, the order of creation was reversed to imply that Eve was created of Adam's rib despite the fact that the concept of Eve does not exist in the Quran.

The question, therefore, is this: How is it possible for a Muslim society to provide identity when almost half of the society, the women, is paralyzed or not actively participating in realizing the Quranic meaning and following Quranic guidance? Because Islam is affirmed to be both a belief and a social structure that is not based on submission but on action, being a Muslim requires active participation and not mere acceptance of teachings.

By the same logic, how can one assume that a Muslim woman has regained her human rights without her direct involvement in the interpretation and implementation of the Platform for Action? History indicates that she was stripped of these rights many times under the disguise of Muslim laws, of state sovereignty, but also of the many standards in interpreting human rights. The strategy, therefore, is to let Muslim women generate the meaning within the framework of self-identity with Islam themselves and for everyone else to recognize the necessity of generating meaning in this way as the operating principle for action.

Islamic Higher Learning in Practice

By understanding the meaning of *taqwa* (of being conscious of Allah) when identifying with Islam, Muslim women can counter the claims of males to their spiritual and intellectual guardianship and the claims of superiority of certain classes, races, and national or cultural views. Mutual guardianship and equality in the decision-making process, particularly in religious and cultural matters, are more in harmony with the concept of developing individual autonomy and self-identity than is merely pushing for equality in access to resources, for example.

The strategy here is to ask Muslim societies to explain the claim of nonseparation of the religious and political domains that has prevented them from validating and implementing the platform in fight of the fact that at least one-half of their population is expected to practice the religion by proxy instead of consciously exacting the divine will by choice and to explain this claim when some of them do not allow women to vote despite the fact that voting is one of the fundamentals in rejecting or accepting Islam and the human trusteeship. Furthermore, one needs to ask how they can claim nonseparation when most of these societies exclude women from Islamic councils while women are members of parliament in some others.

Human rights advocates need to choose among three options as they try to forge special strategies for Muslim societies. The first option is to change misguided, misogynist interpretations, such as that men are in charge of women's moral and intellectual well-being and to modify the claim of the universality of human rights to include the specificity of self-realization and its full meaning in the Islamic sense. The second is to refute the claim that Muslim societies are acting within the Sharia. The third is to change the Sharia, that is, what commonly is translated as "Islamic law."

Because the third choice is neither acceptable nor possible for a Muslim woman who has chosen Islam, one is left with two choices. The simpler and more practical one for a lasting effect is the first choice. For example, the claim of men's moral guardianship of women mainly is based on the concepts of *qawamah* (responsibility toward) and *daraja* (a degree or an edge). To interpret them, one needs to put them in the contexts of their Suras and in the context of the Quranic concept of Viceregency, al-khilafah and the meaning of "God" in such verses as "In the name of Allah, Guardian of the World, the Merciful, the Magnificent" (1:1-2). Although these verses often are quoted in support of men's guardianship of women, qawamah (responsibility toward) in 4:34 only implies a man's domestic and financial obligations toward his wife's biologically essential role of procreation. *Daraja* in 2:228 only indicates an added responsibility for a husband when he initiates the divorce process. Elsewhere I have suggested that the relationship between the meanings of verses 4:34 and 2:228 and Islamic justice and human viceregency is summarized in verse 4:32: "Do not enviously wish for that which God proffered on some and not on others. Men and women, to each belong the works they have personally accomplished." That is, although Islam regards men and women as created for different but complementary biological and domestic functions, it does not specify these functions, nor does it generalize them to cover other intellectual and social roles.

Nasr argues that the sacred law, Sharia, in Islam involves not only principles but also their application to daily life in the form of legal codifications. This argument is valid as long as one understands Sharia as outlined in the Quran and explicated in the prophetic authentic tradition. The argument loses strength, however, once Sharia is extended to include the different juridic and contemporary interpretations as part of the sacred. The Quranic principles affirm the unity of Islamic philosophy despite theological and historical diversity. Each individual needs to be informed that "on no soul God places a burden greater than it could bear" before he or she can practice Islam. One must guard such transcendent principles from becoming limited or replaced by legal codifications, particularly when Muslim religious scholars try to impose one legal code in their attempt to guard the Sharia from Western rationalized interpretations. One must insist that legal codifications are merely human interpretations in specific social and historical conditions and are not on the same level of sacredness as are the principles or the rules of interpretations that facilitated these codes. Moreover, to accept legal codifications as absolute contradicts the central dynamic of the Quran, that is, that it be understood in its simple pristine form and be open for interpretation at all times and places by capable females and males regardless of their backgrounds. Legalized codes cannot substitute for Muslim men and women's agency in the interpretation of the transcendent.

Neither, however, can a blind acceptance of Western scientific, rational interpretations of texts be made into universal principles. For example, the varied meanings of human dignity and human development do not support the universality of the basic human rights principles because they are culture-specific. Similarly, the claim that changes in the economic conditions by themselves will help women is limited and limiting. Full agency is realized only when women have the opportunity to express their views and to share in all decision-making processes.

Islamic Higher Learning in the Platform for Action

Islamic higher learning is fufilled only when one has facilitated the development of the Islamic view of an autonomous spiritual and intellectual individual. My "reading" of the *Quran* and the *Hadith* indicates that Islam established five basic principles to permeate the life of an autonomous individual who can make moral and intellectual choices in a just society:

- The creation of male and female of a single soul.

  The right and obligation to learn, to "be educated in the teaching/legislation," (*al-alaqliqra*, "the clot/read," 96:1-4). Aisha, the Prophet's wife and major transmitter of his tradition, said, "Modesty did not prevent the women of Ansar from learning."
- The right and responsibility to accept or reject Islam by voting, bay'ah. The Prophet Muhammad dedicated a special day for women to discuss Islam with him and to vote on his message and on accepting him as a Muslim community leader.
- The right to receive and dispense inheritance and property.
- Membership in the Islamic sisterhood and brotherhood with no distinction of sex, race, class, or ethnicity.

Within this Islamic perspective of social organization and of education as a means to approximate the ideals of a just society, one can specifically address the role of women and women's education for bringing about gender justice in Muslim societies. Islam's strongest argument in favour of *tawhid* (Oneness of God) is that the believer does not have to resort to the abandonment of logic to maintain her faith. The faith is compatible with any other form of knowledge. Allah created the universe in order to be known, and, therefore, "it is necessary that human beings be given the capacity to recognize and understand the Truth that brought about their existence."

Similarly, the Platform for Action's strongest argument in favour of womens human rights is the individual's right to freedom of choice. Thus, as human rights advocates, women cannot insist on this right without recognizing the specificity of self-identification of Muslim women. Otherwise, "human rights implementation" may sound as if Muslim women were asked to abandon their agency or their beliefs to be able to achieve human dignity. Several studies show how external intervention without women's deep knowledge of what is "Islamic" has deprived women of the agency they had before the intervention. Badran suggests that such intervention could reinforce cultural resistance and promote the use of women as pawns in political manipulations of cultural "authenticity." Thus, human rights advocates cannot assume that the implementation of the Platform in Muslim societies is just another "case study" within one large, uniform philosophical and methodological framework.

Muslim women must be reinstated as agents of their education. They must outline priorities themselves, beginning at home and ending at the mosque. This reinstatement can be facilitated by Changing the paradigm of Islamic studies both in Muslim and Western societies and examining the widespread assumption that "Islam" is impeding women's development. Islamic simplicity dictates that each believer could and should be able to understand the teachings in order to perfect the practice of the system. The idea of ranking and restricting interpretations to certain gender, class, or ethnic groups contradicts the Islàmic recognition that God is the only Guide and the All-Knowing. Thus, to think of Islamic studies exclusively in terms of scholarly and theological activities is as misleading as is the claim by secular human rights advocates that religion and religious interpretations per se are limiting women's freedom of choice.

The mosques not only have to be open to girls and women, but women and girls must be encouraged to frequent mosques and not only for special sermons. They must be told that the belief that Friday prayer is not obligatory for them is a misconception. Schimmel writes that the Friday sermon and the Friday prayer are a duty for the community and that women could be preachers.

One must focus on Muslim women's agency to counter the general misconception that Muslim women are passive and totally oppressed. From within their families Muslim women run kinship networks and neighborhood networks. They influence local politics. Singerman's story shows how powerful the Egyptian women who run such networks have become politically and economically. Eickelman and Piscatori suggest that governments accord these networks de facto autonomy. I argue that one ought to count on women to work for better control of their lives from within their families rather than to encourage them to revolt against their families and communities.

Membership in Islamic councils must be open to capable Muslim women who are learned in Islam. In the past Muslim women were narrators of Hadith, for example, that made them an important part of the *isnad* process, the ascription of an uninterrupted chain of authorities on which a tradition is based, and women were involved in the interpretation of the Quran. It is, therefore, totally unjustified to bar women from Islamic councils today, especially if one keeps in mind that oral instruction was, and still is to a certain extent, the rule not only in teaching of Hadith but also in other Islamic sciences and arts and that this applies even more to the interpretation of Islamic philosophy. In Schimmel's view when one keeps in mind the Sufi insistence upon oral transmission of classical texts for "reading between the lines," one realizes the equal importance of such "reading" to the reading of the actual letters. This Sufi point of view also helps one understand why Shah Walliuldin of Delhi remarked that the books of Sufism are elixir for the elite but poison for the normal believer. Such a remark could also be used to criticize Walliuldin's approach to the education of the believers. Instead of preventing the "normal believers" from reading Sufi books, Walliuldin should have made efforts to uplift the Islamic education of these normal people from less-valid and less-rational readings of Islam provided by the preachers and extremist Sufis to a higher learning of Islam.

By extension, the only way to demystify Muslim women and to correct the wrong images of them as passive and helpless is by opening human rights agencies where Muslim women can speak for themselves even if their perspectives differ from the normative perspective of these agencies.

Muslim men and women must be coached to rethink Islam and to act within a balanced perspective of its first source, the Quran. This perspective must put in their proper place the many layers of *taqlids* (following of precedent) and interpretations and Western discussions of Islam as well. By dispelling the extremist mystics' and other elites' claims that there are hidden meanings that only a select few can know the Quran can become comprehensible even to an illiterate person. To educate the preachers women should attend the mosque regularly and should counter preachers' unfounded claims with clear arguments. Similarly, Muslim women must be involved in debates of the Islamic concept of justice in the face of outside influences. Such debates and encounters do not necessarily call for educated women theologians. After all, the woman who protested the second caliph's imposition of certain restrictions on women's visits to the mosque was acting from her simple understanding of the core of the Islamic message, that is, trusteeship to all.

Muslim women must be encouraged and given the means to educate themselves and others and to define their own identities as autonomous spiritual and intellectual beings. Such education must be facilitated by discussing alternative interpretations of themselves and their places in the community of believers.

In this enterprise community leaders must be involved to provide an environment for inquiry and learning and for building consensus around each step of the Platform. Community-based education that could be similar to already existing models, such as the *kuttab*, the school-like place where boys and girls were, and in many rural areas still are, taught the Quran and basic literary and math skills, and the *madrasah*, the collegelike place that provides higher Islamic education for male and female students.

Human rights activists' programmes must be interpreted within the Quranic understanding of a just human society. Educating human rights advocates in Islamic concepts of justice ought to be as important as educating local and state governments in human rights.

12

International Organizations, Foreign Policy and Islam

Introduction

The historical perspective of the accomplishments and shortcomings of the national machinery, with a brief reference to the case of Egypt; the effect of *CEDAW* on women's rights in Muslim societies; and the influence of foreign policies of donor countries and these policies' compatibility with the Beijing commitments toward gender equality. The dissemination of a wealth of knowledge on women's roles in modern societies led to radical changes in the perception of gender issues and despite prevailing conservative trends worldwide resulted in commitments by a great many governments to advance women's causes. Despite many unsolved problems the Beijing conference was a success.

For this success the NGOs largely must be credited. Their preparatory work proved to be vital in the struggle for gender equality, and their engagement will urgently be needed for the implementation of the Beijing Platform for Action in the future. Another factor in the success was that women were in charge of negotiations and were presiding over the committees and workshops in contrast to earlier women's conferences in which women were mainly represented by men.

This shift in participation reflects the gradual development of the status of women in international diplomacy from Mexico to Beijing. In Mexico and Copenhagen, for example, several male delegates controlled the negotiation process and insisted on introducing controversial subjects totally irrelevant to women's issues to score points in the ideological power plays of the two superpowers. Counting on the women participants' lack of political expertise, these men delegates used the U.N. women's forum for their own national political interests. This usurpation of the negotiation process resulted in divisiveness, hampered the implementation of the final documents, and diffused the momentum that was generated in favour of gender equality.

In contrast, in Beijing the women who headed committees and working groups worked together in harmony and supported each other. For example, they met every evening to decide on a strategy for the following day, and members of the NGO Forum informed the women negotiators of problems or adversarial political moves in advance. The negotiations succeeded despite the many controversial issues under discussion and despite the hard-line positions of certain delegations because women and men worked together and reached agreements without sacrificing women's causes. For example, the working group on health, discussing controversial issues such as abortion, reproductive health, and family planning, managed to reach agreement on more than ninety problematic pending paragraphs that were potentially a great threat to the success of the conference. It is worth noting that this working group was presided over by a woman from a Muslim country, namely myself, who had to work, on the one hand, with tough, religiously traditional Muslim and Catholic men and, on the other hand, with the most liberal delegates from northern European countries.

This empowerment of women through women leaders in negotiating processes was inspiring. Women will need to build on this experience in the implementation of the Platform for Action.

National Machinery

During the preparatory work for the first U.N. Conference on Women in Mexico City in 1975 the idea for setting up so-called national machineries as a vehicle for the advancement of women was formulated. Since then many countries indeed have established different national machineries within different legal frames.

National machinery as defined by the United Nations is any organizational structure established with particular responsibility for the advancement of women and the elimination of discrimination against women at the central national level. It may include governmental, nongovernmental, or joint governmental-NGO bodies and may consist of one or several agencies all of which are recognized by the government as the national machinery for the advancement of women.

Table 12.1. National Machinery, by Region

	Region				
Countries with National Machinery	Africa	Asia and Pacific	Europe and Others	Latin America and Caribbean	Total
Percentage	55.8	41.9	88.9	66.7	61.6
Number	52	43	36	33	164

The recommendations of most U.N. conferences on women, particularly those adopted in Nairobi in 1985, emphasized the importance of the national machinery to monitor and to improve the status of women, to promote and to integrate women's needs and concerns into government policies and programmes, to mobilize grass-roots support, and to provide information at the national and international levels.

The United Nations has undertaken several reviews and appraisals of national machineries. A seminar on national machineries organized by the United Nations in 1987 in Vienna provided qualitative information. In 1989 the first directory on national machineries was prepared; in 1990 the review of the results of the Nairobi conference included a chapter on national machineries; in 1991 a questionnaire collected more detailed information from member states; and in 1993 a second directory was published.

According to the first U.N. directory of national machineries in 1989, 101 countries reported the existence of a national machinery; 54 per cent of developing countries and 89 per cent of developed countries had a national machinery in place. Almost three-quarters of the countries that have signed or ratified the *Convention on the Elimination of All Forms of Discrimination Against Women* have a national machinery in place.

The first directory on national machinery states that although most countries have a national machinery in some form, most of these do not function as effectively as they could and will need more support on all levels to perform their assigned role. Indeed, most national machineries lack a strong technical capacity or are precariously located in the government structure. Frequently, they lack resources for staff and equipment. For example, whereas 90 percent of national machineries in developed countries reported that they had headquarters, only 44 per cent in developing countries did so. Of these, only 20 per cent had more than one computer compared to 65 per cent in developed countries, and no national machinery in developing countries belonged to a computer network.

Table 12.2. Countries with a National Machinery

Countries with National Machinery	Signed or Ratified the Convention	Neither Signed nor Ratified the Convention	Total
Percentage	71.5	37.5	61.6
Number	116	48	164

The directory, published in 1993, provides the following information about 128 states with national machineries.

1. Although many countries have a national machinery located in the government, others still use nongovernmental organizations as national machinery.
2. Although some countries have ministers of women's affairs, others include women's affairs in the title of ministers reporting to the cabinet, such as in the ministries of Youth, Social Affairs, and Education.
3. In some countries lower-level-organizations such as the council for equality, the office of ombudsman for women, or parliamentary commissions are responsible for national machinery tasks.
4. The weakest national machineries are located only as focal points in ministries with other responsibilities.

Just as the structural location of national machineries varies greatly from country to country, so do mandates. Some are dearly delineated, backed by laws, and funded adequately, whereas others are less well integrated and, therefore, are less effective. In Asia many national machineries are nongovernmental because of active women's NGOs. The support for ministries for women's affairs in Europe to a large extent depends on the political party in power and, therefore, can change rather fast.

Although national machineries can be useful tools for the advancement of women, in twenty years many have not been very effective. For a national machinery to be effective and successful it must have a clear identity and a well-defined mandate, an appropriate, firm location within the government structure independent of the interests of political parties, adequate financial and human resources, and it must maintain close working relationships with local women's NGOs.

The Beijing platform recognizes the importance of national machinery by including it in its three objectives, namely: the strengthening of the national machinery; the integration of gender perspectives in legislation, public policies, and programmes; and the generation and dissemination of gender-disaggregated data for planning and evaluation. National machineries further were charged with monitoring the prevailing political trends to prevent any potential setback to women's rights as a result of political and economic changes in the country, particularly the rise of extremist ideologies and any radical and ultraconservative trends.

Moreover, the national machinery must institutionalize women's gains to prevent setbacks such as the weakening of affirmative action in the United States or the abolishment of quotas for seats in the parliament and the municipal councils of Egypt. National machineries must take a proactive rather than a defensive stance by setting new goals for decision making for women in high political levels to prevent setbacks.

One of the weaknesses in the operation of national machineries is the concentration of activities in the capital and in urban areas, which excludes many women. Only if women from all areas and all social backgrounds are reached can a national movement for gender equality be generated.

The U.N. Committee on the Elimination of All Forms of Discrimination Against Women is entitled to monitor governments' compliance with the articles of the convention on women. Its evaluations and criticisms should be acted upon promptly by the national machinery to ensure that the suggestions for the advancement of women at the international level are reflected on the national level. National organizations can promote change by comparing local conditions with international norms and experiences; close partnerships between national and international organizations facilitate the exchange of ideas and experiences and foster women's global solidarity.

Inter-relationships between the National and International Levels

In the 1970s I participated in the drafting of the convention that had affirmative action for the advancement of women as the subject of ARTICLE 4. Egypt was aware of this subject and of the growing trend toward allocating special quotas for women and passed a law in 1979 allowing women a quota of thirty seats, dose to 9 per cent, in the parliament, and 15 per cent to 20 per cent of the seats in local and municipal councils. In 1986, however, the quota system was abolished after a court ruling proclaimed it to be unconstitutional and to represent reverse discrimination. The advocate of this ruling was a conservative antifeminist lawyer on the Supreme Court. Since the quota system was abolished, women's representation in the parliament has fallen to 2.2 per cent.

The national machinery in Egypt was established in 1975 with the preparation for the Mexico conference and has had many ups and downs since then. For example, after the first chairperson was replaced, not much was achieved for women by the national machinery. In 1993 its mandate was renewed and strengthened with a new leadership and the preparation for the Beijing conference. It organized its first general conference in 1994 and its second one in 1996 to discuss the implementation of the Beijing Platform for Action. Egypt's First Lady, Mrs. Mubarak, the president of this committee, announced the main guidelines for action. The most important result of this meeting wag the integration of the policies for the advancement of women with the Five-Year National Development Plan.

The recommendations emphasized among others the importance of women's education and, particularly, the eradication of illiteracy by increasing the number of single-class-schools in rural and remote areas to three thousand and by establishing community schools funded jointly by the government, individual donors, and communities. Furthermore, the general school curriculum is to include information on women's rights to ensure that the new generation of men and women become more aware of gender equality.

A publicity campaign was planned to change traditional attitudes that are detrimental for women, and a review of laws was recommended to remove contradictions in the legal code and laws that could be used to limit the progression toward gender equality.

The current status of women in Egypt must be seen in the light of Egypt's long and complex history, which spans civilizations in which women such as Hatchepsut, Cleopatra, and Shagaret-El-Dorr participated in the governance of the society, and times when women had little input in the political domain. Egypt's many different roots in African, Arab, and Mediterranean traditions, and its geographical position at the crossroads of East and West have enabled it to borrow widely and to be open to new and universal trends. In 1956 Egypt's Constitution gave all women political rights. A series of legislations was passed to promote women's legal and social equality with men. This progressive development was a result of a long reformist evolution in Egypt whose origins go as far back as the mid-nineteenth century when Mohamed Ali Pasha established the first school for girls. At the turn of the twentieth century, several reformists called for the emancipation of women including Mohamed Abdou, Kassem Amin, and Mostafa Abdel Razik. Their writings advocated the importance of women's education as investment for the future of Egypt's society and propagated the slogan "Educating a Woman is Educating a Whole Generation."

Mohamed Abdou and other reformers were well-respected theologians and graduates of the prestigious Islamic University, al-Azhar al-Sharif, the first university in the world and a global centre for Islamic teaching. Graduates of al-Azhar are leading Muslim theologians in many countries in Africa and Asia today. In Egypt their reformist ideology created a climate that favoured women's equality and led to the creation of Egypt's first women's movement, chaired by Hoda Sharawy, the first woman to represent Egypt in international conferences even before Egypt's independence. She led the struggle against veiling in the early 1920s, organized the participation of women in the struggle against the British occupation, and joined the Egyptian revolution of 1919.

Thus, the reformist ideology behind the movement for the emancipation of women in Egypt ultimately came from the highest authority in Islamic theology and jurisprudence, al-Azhar. It was guided by Islamic teaching, which recognizes women's importance for progress, and shows how misconceived and unfounded are today's fundamentalist ideas about women's rights in Islam. If Muslim theologians thought progressively about Muslim women's positions in a Muslim society almost one hundred years ago, one must seriously ask whether modern fundamentalists' contrary claims are not so much related to theology and religion as they are to political goals.

Current Egyptian laws follow the spirit of the constitution in treating men and women much the same. Moreover, several important measures have been taken toward gender equality. These include the ratification of a number of U.N. treaties, including the international *Convention to Eliminate All Forms of Discrimination Against Women* in 1981; the creation of the National Council for Childhood and Motherhood in 1988; the establishment of a Ministry for Population and Family Planning in 1993; the consolidation of departments concerned with women's issues in the Ministries of Social Affairs, Health, and Agriculture; the passing of the law on Childhood and Motherhood in 1996, which goes a very long way toward asserting women's and children's rights; the recent adoption of a law concerning legal procedures in family law, which ensures that decisions in legal disputes are reached promptly; the amendment of family law with the aim of curtailing polygyny. A national law to grant citizenship to children of Egyptian women married to foreigners is currently under review.

Today, Egyptian women hold 12 per cent of all high positions in the diplomatic corps; twelve women ambassadors are in charge of different embassies, missions, or general consulates. Women represent 23 per cent of the total work force, 38 per cent of the informal sector, and 17 per cent of the business community. In the parliament are seventeen women representatives in the Lower House, that is, 2.2 per cent of all representatives, and 4.7 per cent in the Upper

House. (As mentioned earlier, these figures constitute a decline from the 1970s when women constituted 9 per cent of the members of parliament. The decline was the result of a court order that abolished the quota system for women.)

Despite considerable achievements toward gender equality, many problems and obstacles remain, particularly those posed by the resurgence of outdated and backward models of how a society should work and by ideologies about women's roles in it that are propagated under the influence of or in the name of religious extremism. There is strong hope, however, that the fight against this wave of extremism will be won by the Egyptian people, men and women together, who constitute an overwhelming moderate majority, supported by the international community of all those who believe in tolerance, coexistence, and equality. This support and solidarity between international bodies and local women's movements is essential for sustaining the momentum toward gender equality not just in Egypt but everywhere.

Implementation of the Platform for Action in Muslim Societies

The following experience is an example of the linkage between national and international levels of activity and of the need for international support of women's rights in a particular country or region. In 1987 three Muslim governments' reports submitted to *CEDAW* included assertions of practices they called Islamic but which constituted grave breaches of women's rights and were challenged by other Muslim authorities. The first report came from an Asian Muslim country and stated that throwing add in a woman's face for punishment is supported by the Shari'a, Islamic law. The second report was submitted by an African Islamic country and stated that when a husband dies, his wife is considered part of his movable property to be inherited by his brother. This, too, was attributed to Shari'a law. The third report allegedly attributed a great many degrading treatments of women in the delegate's country to Shari'a law.

The only Muslim expert in *CEDAW* at the time challenged the content of these reports and protested against such wrong interpretations of Islam being submitted to the United Nations in official governments' reports from Muslim countries. When questioned about the source of such obvious misrepresentations of Islam, the representatives from these three countries could not provide answers and instead were taken aback because they had not been aware of the problematic content of these passages. *CEDAW*'s experts then decided to request the Economic and Social Council of the United Nations (ECOSOC) to call for the preparation of a compilation of women's rights as stipulated in Islamic scriptures. This compilation was to be done in cooperation with a renowned religious Islamic authority such as al-Azhar and to be made available to *CEDAW*'s members, most of whom had no prior understanding of Islam, to use as a reference in future considerations of various governments' reports regarding basic Muslim women's rights.

This decision never passed ECOSOC because of the strong opposition from representatives of Muslim countries who considered the decision biased against Islam because there were no similar requests for other religions.

The opposition against the decision was instigated by one of the countries whose report had included a controversial claim and had supported it by a for many Muslims blasphemous reference to Islam. Obviously, the country now wanted to shift the blame for the mistake on the committee and its female experts.

The rejection, however, was based also on the fear that this study, once translated into six official U.N. languages and disseminated widely, would, in fact, embarrass many Islamic countries that are known for their hard-line policies against women, policies that now would be declared to be against Islamic teaching. Moreover, it would make it obvious that no unanimity exists among Islamic countries on the interpretation of Islamic scriptures, especially in regard to the Shari'a. Ironically, the *CEDAW* decision, which was aimed at defending Islam and showing it to contain women's rights, was turned around and used as an example of the alleged bias the United Nations, and especially *CEDAW*, has against Islam.

This is a clear case of the old and complicated issue of the interpretation of Islamic scriptures in different cultural settings and of how Muslims and non-Muslims understand Islamic teaching. The issue is not easily settled, especially because centuries ago the religious leaders closed the door to the kind of flexible interpretation of the Sharia that would reflect the actual situation of a society and cultural changes over time.

The difficult problem of the interpretation of Islam and the Sharia raises the following questions: Can the Platform for Action be implemented in Muslim societies at all? How can one help Muslim women who struggle against the rise of extremism? How dangerous are the misconceptions of Islam for women? What is the impact of the media on the next generation? Answers to these questions lie in the wider context of the ongoing debate on Women and Islam with its numerous contradictory and confusing claims.

It is wrong to assume that the status of women is the same in all Muslim societies. Local cultural backgrounds and histories affect the status of women so much, despite a common religion, that there are profound differences even among Arab countries that share the same language and a common identity. One must take respective cultural backgrounds into consideration.

Islam, just like all other religions and faiths, can enrich and enhance the lives of people, including women. It is wrong to assume that Islam itself is against women. Women must correct the widespread misinformation in the world mass media on this point. A clear distinction must be made between the rights and principles as stipulated in the religion and the practices in the name of religion by some Muslim people who interpret Islam to justify misogynist cultural customs.

A complex and serious problem is the imposition by new radical so-called Muslim groups of detrimental ideas about women's and men's allegedly different rights and duties in Islam. Rather than sound theology, this is a political tool to suppress women and to take away their rights as stipulated in religious texts. These rights were preached by Muslim theologians fourteen centuries ago and are similar to those formulated by modern advocates of equal rights movements. People all over the world need to be educated about the basic tenets of Islam to counter the dangerous and self-serving new ideologies of so-called fundamentalist groups. Women need to demonstrate that Islam was, and still is, a force for emancipation that gave women unprecedented rights, such as the right to independent legal and economic identity; to payment for work; to own and inherit property; to learn and to have the liberty of thought and movement; to perform the pilgrimage and to take part in Holy

War; to control important aspects of their lives through marriage contracts in which they can stipulate the right to initiate divorce proceedings, to financial compensation, to monogamy, or to the custody of children, for example. The rights are there, but sadly, women do not know them, or they choose, for many reasons, not to use them. Efforts must be made to teach women their rights and to give them the legal means to use them to their advantage.

The veil and polygyny are the two most obvious and most exploited issues for negative propaganda about Islam. Yet they are trumped-up issues; total veiling is not required by Islam. Indeed, during the pilgrimage to Mecca, the most sacred religious event, women must not cover their faces and their hands in the mosque if their pilgrimage is to be valid. The Quranic injunction on polygyny was used to limit the practice to certain social necessities such as wartime widowhood. Before Islam, the number of wives a man could have was unlimited. Furthermore, there is an explicit Quranic order for a man to have only one wife if he cannot treat his wives absolutely equay.

When talking about Islam, the international media almost exclusively reports on the views of extremists and thereby supports them. Giving the title "Women in Islam" to a large picture of a totally veiled woman in a newspaper is catchy but is stereotyping and misleading. This is a serious problem because it means that the media is taking sides in the ongoing debate between moderates and radicals in the Islamic world at the expense of women's rights. It also means that it tacitly supports the fundamentalist view that the Sharia is a static body of laws against the many Muslim scholars who call for more flexible interpretations.

These practices by the international media jeopardize Muslim women's battles for exercising their rights as stipulated by their religion and will propagate the fundamentalist view of Islam in Muslim countries and abroad. The current media campaign also strengthens the extremists' position by introducing extremist ideas in every aspect of life. Thus, the cultural and religious gap between Muslims and non-Muslims and between mainstream-Muslims and extremists will widen as a result of polarizations of opinions and an increasing lack of tolerance and dialogue between adherents to different religious ideas.

To implement the Beijing recommendations the attitude of the mass media toward Islam in regard to women must be countered and corrected, and the current use of religion as a means to suppress women and other segments of society must be discussed to overcome the dangers that these new movements pose to women. Instead of being told that their religion veils and marginalizes them, women must be educated by the mass media about their rights in Islam.

Implications of the Foreign Policy of Donor Countries

The relevant issues for the foreign policies of donor countries are: human rights, democracy, population issues, and official development assistance.

Human Rights: Although I have great reservations about using human rights arguments, democracy issues, and offical development assistance as political tools in imposing policies of donor countries on recipient countries, such noninvolvement can go too far. Some donor countries' own concerns with women's rights and gender equality not only are not expressed in their foreign policies, but these donors' support of repressive regimes and governments as far as women's rights are concerned is contrary to their commitment to the Beijing recommendations.

Unfortunately, many Western countries and international organizations as well defend the rights of opposition groups, extremists or fundamentalists on the grounds of human rights, whereas the fate of millions of women who suffer under blatant discrimination and physical and mental abuse and violence does not raise similar concerns and does not motivate much international action.

Democracy: The quest of most donor countries to promote democratic political systems in recipient countries does not extend to women. There are few official inquiries into the participation of women in so-called democratic processes or into the extent to which women benefit from the kind of democracy that is sponsored. Because women are badly underrepresented in many political and legal democratic processes, there should be discussions about the workings of democracy and about possible constitutional measures to reach more equitable participation in the democratic process. Donor countries could do a lot more by initiating such debates and by linking their assistance to women's political inclusions.

Population: The population issue is closely related to women's status, their rights, and their prospects for the future. National and international bodies that handle population problems and make decisions about the allocation of resources for population issues, therefore, should give priority to the affected women's perspectives and needs. To be more effective, donor countries' policies regarding population issues should be long term and stable rather than change widely according to the policies of different political parties who win and lose elections.

Official Development Assistance (ODA): Although recently there has been some improvement in how funds are allocated, the ODA still does not give enough attention to women's programmes, especially in areas of basic needs such as health, education, human resource development, economic development, and lending facilities, especially in light of the fact that most women are self-employed and have little access to existing insurance possibilities or governmental programmes for workers.

Radical change is needed in the concept and methods of using aid for gender issues. ODA resources should be used according to a comprehensive plan that would assist rather than duplicate or undermine national efforts at the governmental and nongovernmental levels. Helping the NGOs' activities alone is not enough. Particular responsibilities require governmental intervention. Such activities need bilateral regional and international support.

Women of the Middle East and other Muslim countries are paying the price for some Western foreign policies in the region. Such policies are seen by many as humiliating for Muslims and as biased against the people's customs and religion even in times of peace. They create deep animosity, even hatred, against the West and its cultures and ideologies and against those who support or defend it inside the Muslim countries. The more the West is seen as the force behind campaigns that are locally perceived as being against Islam or humiliating for Muslims, the more difficult it is for women in Muslim countries to exercise rights that are seen as ultimately coming from the West.

Bibliography

Abd Amal al-Rahim. "The Female Image in the Media." Paper presented at the American Cultural Center in Damascus, Syria, March 1996.

Abu J. Nasr, I. Lorfing, and J. Mikati. *Identification and Elimination of Sex Stereotypes in and from School Textbooks: Suggestions for Action in the Arab World*. Paris: UNESCO, 1983.

Abu J. Nasr, N. Khoury, and H. Azzam, eds. *Women, Employment and Development in the Arab World*. Berlin: Mouton, 1985.

Basu Amrita, ed. *The Challenge of Local Feminisms: Women's Movements in Global Perspective*. Boulder, Colo.: Westview Press, 1995.

Berik Günseli, and Nilufer Cagatay. "Industrialization Strategies and Gender Composition of Manufacturing Employment in Turkey." In *Women's Work in the World Economy*, edited by Nancy Folbre et al. Hong Kong: Macmillan, 1992.

Cooke Miriam. *Women Write War: The Centering of the Beirut Decentrists*. Oxford: Centre for Lebanese Studies, 1987.

Cornell V. J. "Tawhid: The Recognition of the One in Islam." In *Islam: A Challenge to Christianity*, edited by Hans Küng and Jürgen Moltmann, 6166. London: SCM Press, 1994.

Desai Netin. *Keeping the Promises*. Women's Environment and Development Organization (WEDO) *Workshop Report*, 8-10. New York, 1996.

Garaudy Roger. *Islam habite notre avenir. Paris: Desclée de Brouwer, 1981. Trans. Abd al-Majid Baroudy, Al-Islam diin al-mustaqbal. Damascus: Dar al-Iman, 1983.*

Hafez Nimat Barazangi. "Educational Reform." In The Oxford Encyclopedia of the Modern Islamic World, vol. 1, edited by John S. Esposito, 406-11. New York: Oxford Univ. Press, 1995.

Ibrahim Sa'ad Eddin. "Thinking of Assassination and the Assassination of Thought." Civil Society (Cairo) 3, no. 35 (1994): 3.

Karam Azza M. Women, Islamism and the State: Contemporary Feminisms in Egypt. London: Macmillan.

Karam Azza M., et al. Islam in een ontzuilde Samenleving. Amsterdam: Royal Tropical Institute Press, 1996.

Lawyers Committee for Human Rights. Beset by Contradictions: Islamization, Legal Reform and Human Rights in Sudan. New York: Lawyers Committee for Human Rights, 1996.

Mehdi Rubya. The Islamization of the Law in Pakistan, 95-108. Chippenham: Nordic Institute of Asian Studies, 1994.

Mernissi Fatima. Beyond the Veil: Male-Female Dynamics in Modern Muslim Society. London: al-Saqi, 1985; Bloomington: Indiana Univ. Press, 1987.

Nasr Seyyed Hossein. "Comments on a Few Theological Issues in the IslamicChristian Dialogue." In Christian-Muslim Encounters, edited by Yvonne Yazbeck Haddad and Wadi Zaidan Haddad, 457-67. Gainesville: Univ. of Florida Press, 1995.

Sadowski Yahya. "The New Orientalism and the Democracy Debate." Middle East Report 183 (1993): 14-26.

Sarehane Fatna. "Legislation comparée: Maroc, le statut personnel: Droit commun, capacité, mariage, filiation." Pt. 2-1. N.p.: Editions Techniques-JurisClasseurs, 1993.

Singerman Diane. Avenues of Participation: Family, Politics, and Networks in Urban Quarters of Cairo. Princeton, N.J.: Princeton Univ. Press, 1955.

Slyomovics Susan. "Hasiba Ben Bouali, If You Could See Our Algeria: Women and Public Space in Algeria," Middle East Report 192 (Jan.-Feb. 1995): 813.

Zipes Jack D. Arabian Nights. New York: Signet Classic, 1991.

INDEX

A

Agnatic Heirs, 121
Allah, 12
Al-Zamakhshari, 20
Amount of the Bride-Price, 181
Arab-Islamic Renaissance, 42

B

Batil Marriage, 99
Bride-Price in Marriage, 179
Burqa, 75

C

Caliphs Are Above the Law, 196
Child Care, 38
City of Islam, 42
Classification of Marriage, 99
Conditions for Marriage, 164
Content of Islamic Higher Learning, 208
Context and Chronology in Quranic Social Reforms for Women, 27
Convention on the Elimination of All forms of Discrimination against Women (CEDAW), 63

D

Daraba Allah Mathalan, 25
Darajah, 14
Darajat, 16
Demands Hierarchy, 29
Discrimination against Women in Penal Laws, 194
Disobedience to the Husband, 24
Disruption of Marital Harmony, 23
Distinction Between Shariah and Fiqh, 136
Individuals, 55
Distinctive Female Characters in the Quran, 57
Divorce, 28, 108
Dower Rights, 104
Duties of the Wife 103

E

Education and Islamic Higher Learning, 211
Extraneous Sources, 156

Extra-Quranic, 14

F

Faddala, 15
False Accusation and the
 Controversy Surrounding, 199
 Allegations and Oath, 196
Family Law, 95
Family Protection Act, 161
Fasid Marriage, 100
Female Genital Mutilation (FGM), 70
 Infantícíde Ín Pre-Islamic Arabia, 86
First Century Vacuum, 143
First Injunction: Confine Lewd Women, 188
Front Des forces Socialistes (FFS), 45
 of Socialist forces, 44
Functional Distinctions on Earth, 13
Fundamentalism and Women's Rights, 40

G

God-Conscious Piety, 13
Gross National Product (GNP), 91
Guard their Sex Organs, 81
Guardianship in Marriage, 98

H

Hadiths, 78
Higher Council for Islamic Affairs, 71

I

Ibadat (Worship), 97
Iddah, 102
Ijab, 98
Ijtihad *vs.* Taqlid, 134
Implementation of the Platform for Action in Muslim Societies, 229
Implications of the foreign Policy of Donor Countries, 233
Industrial Revolution, 40
Inheritance, 35, 117
International Organizations, foreign Policy and Islam, 221
Interrelationships between the National and International Levels, 226
Intra-Quranic, 14
Islam today: Economic Disadvantages of Inequality, 91
Islamic Higher Learning in Muslim Women, 204
 in Practice, 214
 in the Platform for Action, 217

K

Khilafah, 33
Khul and Mubaraah (Mutual Divorce), 113

L

Legal Age for Marriage, 176
 Methodology for Reform in Islam, 133
Lessons from Dar Al-Islam, 41
 from the City of Women, 44

Lian and Faskh (Divorce by Judicial Process), 113

M

Ma'ruf, 18
Maintenance Rights, 106
Male Authority, 36
  Sexual Insecurity, 79
Marriage, 97
  and Family Laws Commission of 1955, 135
Maze of Restrictions against Women, 75
Middle Assyrian Law, 89
Muakhkhar, 105
Muamalat (Social Relations), 97
Muqaddam, 105
Muslim Family Law, 95
  Law and Women, 127
  Societies and Women, 62

N

National Machinery, 222
New World Order, 40
Nikah, 97
Nushuz, 23

O

Obligatory Bequest, 150
Option of Puberty, 99
Origins of Muhammadan Jurisprudence, 142

P

Pakistan's Marriage and Family Laws Commission, 149
Patriarchy, 29
Polygamy, 31
Primitive Marriage Laws, 165
Property Rights, 104
Prophetic Sunnah, 144
Punishments for Sexual Misconduct in Islam, 187
Purdah, 73

Q

Qabul, 98
Qawwam, 19
Qawwamuna 'Ala, 19
Qiwamah, 22
Quran Teaches the Reader through the Events in the Lives, 49
Quranic Heirs, 119
  Reforms, 95
  Utopia, 11
  View of Woman, 48

R

Rassemblement Culture Et Democracie (RCD), 45
Ray and Qiyas, 147
Regulations of Marriage Agreements, 103
Rights and Roles of Woman in Islam, 11
Risalah, 14

S

Sahih Marriage, 100
Satans, 80
Sayyid Qutb, 21
Self-Exertion, 147
Significance of the Women Mentioned or Referred to in the Quran, 51

Son of Mary, 58
Status of Woman in the Pre-Islamic Period, 84
Stoning, 190
Sunnah of the Prophet, 141
Surat-Al-Tahrim, 52
Syrian Law of Personal Status, 155

T

Tafdil, 15
Talaq Al-Tafwid (Delegated Divorce), 112
    Proper, 109
Taqwa, 13
The Era of Sterility, 134
    Will of Allah, 74
Tradition and Change, 133
Treatment of Women Based onthe Quran, 78
Tunisian Law of Personal Status, 155
Types of Marriage, 169

U

Ummah, 97
Universal Declaration of Human Rights, 40
    Human Rights, 41
Usul Al-Fiqh (Sources of Law) and Islamic Reform, 136
Uterine Heirs, 121

V

Veíl and Marriage, 83
Veíl as a Check on Male Sexual Desíre, 79
Veíl in the Pre-Islamic Period, 88

W

Wahy, 14
Weltanschauung, 12
Widow's Right of Retention, 105
Witness, 33
WLUML and Muslim Laws, 128
    and the Platform for Action, 130
Woman as an Individual, 53
    is Not Just Biology, 13
    Seclusion in Islam, 72
Women in Ancient Egypt, 166
    in Babylonia, 167
    in Elam, 168
    in Pre-Islamic Arabia, 96
    Living Under Muslim Laws (WLUML), 128
    of India, 169
World Community, 40